SECRET
PIGEON
SERVICE

SECRET PIGEON SERVICE

OPERATION COLUMBA, RESISTANCE AND THE STRUGGLE TO LIBERATE EUROPE

GORDON CORERA

WILLIAM COLLINS

William Collins
An imprint of HarperCollins*Publishers*
1 London Bridge Street
London SE1 9GF
www.WilliamCollinsBooks.com

First published in Great Britain by William Collins in 2018

1

Map © Martin Brown

A catalogue record for this book is
available from the British Library

ISBN 978-0-00-822030-3 (hardback)
ISBN 978-0-00-822031-0 (trade paperback)

Printed and bound in Great Britain by
CPI Group (UK) Ltd, Croydon, CR0 4YY

MIX
Paper from
responsible sources
FSC® C007454

This book is produced from independently certified FSC paper
to ensure responsible forest management

For more information visit: www.harpercollins.co.uk/green

In memory of Leopold Vindictive
and others who made their choice.

Contents

Map   ix

Prologue   1
Introduction   5

ONE: Birth   13

TWO: The Special Pigeon Service   25

THREE: Leopold Vindictive   45

FOUR: Arrival   61

FIVE: Listening   75

SIX: Battle of the Skies   86

SEVEN: Reaching Out   100

EIGHT: Resistance   112

NINE: Secret Agents   125

TEN: Undercover   146

ELEVEN: Battle of the Skies II   160

TWELVE: Capture   172

THIRTEEN: Interrogation and Infiltration   181

FOURTEEN: The Viscount   200

FIFTEEN: Trials and Tribulations   222

SIXTEEN: Deception   236

SEVENTEEN: The Americans are Coming   247

EIGHTEEN: Fates   271

   Acknowledgements   287
   References   289
   List of Illustrations   313
   Index   315

Prologue

The Belgian farmer could see there was something odd in his field, something that did not belong there. It was early on a July morning in 1941, just over a year after Nazi tanks had swept through the country. As he stepped closer the farmer could make out that the unfamiliar object was a small container with a length of white material attached. Picking it up, he realized the material was a parachute – but one too small for a man. Inside the box he could see something moving and a pair of eyes that peeped out at him through a small opening. Next came the unmistakable sound of a pigeon cooing. Attached to the side of the container was a message – a request for help. The farmer decided this was something that he needed to consult his wife about.

It was a moment of peril – one that many a British pigeon did not survive. The message made clear that this was no innocent pigeon but a very dangerous bird. It was a spy pigeon that could get the farmer and his wife killed. At this crossroads in the war, many faced with the same discovery across north-western Europe would decide it was better that the pigeon died than they did. Often villagers would make the choice more palatable by roasting and eating the bird. Others went straight to the local police station or to their Nazi occupiers and took the reward on offer for surrendering one of these pigeons. That July morning, half a dozen other birds dropped in nearby Belgian fields would be handed over to the authorities out of fear or greed.

But this farmer and his wife were not like the others. And so the first in a series of small choices was made. The wife set off by bicycle, hiding the container in a sack of potatoes. She had an idea where to go. The small local town of Lichtervelde was, like Belgium as a whole, divided by Nazi occupation. The split was delineated by alcohol. Those who frequented a local pub called De Keizer were known as whites – they thought of themselves as 'patriots' – meaning they were against the occupation. Meanwhile those who frequented De Zwaan were blacks – nationalists who often wore black shirts and sympathized with the Nazis. Everyone knew who was who and what side they were on.

The farmer's wife parked her cycle by a grocery shop on a corner a few streets from the centre of town. She carried in the sack of potatoes – nothing suspicious, since it was part of the regular drop-off of supplies for the shop's owners. But she also handed over the spy pigeon to the family who ran the store. Why them? For two reasons. Everyone knew the Debaillie family were patriots – three brothers and two sisters, plus assorted relatives sent to them for safety during the war. But there was another reason. One of the brothers, Michel, was a pigeon fancier.

The brothers and sisters gathered round as Michel – gangly, with a mop of unruly curly hair – carefully took the bird out. Like any pigeon fancier, he knew how to hold it tenderly but firmly. With the bird were a small sack of feed, two sheets of fine rice paper, a pencil, a resistance newspaper and a questionnaire. The questionnaire, like the pigeon, was from England. It asked for help: specific and dangerous help.

It was time for another decision, one that would shape the course of the lives of this family and others. To help or not to help? To spy or not to spy? To resist or not to resist? Not all were sure. Michel's younger brother wanted to act. The elder thought it was dangerous. But collectively, they made their choice. If they were patriots, they were patriots.

What did they know about spying? Nothing, really. But they had some friends who might be able to help. One was a former soldier from the First World War who had a fascination with military maps. The other, more surprisingly, was a priest. By the next day, these two had arrived in the corner shop and were inducted into the secret of the pigeon. An amateur spy network, consisting of a band of friends, had been born, driven by a desire to do something about the Nazi occupation that blighted their homeland. For the first friend, the former soldier, the bird was a thing of beauty that he marvelled at, reminding him of the pheasants he kept at home. For the priest, the rice paper was what lured him in. It was like the type of paper on which he had learnt to write characters in China a decade and a half earlier. Like the paper he had used to draw maps of German positions in the last war. And so, he knew, the paper and the pigeon were drawing him into the world of espionage – to make him once again priest, patriot and spy.

Introduction

L ike the farmer in the field, I stumbled across the oddities of Operation Columba by chance one morning. I was covering a quirky news story about a dead pigeon's leg found in a chimney in Surrey. Attached to the bony leg was a message which had stumped GCHQ's top code-breakers. They had been unable to decipher what the seemingly random series of letters meant. No one was even sure who the pigeon had been sent by, and everyone seemed quite surprised to find that pigeons had been used in the Second World War.

Perhaps there was some clue in the National Archives in Kew which could unlock this pigeon's secrets? I spent a morning pulling up any and every file that looked as if it might relate to pigeon messages in the Second World War. There were more than I thought, and it was a bewildering induction into a world I had never even known existed. But amidst the interminable accounts of which department should pay for pigeon feed, or what rank of personnel were required for a particular RAF loft, one file that landed on my desk immediately stood out.

Apart from the dates, the front cover bore only two words. One was 'Secret'; the other, in elegant handwriting, was 'Columba'. At the top was a photo of a pigeon someone had cut out. Just below the pigeon was a cartoon – also cut out, this time from a newspaper – of Hitler lying prostrate on the floor. This gave the impression that the pigeon had done on the Führer what pigeons do, leading him to fall over. At the bottom of the cover was another cartoon, this one of an RAF plane flown by Winston Churchill with a familiar cigar in his mouth and his fingers held up in his 'V for Victory' sign. The file clearly contained details of a secret operation. But it looked utterly unlike any I had seen before. What kind of people would, in the midst of war, encase the contents of their clandestine work in such colourful – even playful – packaging?

Loosening the ribbon that bound the file, I uncovered riches inside. The file had nothing to do with the secret message found in the chimney. But it was far more interesting. The riches came in the form of tiny pink slips of paper. These were messages from ordinary people living under Nazi rule in occupied Europe that had been brought back by pigeon. They were filled with the day-to-day realities of wartime and offered a remarkable insight into the small frustrations and dark tragedies of life under occupation. And then I came across message number thirty-seven. It was unlike everything else. All the other messages had been written up into formal notes, but in this case a copy of the original message had been included in the archive, clearly because it was something special. It looked more like a work of art than an official document. There was tiny, beautiful inky writing, too small to read with the naked eye and densely packed into an unimaginably small space. A swirling symbol as a signature. And maps, detailed colourful maps. Most of the other messages produced intelligence reports that were half a page or perhaps a page long. Message 37 – rolled up tightly into the size of a postage stamp so it could fit into a cylinder attached to a pigeon's leg – produced an astonishing twelve pages of raw intelligence. And it had clearly had a profound impact on the team running Columba. The intelligence must have left an impression on everyone who saw it – and many did as it was passed around the highest levels of government, many referring to it in almost reverential terms.

But there was a mystery. Who had written it? And what had happened to them? The files had no answer. There was only a code-name – Leopold Vindictive – on the message. Other documents contained confusing references to attempts to contact the writer after the message had been received. In none of them could I find a name. Nor was there any reference to the author in the history books I consulted. I knew I had to find out. The quest became something of an obsession. Who or what was Leopold Vindictive? And what was his – or her – fate?

Three years after first opening that file, I found my answer in Belgium. The answers lay partly with the families of those who had been members of Leopold Vindictive and who had preserved their story. In one house in a small town, a family opened up a metal keepsake box. Inside was a treasure trove of photos, maps and – most startlingly – the raw intelligence that had been collected to send back to Britain. Some of it had formed the basis for my message 37, but even more surprisingly, there was much more that had never made it over the Channel. Alongside those artefacts, I found a human story more dramatic and more powerful than I imagined. It is a story which has not been told before and which has had to be pieced together from personal accounts and archives in Britain and Belgium. It is the story that forms the centrepiece of this book, around which the wider story of the operation called Columba is told.

The pigeon is not the most obvious subject for someone inter-ested in intelligence to write about. It is fair to say that the birds had not exactly stirred my interest before. Pigeons have a bad name. Quite literally, since if we preferred to call them by their proper name – doves, or to be more precise rock doves (or, most formally,

Columba livia) – they might be seen in a less negative light. Our perception of the pigeon is coloured by the times as children we have chased them or as adults have evaded their droppings. But our experience of 'feral' pigeons has obscured from us the truth that some pigeons are a form of superhero. Imagine being blindfolded and then taken hundreds of miles from home – perhaps even to another country across the sea. And then suddenly having the blindfold removed and, despite not having the slightest idea where you are, racing home at top speed. Even if home is six hundred miles away. That is not normal. Just like the super-powers of comic-book heroes, the homing instinct of pigeons is something that scientists cannot explain. They have tried over the years, with theories about magnetic fields and the sun, but no one has satisfactorily managed it.

It is a strangely comfy super-power though. The pigeon is not on a mission to save the world. It just wants to go home. From the age of six weeks, pigeons can be taught to 'home' to the loft from which they make their first flight, because they understand that is where they will find food, water and company. Pigeons can be picky in their journey – they do not like to fly at night or to cross water, often flying along the coast to find the shortest point at which to cross a body like the English Channel. But they are ultimately single-minded in simply wanting to get back to where they belong. Amidst the horrors of wartime, this longing has a particular resonance.

Over the course of human history, this super-power has been recognized by people who have learnt to employ it for communication by releasing pigeons to send messages home. Noah released a dove from the Ark to bring back reports of whether the flood waters had receded. In Ancient Greece, the names of winners in the original Olympic Games were sent to distant towns by pigeon. Julius Caesar used birds during the conquest of Gaul (the Romans had, at various times, a fad for breeding pigeons, but that seems largely to have been in order to eat them). The Sultan of Baghdad used a pigeon post around 1150. In the nineteenth century, Julius Reuter began a news service using pigeons to send messages between Brussels and Germany. In Paris, pigeons were the only form of contact with the outside world during its siege in 1870. A manned hot-air balloon flew out of the city under fire carrying pigeons. Friends and family (including those in Britain) could post their letters to the city of Tours, where they would be photographed and then reduced to the point where one of the pigeons could be loaded with a film containing 2,500 messages before it flew home to Paris. A magic lantern would project the messages onto a screen so they could be copied out and sent to the recipients.

The modern sport of pigeon racing began at the start of the nineteenth century in Belgium. Clubs were formed as pigeons were carefully selected and bred to improve their abilities. The breeding extended their range from 40 miles to 200 miles and then upwards to 600 miles or more. The peak popularity of the sport came in the years before and after the Second World War; at least a quarter of a million Belgians were involved, and one in nine families had a pigeon. Lofts were present in almost every small town and village in northern France and the Low Countries, across much of Britain and in the United States.

Breeding pigeons to improve their ability (or their looks) was honed to a fine art by pigeon fanciers, or – to give them their proper name – the *fancy*. Pigeon keeping has come to be seen as a working-class preserve, the 'poor man's racehorse', a sport offering the chance to train an animal, enjoy a social life around meetings and even perhaps win a bit of money on the side. Historically, it was also a sport for the well-off, which is why so many country houses had dovecotes and pigeon lofts. The Queen still has her own pigeon loft at her estate in Sandringham, the first pigeons a gift from the

Belgian king. At the start of the Second World War, these pigeon owners – rich and poor alike – were called on to play their part in a remarkable and little-known volunteer effort. Total war demanded sacrifice, and pigeons and their owners played their part.

Pigeons did not win the war. People did. And this story is not so much about the birds as about the people who sent and received the pigeons of Columba. Yet, in a war that began with Blitzkrieg and ended with the atomic bomb, pigeons had a unique place when it came to intelligence gathering. Intelligence involves understanding your enemy – the disposition and composition of their forces, the lie of the land and the mood of the people. There are many ways of finding this out, the oldest being to use human spies who can see what is happening. But in this war there was a crucial challenge. How did your agents get the information back from behind enemy lines? Long before modern communications technology, the near-miraculous ability of trained pigeons to return to their home loft offered an unusual but highly effective way of receiving news and communicating.

Columba ran from April 1941 until September 1944. A total of 16,554 pigeons would be dropped in an arc from Copenhagen in Denmark to Bordeaux in the South of France. Casualties were heavy. Some were lost on planes shot down before they had a chance to be released. Some lay unfound in a field. Others fell into enemy hands. Some were eaten by hungry locals. Others were released but never made it back. The pigeons had to race through storms and battle against their nemesis – the hawk – to come home with their precious cargo. They returned with their messages to a quirky and quarrelsome band of British spymasters-cum-pigeon fanciers who did their best to prove the worth of their special operation against bureaucratic hindrances, institutional scepticism and bitter personal rivalries. The story of Columba – and particularly that of its most important message – does not always shine a particularly happy light on the inner workings of British intelligence, revealing divisions often overlooked in rose-tinted accounts of the war. The harsh reality is that brave men and women in the field were sometimes let down by London.

The messages Columba's pigeons carried, though, would prove their worth. Messages like number 37 provided vital intelligence on Nazi plans to invade England during its darkest hour. Others would bring news of the latest German weapons and would pave the way for D-Day and victory in May 1945. Still other messages were more personal, like the letter from a crashed RAF airman to his mother.

Who were the people who provided this rich seam of intelligence? Some were trained agents. But most were simply local villagers who made a choice to undertake their own small act of resistance. As a result, their messages – sometimes tragic, sometimes comic – provide a unique and untapped insight into the realities of daily life under Nazi occupation, from the struggles over food to the attitude towards collaborators, and even the often terrible impact of Allied bombing on those living under occupation. They offer the authentic voice of the villagers of rural France, Belgium and the Netherlands and their calls to Britain for help.

The pigeon was simply doing what it did by its nature. It knew nothing of the war that raged around it. But for those involved in Columba, the values of sacrifice, duty and a love of home all came to be embodied in the humble pigeon's flight. The living creatures offered a unique bond. For the British commando dropped with a pigeon behind enemy lines and in fear of his life, the sight of the bird flying off to a suburban garden with a message that he was safe offered a connection to home from a dangerous foreign field. And for a Frenchman or woman or a Belgian living under occupation, there was the knowledge that the pigeon that they released up into the sky was racing back to its home, bearing their message, to a land still free. This was the secret of Columba.

CHAPTER ONE

Birth

The pigeon that fell in the farmer's field near Lichtervelde in July 1941 had begun its journey a day and a half earlier. Home was a loft in a large garden on Lattice Avenue, a quiet suburban street in Ipswich full of recently built houses. The bird had been plucked from its loft and handed over by its owner. Owners were told nothing of where a bird was going or what it would be doing. All they knew was that it was something secret for the war effort.

Soon the bird had company. Our pigeon and its fellow birds were driven in a van about forty miles to Newmarket racecourse. There each pigeon was placed in its own special box with a parachute attached. A tiny green Bakelite cylinder – about the size of a pen top – was placed around its leg.

Newmarket was home to a top secret RAF squadron whose job was to carry out 'Special Duties' for British intelligence. In the summer of 1940, MI6 had approached the Air Ministry to ask if it could help drop agents behind enemy lines. The first attempt to land an agent in Belgium using a small Lysander plane ended in disaster on 18 August 1940. The plane was unable to touch down and was lost on its return flight, killing both pilot and agent. But the RAF persisted and began to use a mix of Lysander landings and parachute drops to deliver agents. The crews were trained in the dangerous task of night-flying over enemy territory using moonlight. The hours before take-off would be spent memorizing the location of rivers, lakes, railway lines and forests. The moonlight allowed them to read their maps and guide themselves by the landmarks they could see below.

The drop of our pigeon on that July night was a minor add-on to the primary secret mission of parachuting two agents into Belgium. The pilots, Ron Hockey and Ashley Jackson, took off in their Whitley from the racecourse and headed over the Channel into Nazi-occupied Europe. Enemy searchlights lit up the plane as it reached Nieuport on the Belgian coast – not far from Dunkirk, where the previous year the little boats had played a vital part in rescuing the British Expeditionary Force from destruction. Anti-aircraft fire opened up from the ground but the pilots pressed on. They headed inland towards Charleroi, south of Brussels. As they did, they passed over a field in Ardoye, near Lichtervelde. This was our pigeon's moment.

The flaps of the aircraft were lowered and one of the team grabbed the container. The best height from which to drop was between 600 and 1,000 feet, at a speed of about 180 miles an hour. The pigeon was rudely ejected. 'We tried to be very humane and give them a good drop,' an RAF pilot remembered of the process.

The plane went on to Namur and St Hubert but the crew realized they were lost and had to abandon the agent drop, returning home after a five-hour trip. The next night they tried again but the mission went disastrously wrong. The parachute of one of the agents caught in the plane as he leapt out over Belgium. He was left twirling out of the back like a puppet on a string. The crew were unable to reach him as his body repeatedly slammed against the side of the aircraft. By the time they returned to Britain, he was dead and his battered body was dropped into the sea the next night.

Crews, as well as agents, took enormous risks – their life expectancy was lower even than that of those who flew bombing missions over Germany – and with their gallows humour they enjoyed regaling each other with stories of derring-do. They found Columba a rather amusing and odd little sideshow. 'Pigeons were dropped in a small parachute container, their heads just visible through the top of it,' one pilot recalled. An agent might sometimes have second thoughts about parachuting into some dark, snowy wilderness but the pigeons were given no choice. 'I doubt if any of them survived,' the pilot reflected.

But the bird dropped near Lichtervelde did make it. The primary mission of that flight to drop agents might have failed, but the pilots would not have known that the train of events set in motion by the pigeon they had pushed out would end up with intelligence landing on Churchill's desk. The parachute deployed and the pigeon fell gently into the dark field, ready to be discovered by a farmer the next morning.

This was Columba – the Secret Pigeon Service.

The driving force behind the use of pigeons in the Second World War were two men with experience of the previous war. One was a leading member of the 'fancy' – the community of pigeon fanciers in the country – whose ambition would drive deep fissures within the pigeon world. The other was a washed-up spy looking for one more chance to make a difference.

The name of Osman is to pigeon racing the equivalent of the Kennedys in American politics – a family dynasty stretching back for decades. The founder of that dynasty was Lieutenant Colonel Alfred Henry Osman. Stout, with a proud moustache, Osman had abandoned a career as a lawyer to found the publication the *Racing Pigeon* in 1898. In the First World War, he brought his personal passion to bear as the leading light in all matters pigeon. A hundred thousand pigeons were bred for use in the war. First deployed on trawlers commandeered to carry out minesweeping in the North Sea, one brought news of a Zeppelin heading towards Britain. Another was released by a skipper who lay mortally wounded on deck after a U-boat attack, allowing his crew to be rescued.

Pigeon use quickly expanded across all the services. The Army used them for communicating short distances from the front line, especially when cables had been cut or visual signalling was impossible owing to smoke, or when a runner carrying a message might be shot. 'If it became necessary immediately to discard every line and method of communications used on the front, except one, and it were left to me to select that one method, I should unhesitatingly choose the pigeons,' wrote Major General Fowler, Chief of Signals and Communications of the British Army, after the war. 'When the battle rages and everything gives way to barrage and machine gun fire, to say nothing of gas attacks and bombings, it is to the pigeon that we go for succour.'

Belgium had the best pigeon service but had destroyed many of its birds at the start of the war to prevent them falling into German hands. The French released five thousand birds during the Battle of the Somme. The Americans took home and eventually stuffed one bird that had arrived badly wounded with a message that saved a battalion trapped behind enemy lines.

The British Army Pigeon Service was disbanded not long after the war. But as the 1930s turned darker and the threat of another war loomed, there were those from the fancy who saw themselves as voices in the wilderness, just like those calling for rearmament with tanks and aeroplanes. They urgently pressed the authorities to prepare to make use of pigeons once again. The leading advocate was Alfred Osman's son, William. His poor eyesight meant he had been rejected from regular service in the First World War but he had worked with his father. On Alfred's death in 1930, William inherited

his father's mantle as editor of the *Racing Pigeon* and leading propon-
ent of the birds' value in times of war. In 1937, he wrote to the
Secretary of the Committee on Imperial Defence saying it was a
mistake not to prepare pigeon plans. The Army said it saw little need,
apart perhaps from their use for contact with isolated garrisons. The
RAF thought they might need a hundred or so birds as an alternative means of communication – for instance if a plane crashed or a
radio was jammed. But that could be organized when war began.

Osman kept pressing. At over six foot, he had the bearing of an
old-fashioned military officer and the manner to go with it – abrupt
in a way that could easily be interpreted as rude. He did not suffer
fools gladly. The next year he attended a meeting of the Committee
on Imperial Defence, explaining that it was a blunder not to have
maintained a compulsory register of pigeon owners. His profound
knowledge of pigeons was clear but there was also an element of
self-interest – he proposed that an appeal for volunteers could be
made through the *Racing Pigeon*, the newspaper he edited. It was
agreed that a committee of four – including Osman – should start
a National Pigeon Service, the NPS. It was to be riven by bitter
infighting.

An immense voluntary effort was at the heart of Britain's wartime
pigeon operations. It is hard to appreciate just how popular a sport
pigeon fancying was at the time. There were a quarter of a million
people involved, with at least 70,000 lofts, mainly concentrated in
working-class areas. At the outbreak of war, all pigeons had to be
registered. In Plymouth, Bert Woodman went to the city police to
collect his permit to keep his pigeons. A middle-aged local food
factory manager, he was typical of the working men who would
play their part. The regime was strict: all foreign birds and those
without a ring which identified their owner were destroyed. 'There
was a terrible slaughter,' Woodman remembered. Registration was
about control, but it also offered a route for those like Bert Woodman

to volunteer for the new NPS. Two thousand signed up at first, but the membership would grow to include 18,000 lofts. NPS members agreed to offer at least twenty birds a month for national service and membership was the only way a fancier could legally obtain food for his pigeons. Members were organized into local pigeon supply groups led by a pigeon supply officer – Bert Woodman would take on the role in Plymouth, where he also acted as adviser to the police. Membership offered a way to make a difference and was one of the many ways in which the Second World War became 'the people's war' in which so many contributed. For one man, too old to fight but who had lost his brother in the last war, handing over his pigeons meant he could feel he was doing something for his brother's memory. Meanwhile, a Nottinghamshire miner's children remember always being late for school on a Tuesday, as this was the day their dad was down the pit early and they had to excitedly wait for someone to come and pick up his pigeons for some kind of secret work. Pigeon keeping had been a largely male pastime, but many women also took over a husband's or son's loft as their loved ones served far away.

The Air Ministry was given the overall co-ordinating role for all matters pigeon, including the supervision of the NPS. Its pigeon section was run by the influential but insecure William Dex Lea Rayner, who was manoeuvred into the job by Osman. Another veteran pigeoneer of the First World War, Rayner had gone on to run military pigeon operations in Ireland (soldiers battling against Irish Republicans would sometimes send news by pigeon that they were under attack). He then operated his own pigeon stud list in Norwich before becoming a somewhat hard-up dance band manager. Balding, with an oval face and sharp nose, he was bird-like in looks and was determined to maintain his position as pigeon supremo. He would be at the centre of 'pigeon politics' and some monumental feuds. This was especially the case once the Army –

rather than Rayner's own RAF – moved into the pigeon business when it saw the particular value of the birds in intelligence work. The Army, not the RAF, would be Columba's master.

Osman had ensured that the humble pigeon had its place in the machinery of war. But he was not inside the spy world. And the pigeon's specific role in Columba – as a tool to get intelligence back from ordinary people behind enemy lines – was established thanks to the vision of Rex Pearson, a veteran of military intelligence in the previous war. But as the Second World War began, Pearson was a spy without a mission or role.

In the inter-war years, Pearson had – to all appearances – left the intelligence game for a career in business. In Switzerland he had become the representative for the British firm Unilever. But that was not the full picture. In the mid-1930s, he had resumed his clandestine life. He was recruited into the 'Z' organization. 'Z' was the brainchild of Claude Dansey, a powerful figure within MI6. Some called him 'Uncle Claude' because, at first sight, Dansey looked like an elderly uncle, white-haired and with a general air of benevolence. That impression never lasted for those who got to know him. Dansey was an acerbic, sharp operator whose penchant for secrecy and intrigue made him as many enemies as admirers and left junior officers terrified of him. He had achieved his lofty position by trusting nobody. In the thirties, he had realized that the Germans had worked out MI6's use of the Passport Control Office in British embassies to hide its undercover officers. That made MI6 officers easy to identify. So Dansey set about building his own network across the continent, using businessmen.

The Z organization was a parallel intelligence network and Pearson – a colleague of Dansey's from military intelligence in the First World War – was Z's man in Zurich. Dansey himself moved to Switzerland to run the network late in the decade. But in November 1939 he returned to London to supervise all MI6's European operations, leaving Pearson in charge in Switzerland. The results were disastrous. Chaos ensued as Pearson proved not to be up to the job. At one point he managed to send two different officers to the same rendezvous with a contact. His catastrophic performance may also have stemmed from the fact that he had a drink problem. Heavy drinking was common at the time, but Pearson's seems to have been bad enough to have an adverse impact on his work. In February 1940, another MI6 officer was sent out to Switzerland to replace him.

Pearson returned to London, his intelligence career in apparent ruins just as the war was beginning. But in November 1940, he approached Military Intelligence with an idea. In the last two years of the First World War, he had been involved in a clever intelligence operation that he wanted to reprise. It involved pigeons. He was met, perhaps unsurprisingly, with a degree of bewilderment bordering on annoyance from the higher-ups. Pigeons were an 'outmoded' weapon in Britain's armoury, he was told. But Pearson persisted, and explained to his superiors what he had got up to in the last war.

The first lesson from that war was that you could use pigeons for the core business of intelligence gathering. The intelligence the military wanted included things like the disposition and movement of enemy forces. If train-loads of soldiers were seen heading to a particular station, for instance, that might mean the Germans were about to make a push on the front at that point. Networks of agents had emerged, especially in Belgium, to collect this information in the previous war but the biggest challenge had been getting their information back from the other side. MI6 had employed couriers and specialist *passeurs* (line crossers), whose hazardous work involved cutting and crawling through barbed wire, wearing rubber boots to avoid being electrocuted while carrying details of German forces.

Inventiveness was at a premium. A colleague of Pearson had

developed a system in which messages were written in invisible ink on banknotes and dropped in offertory boxes in Catholic churches, which were allowed to be taken across the front lines. Another officer was convinced that by standing in front of an oven and moving back and forth he could send 'infra-red rays' to signal with Morse code. Animals were another possibility. The pigeon with its homing instinct seemed an attractive option, and it was soon employed to carry intelligence back from agents.

But Pearson explained that he had been involved in a further innovation. What about not only using pigeons to send back intelligence from existing agents, but to actually recruit people to gather intelligence in the first place? There were sympathetic people on the other side who wanted to help. The challenge was finding them and then getting their intelligence back. In the First World War small hydrogen balloons had been sent out downwind from the British side of the front lines to any district where it was thought German forces were concentrated. Normally seven balloons were released in a night, each holding four carrier pigeons in their own basket with a parachute. At first, the baskets were attached to a cross-shaped device with an alarm clock in the middle. When it reached the right hour and rang it would release the parachutes. Later, a slow-burning fuse was employed.

Attached to the pigeons was an envelope containing a patriotic appeal and a questionnaire asking whether the Germans were present, and in what numbers. This could be filled in by locals and then clipped back onto the pigeon's leg. By breakfast time, a quarter of the pigeons released at night had normally returned, half with messages. It bothered the Germans enormously. The chief of the German Intelligence Service had griped about their use and fourteen days' leave were promised to any German soldier who shot a pigeon down. At least eleven were shot and found to be carrying important military information.

Pearson had been in charge of all balloon operations in France by the end of the First World War. Now he wanted to do it again. And better.

What Pearson had in mind this time round was much more ambitious. In the previous war, the pigeons had typically flown only fifteen or twenty miles across the front lines. Balloons dependent on the wind might be fine for delivering pigeons over enemy lines that you were sometimes close enough to observe. But in this new war, the challenge was much greater. Pearson wanted to see if pigeons could make it all the way from occupied Europe, over the Channel or North Sea and back home to England. The challenge of getting the pigeons to the target zone in the first place could be solved by dropping them from planes rather than balloons. The chances of their return home would depend entirely on the skill of the birds.

Pearson pressed his case, against considerable resistance. His old service MI6 (officially designated the Secret Intelligence Service, or SIS), which recruited agents to provide information abroad, was dismissive. It thought so little of the prospects that it said it wanted absolutely nothing to do with the idea and refused to co-operate. But Military Intelligence – based at the War Office and reporting to the Army, separate from MI6, which reported to the Foreign Office – eventually relented. It was a long shot but Columba, as the service was christened, offered the tantalizing chance to establish contact with untapped sources which Britain could reach by no other means. Pearson was appointed officer in charge of the Special Continental Section of the Army Pigeon Service, and soon a grandly titled 'Special Section (Carrier Pigeon)' team was set up in the Royal Corps of Signals. He would organize the logistics. Any messages that arrived back were to be sent on to a Military Intelligence team at the War Office. This meant Columba was rooted in the Army and not in the RAF – a source of abiding tension.

The first experimental pigeon drops took place at the end of 1940. Pigeon owners were told as little as possible about why their birds were needed. Early trials focused on how to transport the pigeons, and whether 'head down' or 'tail down' was better to avoid tail feathers being frayed. By January, a new container made their journey somewhat more comfortable as six birds were dropped from a Lysander plane at 130 feet. The parachute opened perfectly and the landing was gentle, but the container rolled over two or three times after reaching the ground. The pigeons did not appear 'unduly frightened', it was noted. They were given two minutes to recover before being liberated. Visibility was poor, so the birds circled for nine minutes or so trying to get their bearings before heading off to Aldershot. They covered ten miles in about fifteen minutes.

By April 1941, Columba was ready. Each container would be attached to a three-and-a-half-foot parachute. On the outside of the container was an envelope with a questionnaire, some rice paper for the return message and – thoughtfully – a pencil, as well as a bag containing ½ lb of pigeon food. Instructions explained that the parachute must be disposed of, and that the pigeon should be fed an eggcupful of corn a day and allowed to stretch its wings a little.

The questionnaire would be in French or Dutch, depending on the drop site. It included a run-down of the information Britain sought, compiled by the organizations that were customers of Columba's information – Military Intelligence, the Air Ministry, the Admiralty and the BBC. Top priority was anything on a planned invasion of England, followed by details of any troops in the area, enemy morale, significant addresses the Germans were using, the location of aerodromes, the effect of any recent bombs dropped by the Allies, and finally – in an example of early audience research – the extent to which people could hear BBC radio clearly and their views of the service it provided. It ended with the words: 'Thank you. Take courage. We will not forget you.'

Instructions showed how to correctly clip the small green cylinder onto the pigeon's leg again once the questionnaire had been filled in. Also enclosed was a copy of the latest edition of either a French, Belgian or Dutch resistance newspaper printed in London (or in some cases the *Daily Mail*). The idea was that this would provide assurance to the recipient that the bird had come from England and would return there when released.

No one was quite sure it would work. One official reckoned there were four options for a pigeon. It might not be found and simply die. It might be picked up by a local, as hoped, and a message sent back. Or it could be picked up by the Germans and dispatched back with a fake message. There was a final option – 'they may be picked up by a hungry patriot and find themselves in a pigeon pie.' The scepticism was shared by the RAF pilots who were asked to drop the birds. Perhaps reflecting their own sense of humour, they were convinced that any questionnaires that did come back would be filled with obscene messages from the Germans. But most, they thought, would not even get that far. 'In our jaundiced opinion most of them ended up on the dining table!' a pilot reckoned. That may have been true for many of the birds. But not all.

On the night of 8 April, an RAF Whitley took off from Newmarket making for Belgium on Columba's first run. The plane was attacked by anti-aircraft fire near Zeebrugge but the Germans on the ground were wide of the mark. The rear gunner on the RAF flight even managed to take out one of the searchlights. The plane headed for the Franco-Belgian border and the dispatcher was told to 'commence operations'. The pigeons in their containers were pushed out.

At Columba's HQ in the War Office, they sat and waited.

CHAPTER TWO

The Special Pigeon Service

I n the bowels of the War Office, two men waited anxiously for the first signs that Columba would work. Everyone has heard of MI5 and MI6, the domestic and foreign intelligence services that survive to this day. Some may even have heard of MI9 – the wartime department that helped Allied servicemen escape from behind enemy lines. But few will have heard of MI14 – let alone its subsection MI14(d) and its 'Special Continental Pigeon Service'. Perhaps that subsection's lack of fame is understandable, given that in 1941 it comprised a crack team of just two. But the little-known MI14 department to which those men belonged had arguably one of the most important tasks of the war. Its mission was the first priority of intelligence – to know your enemy.

As war began in 1939, the entire staff devoted to evaluating information about the Nazi war effort and its day-to-day battle strategy amounted to a grand total of five officers across MI14. The initial estimates of German military strength were way off the mark – Britain thought the Germans had 1,400 medium tanks, for example, when there were only 300. That kind of knowledge had serious repercussions when it came to understanding the fight that lay ahead, and whether and how it might be won.

Initially operational intelligence on the enemy sat within the department known as MI3, which was broken down into different departments. MI3b looked at Italy, while MI3c looked after the Soviet Union and was staffed by two Russian-speaking former brewers who despised the USSR more than they did the Germans, and who were consistently wrong on every issue. Intelligence on Germany became so important that it merited its own separate team, and so it was hived off to become MI14. Initially the small team consisted of a rich array of old-timers from the First World War who were not quite up to it, alongside a new batch of often eccentric but more talented younger men.

MI14 was itself broken up into smaller units populated by an array of oddballs and professors who had come into the military from civilian, often academic, life. One section investigated German strategy and intentions. Another, led by a former England cricket captain, looked at German anti-aircraft positions. A professor who had studied the Roman army's order of battle two thousand years ago now did the same for the Wehrmacht, the German army. As seems customary in British intelligence, MI14 even had its own Soviet mole in Leo Long. He had been recruited at Cambridge and was, unbeknownst to his colleagues, passing on their secrets to Moscow via Anthony Blunt. The teams worked all hours dealing with a constant stream of queries and requests from different parts of the armed services. Which were the best targets to attack in Germany by air? Where was this or that Panzer division? How was the Germany army reacting to British propaganda?

The specific task of MI14(d) was to understand the German occupation of Western Europe, including the deployment of its forces and the work of its secret services. And it was in this team that Columba found its home.

Brian Melland was the man in MI14(d) who oversaw Columba for much of its life. Melland was described by a colleague as a 'theatrical character'. He was a convivial figure, a brilliant comic and mimic round the dinner table, but could quickly go from fooling around to focusing on the most serious matters with a fiery moral indignation. The theatrical description, moreover, was literally rather than just figuratively true. He had been born in 1904 in Paris, where his father had fallen in love with a French pianist. After studying French and German at Cambridge, he had begun a rather conventional career with Shell Oil. But after five years he realized he was bored and gave it up for his first love, acting. He spent eight years before the war treading the boards as a professional actor in repertory theatre in Manchester. He was married in 1938 and his son was born just as the war was beginning. Melland had hoped to join the Navy, but when that did not work out he walked across the road to the War Office; thanks to his language skills, they put him straight into Military Intelligence. With his dark hair parted on the side he was handsome but also smart and diligent. He would become the leading British expert on the German military and the go-to man on German documents. This meant he became involved in interrogating captured Germans. In the summer of 1941, just as Columba was starting up, a secretary came in to his office. In her strong cockney accent, she said there was a 'Mr S' who Melland needed to go and see urgently. It turned out she meant Rudolf Hess – the Deputy Führer, who had just landed in Britain.

The second member of MI14(d)'s double act was L. H. F. 'Sandy' Sanderson. He had joined MI14 in January 1940 after being told he was too old to return to the Highland Division, with whom he had served in the First World War. However, the fact that he spoke excellent German would be put to good use. Lean and moustachioed, Sanderson had served as a business executive between the wars. 'He looked like a friendly, alert terrier,' recalled Noel Annan, who had been recruited into MI14 as a 24-year-old on New Year's Day 1941. It can be surprising to realize the inexperience of the quickly expanding British intelligence world in the early years of war. But in some cases, it drew in people who brought their own skills and experience. That was true of Melland and Sanderson.

The MI14 team, whose initial five officers would grow to more than fifty, lived what Sanderson called a 'troglodyte existence' in the bowels of the War Office. This created something of a bunker mentality, especially as their job was to immerse themselves in their enemy's thinking. They sometimes feared that their combination of dedication and humour might lead to confusion and even suspicion among those not part of the team. 'We had in this large basement a great picture on the wall of Hitler with the inscription "Heil dem Führer",' Sanderson later recalled. 'We often spoke German among ourselves for fun or practice and I wondered what a British passer-by in Whitehall would have thought, had he witnessed the scene.'

Amidst the humour and camaraderie, MI14's work could not have been more serious. In six weeks of May and June 1940, France, Belgium and the Netherlands had all collapsed. There was now one crucial question to which everyone from Churchill down to the man on the street wanted the answer. Was Britain next? Were the Germans about to invade? This became the overriding mission for MI14 in its early days. Few tasks could have been more important. The fear was that the Germans would simply follow through and head over the Channel. At the end of May 1940, an urgent telegram went to coastal stations saying all defences had to be manned through the night since an invasion was considered imminent.

From June 1940, Sanderson was made responsible for all Army intelligence relating to the invasion of the UK. He was the only officer on the 'Invasion Warning Committee' who worked full time looking for 'indicators' – warning signs that meant the worst was about to begin. The committee met every day at noon at the Admiralty and at one o'clock would issue a single sheet of paper that summarized all the intelligence which had come in over the last twenty-four hours. It aimed to answer three simple questions: where, when and how would an invasion take place? That piece of paper would go up to the Chiefs of Staff and to the Prime Minister himself. The team would hold their breath for any outbursts from Churchill. Normally, by 3 p.m. they knew they could breathe out if nothing had been heard.

In June 1940, Churchill had prepared the public for the possibility that German troops might arrive over the Channel. 'We shall fight on the beaches, we shall fight on the landing grounds,' he had promised a nervous but resolute nation. The message is now remembered as one of defiance, but it was also designed to prepare the public for what many then thought inevitable. Posters were put up for public consumption entitled 'If the Invader comes – what to do and how to do it'. The advice was simply to stay put.

The last invasion of the country had been in 1066, and Sanderson felt the public had no idea what total war would be like as ravaging armies moved across the British countryside. 'Confusion and bewilderment might have led to disaster,' he believed. 'We felt that if we held out for a week we should do well.' For all Churchill's talk, the secret British assessment was that if the Germans did manage to gain a foothold in Britain, there would be no chance of driving them back into the sea. The country would be lost. The Army was short of equipment and the Home Guard was not far off their depiction in *Dad's Army*, relying on pitchforks and golf clubs as weapons. Sanderson compiled a top secret handbook to help defending British forces know what to expect (although it did not remain so very secret, since someone managed to leave a copy in a public lavatory in Dublin and an Irishman handed it to the German embassy). The Army prepared an emergency pigeon service which would provide communications for defensive lines if all other links between HQ and forward units were cut.

There were also farcical attempts to undermine German morale. English phrase books were dropped by air upon German troops in France containing what seem comical phrases such as 'We are sea-sick – where is the basin?', 'See how briskly our Captain burns!' and 'Why is the Führer not coming with us?' But there was little hiding the fact that the situation was desperate. If the Germans seized the moment, it might all be over.

On 16 July 1940, Hitler issued Directive No. 16, ordering his armed forces to prepare plans for Operation Sealion – the invasion. The German navy had been considering the challenge for close to a year. They reckoned if they could get an initial ten divisions, or about 110,000, men over a bridgehead they could drive west of London to cut the capital off, forcing its surrender. German spies reported back to the High Command details of coastal defences between Dover and Brighton. The Germans also planned their own deception operation – as the British would later manage – in which they would feed false radio traffic and intelligence to make it look as if a landing was about to take place in the north-east of England to send defending forces the wrong way. The German D-Day was initially planned for September 1940.

The job of Sanderson and the MI14 team was to provide warning. They had said an attack on the Low Countries was probable. But they had never spotted any signs that it was actually beginning. Britain had been completely blind to the attack on Norway as well. The fear that there would be no warning when it was Britain's turn haunted the team at the War Office. They were convinced Germany had completed all the necessary arrangements.

The British had no spy inside Berlin who could tell them when the order was given, so Sanderson's job was to scour whatever scraps of intelligence he could get his hands on to find any so-called indicators. For instance, the Germans would need barges and other vessels to carry troops across the Channel, and so any sign of increased activity at ports in Belgium and France might be a give-away (there were plans to bomb the ports if sufficient warning was received). Every moment mattered and might make the difference between the country's survival and its capitulation.

The sources Sanderson and MI14 could turn to for insights into German plans were scant. The intelligence picture was parlous. The pickings were so slim that at one point MI14 were instructed to see if an astrologer and water diviner, 'Smokey Joe' from Yorkshire, might be able to help. The Enigma decrypts from Bletchley Park would eventually transform understanding of Germany's actions, but at the start of the war that effort was only just beginning and was yet to bear much fruit. In the dark early days there were only two real sources.

The first was age-old – human intelligence, courtesy of MI6. But their networks were an absolute mess at the start of the war. In November 1939, two MI6 officers had fallen into a Nazi trap and been captured at Venlo on the Dutch border. They were interrogated, with the result that much of the secret service's work in Western Europe was compromised. The Nazi thrust through Belgium, the Netherlands and then France had compounded the disaster for MI6. No one had expected that those countries would collapse so quickly and so no one had prepared for the gathering of intelligence through underground networks under occupation. Almost all of MI6's existing networks had been rolled up and it had to start virtually from scratch. Dansey and MI6 were all too aware of the pressure they were under to deliver – especially since they now had competition from the newly formed Special Operations Executive (SOE), which was making a lot of noise carrying out orders to 'set Europe ablaze'.

The reputation of MI6 – fuelled by thriller writers even then – might have been fearsome, but the reality did not always match up. Brain power was often lacking, as the emphasis was on a kind of schoolboy cunning. Hundreds of reports from MI6 regularly passed through Sanderson's tray in a single week, but many were likely to be rubbish. Some of the reporting Sanderson saw from MI6 was 'quite ludicrous', he thought. One report in 1940 suggested German troops in Norway were training to swim ashore wearing green watertight suits and had been heard practising on Scottish bagpipes. There was absolutely no reliable source in France reporting anything to MI6 until late November 1940.

Belgium, with its busy ports, was always likely to be a key staging post for an invasion of Britain. But MI14 was unconvinced by the reports that came in during the early months of the war. 'Unfortunately, neither the agent in Belgium nor the agent in France inspire full confidence,' the team noted of MI6's offerings. 'The agent in Belgium may be described as enthusiastic, as well as painstaking; his frequent reports are alarmist in tone (some of his prophecies have already been disproved), and he has provided very few identifications.' Along with the French agent, the two 'can only be classed as among the least reliable of our whole body of sources'.

A second source of intelligence for MI14 was new. Aerial reconnaissance was just emerging. From photographs taken at a height of 30,000 feet, Sanderson recalled, an interpreter in one case was able not only to see a football stadium on the ground but also provide a useful match commentary, reporting that during the interval of nine seconds between three photos, the team at the end closest to a gasworks was being severely pressed by the other side as the opposition moved the ball a good twenty-five yards forward. MI14's specialist would use photos to count the number of barges at Channel ports and look for changes. But there were limits to what could be seen from the skies. Interpretation by analysts was often tricky and filled with ambiguity. Bad weather sometimes meant there were many days when no flights could be made. The irregular timing of reconnaissance missions also made it hard sometimes to know from the pictures obtained what was changing and why. Movements on land were harder to spot than those of ships, since they often took place at night. There was also the risk of reconnaissance planes being shot down.

Air reconnaissance and 'special methods' – a code for intercepts – might provide indications, but agents were the best means of reporting German intentions and identifying what the signs meant. There were at least fourteen ports that the Germans might use. Since August 1940, MI14 had been pressing MI6 forcibly to try and have agents placed in these ports with some means of communication, but so far it had failed to deliver. There were people in occupied Europe willing to help, and Dansey and MI6 were trying to drop or land agents into Europe to contact them, but the going was slow.

The biggest problem with human intelligence sources (other than the reliability of the source itself) was the delay before the information arrived in London. Getting agents in and out at the start of the war was difficult and dangerous. Radios were in their infancy and so intelligence often had to be smuggled out by hand, passing from courier to courier. This meant it could take months, and by the time it arrived an item of intelligence which might have once been valuable could be out of date. One MI6 officer complained that although he was receiving lots of reports from Belgium, the information 'has been so old that they have become valueless'. The average time it took in the middle of the war for an agent's report to reach MI6 was nearly a third of a year. This was frustrating to analysts in London hungry for intelligence to help inform their decisions and improve their understanding of the enemy's capabilities.

★ ★ ★

In the summer of 1940, the Luftwaffe had begun its campaign to destroy Britain's defences – first targeting the RAF itself and then, in what became known as the Blitz, the capital city and other targets. In Plymouth, Bert Woodman watched as incendiaries rained down on the city, anti-aircraft guns roared in response and tracers lit up the sky. As local pigeon supply officer and also an ARP warden, he found his pigeons in high demand, as police needed them in order to communicate when the telephone lines went down. The damage was fearful. 'The bomber will always get through,' pre-war Prime Minister Stanley Baldwin had warned, and for a while it was feared he might be right. As war approached, desperate ideas had been thrown around to stop raids at night, when it was much harder to spot incoming bombers, one serious idea being to floodlight the whole of southern England. Technical intelligence on Germany's weapons – especially in the air – was vital.

MI6 as a whole was sceptical about pigeons as a method of gathering intelligence, but one person who worked at its headquarters would become Columba's greatest champion as he struggled to combat Germany's aerial power. He was not a spy but a scientist. When war began, Reginald Jones – usually known as R. V. Jones – was one of those impatient new men who would rise fast because he understood how much warfare had changed. Jones, from a middle-class background in South London, had by the age of seventeen built a radio set that could pick up transmissions from Australia. He was ambitious and difficult to work with, but he knew what he was doing.

As fears of invasion gripped the country, Jones was sent from the Air Ministry to MI6 as a scientific adviser in its Air Branch. His mission was to detect as early as possible any new German weapon that might change the course of the war. Panic had gripped the intelligence community when Hitler made a speech claiming he had a secret weapon against which no defence could stand. Jones was ordered to find out what this mysterious weapon might be. MI6 files were crammed with wild rumours of 'death rays'. One inventor had been paid by MI6 to see if he could live up to his promise of developing such a ray, but his invention proved only useful for preserving fruit. Eventually, Jones asked for a new translation of Hitler's speech that had started all the fuss. He discovered that the context of the word for weapon (*Waffe*) had been mistranslated; what Hitler was referring to was his 'Luftwaffe' or air force, against which no one could prevail. His inquiries though had taught him two lessons. First, the spies barely understood science. And second, the Germans knew the war in the air would be pivotal and were far ahead in utilizing the latest technology.

Jones found the old hands at Bomber Command complacently arguing that the use of their standard flying instruments along with a quick glance at the sky was enough to find targets. Jones did not make himself popular when he asked why, if this was the case, so many British bombers flew into hills during practice flights. And when German bombers began their onslaught, they seemed uncannily accurate – at least compared to the British – in finding their targets. What followed became known as 'the Battle of the Beams'. Through a series of clues and intelligence leads, Jones was able to work out that the Germans had discovered a successful way of guiding their bombers by means of radio beams, which the planes were able to follow. Aged just twenty-eight, Jones found himself briefing Churchill in the Cabinet Room, rebutting hostile questioning from those round the table who doubted his ideas (including his former tutor, who was the Prime Minister's scientific adviser). But he won the argument, and Britain began developing counter-measures by broadcasting their own beams to confuse the Germans' navigation. At the same time, the development of radar helped the RAF scramble to meet the German threat as the Luftwaffe began their campaign against Britain. It was the start of a scientific cat-and-mouse game that would last throughout the war.

Jones's forte was solving intelligence puzzles. In his hand would be a jigsaw piece that looked curious – say, a report of some kind of unusual German activity. First he had to find other pieces that might fit alongside it. Jones described an intelligence analyst as like a human with various senses – eyes in the sky in the form of aerial reconnaissance, ears listening at Bletchley, hands that could reach out from the Secret Service. When the ears heard an unusual noise, then the eyes would turn towards the sound to find out more. Jones was hungry for every snippet of intelligence that might help him understand German technology but, as with MI14, the sources were scant. Pigeons would play their part.

The RAF's victory in the Battle of Britain meant the summer of 1940 passed without invasion. The Luftwaffe had proved a fearsome weapon but not, as Hitler had claimed, one against which it was impossible to prevail. The German navy had insisted that air super-iority was a vital prerequisite for invasion. Nor had there been enough time to prepare the right type of craft to transport the Wehrmacht over the Channel. But the leadership of MI14 remained convinced that invasion was likely in 1941.

Their job of detecting preparations was complicated by a German decision to keep up the constant menace of the possibility of inva-sion, so as to maintain pressure on Britain. This meant Germany was ensuring that activity was visible and that fake intelligence was passed to Britain through military attachés and other channels. As the spring of 1941 began, the fear that German landing craft would soon be arriving on the British coast was still real. Sources reported details of preparations such as the training of parachutists, and even the intensive manufacture of gas. By May 1941, MI14 were still seeing reports of a possible invasion, with June to August appearing to be the most likely time. Reports from Belgium talked of the training of troops wearing British uniforms and the possible construction of barges.

The reality was that Germany had backed away – but no one in London knew that for sure, partly because the intelligence picture remained so poor. Details of the German military in Belgium and the Netherlands remained 'very unsatisfactory', the Director of Military Intelligence told MI6 in February. 'We have no confirmed evidence of the number of divisions located at any time in these countries … With invasion more than likely at any time after a month from now this is a most serious situation.'

From the spring of 1941, there was a new source for the analysts in London – Columba. For Brian Melland and Sandy Sanderson at MI14, Columba was not a source whose reports were passed on to them like the human intelligence of MI6. It was their own source. Rex Pearson looked after the logistics, but Melland and Sanderson were given the job of overseeing the operation. They were the ones who decided what questions would be asked in the questionnaire; in what areas the pigeons would be dropped; and who evaluated the material when it came back. They were able to handle the resulting intelligence direct. And – most remarkably – it was intelligence so fresh you could almost smell it. It would be in their hands within hours or days of someone observing something.

Two days after the initial drop in April, the phone rang at the War Office. On 10 April the first bird had made its way home to Kent. Columba message number one was phoned back to Melland and Sanderson at the War Office at 10.30 a.m.

The message was from a small village called Le Briel in the commune of Herzeele in northern France, not far from the Belgian border. It might have been short but it contained real information. 'Pigeon found Wednesday 9th at 8am', it began. 'The German troop movements are always at night. There are 50 Germans in every Commune. There is a large munitions dump at Herzeele 200 metres from the Railway station. Yesterday, a convoy of Horse Artillery passed towards Dunkirk via Bambesque and another to Hasebrouck. The Bosches do not mention an invasion of England. Their morale is not too good. The RAF have never bombed these parts. They should come to bomb the brick works as the proprietor is a …' The next word is written up as 'illegible' by the translator, but one wonders if that was actually to avoid the blushes caused by a cruder word the Frenchman might have used about a collaborator.

And then the message ended with one of those phrases that spoke of something in the spirit during those dark days in France. 'I await your return, I am and remain a Frenchman.' It was signed 'ABCD34'. This was precisely the type of intelligence the team had been after. It was a good start, a relief for the team who had backed Columba.

That same day at 3 p.m. came message number two, this time unsigned, from Flanders. 'There are only a few troops here and no petrol dumps, but yesterday some artillery arrived and the men say they are going to Yugoslavia where other troops and wagons are also moving.' Columba was working, although it took another nine days for the next message to arrive.

The next drop took place on 6 May and was less successful. One message simply brought greetings from West Flanders. Below was the slightly forlorn comment: 'Through a mishap this bird lost the questionnaire en route as did a number of others which have returned empty.' Another from the same batch mentioned some aerodromes but, as would often be the case, provided too little detail to locate them.

Resistance is often portrayed as a stark choice. A choice between a life of danger on the run or one of collaboration. But in reality, it was a much broader spectrum. People could and did resist in small ways and large. That was evident from those who chose to take the risk to send a message back via Columba. Some of those early messages were short – 'No troops here' was all one said, without even saying even roughly where 'here' was. Others wrote just a few lines with a plea for help, while making clear the individual understood the risks involved. 'Although this may cost me my head if one of the damned Boches saw me take the bird to my house, I will release the pigeon again with information for you,' they wrote.

Most pigeons were found early in the morning by farmers tending their land. The messages sometimes showed daily rural life continuing as if war had barely intruded. 'I found this pigeon on the 6th early in the morning while I was cutting clover for the animals and I have looked after it well and given it food and drink and am now anxious to know if the little animal reaches its loft … Hoping that I have possibly rendered you some service.' Often the finders were illiterate or unsure of what to do and would confide in a local priest, schoolmaster or someone else whom they trusted. That was often when the best intelligence came.

In some cases the pigeons found their way to people already trying to organize some kind of resistance. In July 1941, a writer said he was part of a group of eleven patriots in a position to give important information. A parachutist who had recently been dropped above Carpiquet in Caen was safe and sound but the person who had sheltered him had been denounced and was going to be shot. 'From now onwards we will take direct action against such person in striking down anyone who betrays,' they wrote. Columba was revealing that there were many in Europe who wanted to do something – some were willing to send a short message back, while others were already looking for ways to do more. There was potential there to be tapped.

Food was one recurring theme. The Germans took around 70 per cent of pre-war food production and the results were severe.

Messages spoke of hunger and starvation. One writer in May said the pork butchers had all been closed because all the pigs had been sent to Germany and there was precious little other meat. 'If it lasts much longer we must starve,' one Belgian wrote, 'try to free us as quickly as possible.' In Brussels a writer said that the rations for the previous month had been 5 kilos of potatoes plus 225 grams of bread per day: 'too much to starve but not enough to live.' Potatoes were being requisitioned to be sent to Germany, they wrote, so people would dig them up and eat them before they were ripe. There were complaints of some French peasants profiteering and selling on butter and eggs to the Germans at high prices. Also evident were signs of small acts of resistance. One writer in Flanders recorded that a local farmer had hung a dead hen outside with a written note on it saying he would rather his hens were dead than lay eggs for the Germans. (The same author ended his message with the phrase 'I do hope this is not a German pigeon'.)

A few weeks after Columba began, a message recorded that everyone had heard the 'startling news about Hess' – the Deputy Führer who had landed in England on some kind of bizarre mission in May and was now in custody. The Columba message noted it had made a 'big impression on the Boches'. Another said that the German soldiers tried to listen to the English wireless to hear what had happened and did not believe the claims on German radio about the Deputy Führer's mental illness. The morale of the Germans was not always good. One message that summer reported that sixteen pilots near Passchendaele being trained at an aerodrome were imprisoned for not flying, while one had actually taken off with his aeroplane and fled. Another writer talked of his conversations with the German soldiers. 'When we talk to a soldier he dares to give his view they are all tired [of the situation] – but then he keeps looking round to see if another soldier is not approaching for they have no confidence in each other.'

One pigeon from Folkestone was found by a fellow pigeon lover in northern France. The English pigeon 'could hardly have come into better hands', he wrote in a detailed message tinged with sadness. He provided a long note full of details of life and of whatever movements he had seen, including the location of German telephone exchanges. He suggested that the Germans were convinced the British would not dare try a landing and could easily be defeated if the British did come. He did not want compensation for his efforts. He was just serving his country. But there was another reason. 'This is a means for me to avenge myself for my son, whom they have killed.' His son could not be replaced, but he did say that after the war he would like to replace all his own pigeons, which had also been killed.

Each pigeon was an act of resistance, however small – the risk of a life for the chance of contact with distant Britain. A bond was being created between the sender of a message in a small rural village and the official reading it in London's War Office. But could Columba provide real, hard intelligence, more than just scraps and colour? The first sign that it might arrived in June.

Top of the list of questions to which Melland and Sanderson wanted answers was whether the finder of a pigeon knew anything of possible plans for the invasion of England. The seventh Columba message pointed to just that. 'The attack on England will occur very soon, unforeseen and terrible,' it warned in spring 1941, saying ships were being prepared in the Grand Canal in Belgium and four new aerodromes would be completed in the next few days. Docks which had been bombed were being repaired. Sanderson would find pigeons among the best sources for invasion intelligence, sometimes noting when they corroborated other sources or failed to back up reports from MI6 agents whom he was not sure about. 'Valuable reports continue to arrive by pigeon,' the official indicator's document noted, adding that the troops did not hold out much enthusiasm for the possibility but that large-scale exercises still seemed to be taking place. In May and June 1941 sources were still suggesting that an invasion was possible, and that exercises were occurring and logistics like barges being put in place.

A pigeon from Cambridge fell in Huines near the Channel coast on 14 June 1941 and was liberated from Pontorson on the 17th. It had an unusual journey back. It was found in Penzance on 20 June. A military officer opened the message and 'with great zeal' translated it himself. It took a further three days for it to be transmitted by a wireless officer to the War Office, leading to an angry letter explaining that in future any pigeon container found with a coloured disc was to be sent immediately by dispatch rider.

The annoyance arose because that message from Pontorson – Columba message 19 – was one of the first to show what the operation might be capable of achieving, especially when it came to the challenge of warning of possible invasion. It contained rich detail of troop movements out of Brittany and the use of nine motor barges near Mont St Michel for embarkation practice. It pointed to an airfield at Caen where the planes were housed in specially camouflaged hangars. Details of anti-aircraft positions were given, and the writer offered specific suggestions of where to bomb. They also warned of fifth columns in England, having heard a drunken officer say that they were dropping parachutists in English uniform who spoke the language. There was even a special instruction centre in Brest to train them. He also wrote that a letter the previous day from a German officer to a female collaborator had indicated that an invasion was to come about next week. This was precisely the kind of information Sanderson was looking for.

The author was highly motivated. 'The population here is 95% with you and hopes for deliverance. They vomit Darlan [the French admiral who collaborated in the Vichy regime] and his clique of traitors; we are ashamed to be represented in the eyes of the world by such a band of bastards. There are some "swine" here too, as everywhere but I've got them listed.' The author went on to name the specific hotel keepers at Mont St Michel who 'fight each other as to who shall make the most fuss of the Boches'. This scandal should be broadcast, he suggested, on the BBC, which he said he could hear very well. On Sunday, 15 June, he reported, there had been violent riots in Rennes when the people tried to commemorate those who died in the fall of France. The Germans and the police drove back the crowd to the Place du Palais where the Marseillaise was sung 'with great fervour' and accompanied by cries of 'death to Ripert' – the prefect nominated by the Vichy government to the area. Reprisals had come thick and fast afterwards, but the plan was to repeat the demonstrations on the night of the 17th – the very night the individual was writing the message. He ended with 'Vive La France, Vive L'Angleterre and Vive de Gaulle'. The writer, who signed himself Arvor 114, asked for more pigeons and gave a specific location in a marsh near a railway line.

The Columba team analysed the message carefully. It was unusually detailed. How, when travel restrictions were in place, could someone living in Pontorson be in a position to report on events as distant as Caen in one direction and Beaumont-Hague in the other? Could it be a plant? They went through the details paragraph by paragraph. The troop movements, they judged, matched those of message number 18 and the train movements also seemed about right. The claim of poor morale in the area was supported by an MI6 source. Other information was considered fairly likely to be true or 'sensible'. They carefully examined the request to name certain collaborators on air. Could this be an attempt to implicate genuine members of the resistance? 'On the whole, we think not,' was the verdict.

One or two points were considered unlikely to be true, but the writer's wide-ranging knowledge could be explained by travel entailed in his job or by information being passed on from others. That would be similar to the way MI6 sources often reported, and 'the information he has supplied us is certainly well up to their standard,' the Columba team noted. The decision was made to consider the message valid and drop more pigeons in the marsh where they had been requested.

On 2 July 1941, the results from Columba's initial foray were written up. Over three months, 221 birds had been released over Flanders, Normandy and Brittany. Forty-six returned, 19 with messages, 17 of which contained information. And this information had already shown its value. The six messages from Normandy and Brittany helped identify two German infantry regiments and also the movement of troops away from Cherbourg and Brittany. This was especially interesting since there had been few such indications from MI6 sources. What was particularly special about Columba was that intelligence would be in the hands of those hungry for information within hours of a message being written. This was unique among sources of intelligence, and the freshness of the information was something London would frequently marvel at. 'I think this form of intelligence is most valuable and has great possibility and should be encouraged,' the Deputy Director of Military Intelligence wrote. It was noted that it was an economical operation. The RAF planes were going across the Channel anyway and the main contribution was that of the pigeon owners themselves, who gave of their time and their birds freely. Columba was up and running. And within days of that first summary of its efforts, its most important message would arrive.

CHAPTER THREE

Leopold Vindictive

The Debaillie family gathered in the large building in Lichtervelde that doubled up as a grocery store and a family house. A local farmer had found the pigeon in the field that July morning in 1941 and his wife had brought it to them hidden in a sack of potatoes. It was just over a year since the Nazi war machine had swept through Belgium and the farmer had taken it to the Debaillies because he knew they were patriots. But now the family had to decide what being a patriot really meant.

Their task was initially to decide the pigeon's fate – and perhaps with it, their own. The decision was far from easy. The three brothers, Gabriel, Arseen and Michel, and two sisters, Marie and Margaret, deliberated over what to do with the bird. Two of the brothers differed. Gabriel thought it best not to get involved. It was true the family were 'patriots' who hated the Germans, rather than 'blacks', but they had never engaged in any overt act of resistance. The risk was too great. They had too much to lose. But Arseen felt the need to act. He was the most ambitious of the brothers and the keenest to take risks. The pigeon had come to them with a call for help and they should not turn it away – it was their duty. Even though he was the youngest brother, he got his way. Margaret, the younger of the sisters, backed him, whilst her elder sister Marie was more cautious.

Once the decision had been made, there was no reluctance or dissent on the part of the other members of the family. They were and remained united. Their father, the founder of the business, had died a few years earlier and the siblings were a close-knit family who ran the concern together and knew they could trust each other. Spying would be a family affair. But what were they actually going to do? They knew that to make the most of the opportunity that the pigeon had brought their way, they needed help. And so they turned to two friends. One was Hector Joye from Bruges, who spoke English and loved military maps. The other was a Catholic priest, Father Joseph Raskin. The Debaillies knew Raskin through another brother of theirs who was a missionary in China. He had been taught by Raskin and had invited the older priest to stay with the family before the war. The priest had become a frequent over-night house-guest, with his own regular room. The two sisters, Marie, aged 48, and Margaret, nearly 40, were particularly devoted to Raskin. In turn, Raskin was a friend of Hector Joye, having presided over his wedding. So the circle of trust between the friends was complete. This was the way many early resistance groups were born – not as soldiers or spies but as groups of friends who felt such deep anger at the occupation of their homeland that they were willing to accept the risk of trying to do something about it. The bonds of friendship offered trust and some degree of protection but this often had to compensate for a lack of experience in the world of espionage against a formidable enemy.

Within a day of the pigeon's arrival, the budding spy ring had gathered in Lichtervelde. Joseph Raskin would be the central figure. For all his outward trappings of a priest, it was as if everything in his life up to this point had prepared him for his career as a spy.

Raskin had been born in 1892 in a comfortable, detached house in Stevoort, a village of a few hundred families who all knew each other. His father had become a teacher and then principal of a local primary school. Joseph was the eldest of eleven siblings – the one they all looked up to and idolized. Culture and Catholicism were the defining characteristics of a family who would pray, sing, draw and read poetry together. From the time he was a small child and grabbed a rattle or moved to the piano, it was clear Joseph had a love of and gift for music. But the church came first. The headmaster of Joseph's school had a brother who was a missionary and his letters from far-off lands would be read out to the pupils. That inspired Joseph to follow in his footsteps, and in 1909 he left home and joined a Belgian missionary organization called CICM – known as the missionaries of Scheut or Scheutists, after the neighbourhood of Anderlecht in Brussels where they were based. It was a strict regime – up at 5 a.m., asleep at 9 p.m., the hours between filled with prayer, study and communal living. Family visits were limited, but when Joseph returned for a few days' holiday in 1912, his siblings found he had grown up. He was still not tall, and he continued to walk with a slight stoop that had been there from childhood, but now he proudly sported a short beard, much to their amusement. Joseph and his youngest brother would become missionaries and another brother a priest. Two of the sisters would become nuns.

When Germany declared war on Belgium on 4 August 1914, Raskin had just been ordained a sub-deacon, but he was not immune from the patriotic fervour sweeping Europe. God and country were intertwined for many at that time. But Raskin's family were about to see up close what war really meant.

The family had moved to the town of Aarschot a few years earlier, when Raskin's father became a school inspector. It was a small town but would become famous both in Belgium and Britain for the events of August 1914. As the Belgian army retreated, two Belgian regiments acted as a rearguard in the town and held up the German advance, much to the anger of German commanders. In their house, Raskin's younger siblings hid in the basement and sat fearfully around a single lamp, occasionally going upstairs to peek at events from behind the curtains. When the town fell, twenty captured Belgian soldiers were shot and thrown into the river. That evening a German brigade commander was shot while standing on a balcony on the square – perhaps killed by the ricochet of a bullet fired by his own soldiers. But the Germans treated the death as an assassination and began heavy reprisals aimed at what they saw as resistance from the local population. Men were rounded up in the marketplace and then taken to a field where they were executed. In all, 156 civilians were killed over the following days. Women were said to have been victimized. The events in Aarschot were pivotal in what came to be known in Britain as 'the rape of Belgium', an episode ably exploited by British propagandists as their country responded to the attack on neutral Belgium by joining the war. The British spy and author William Le Queux wrote graphically of babies being bayoneted and women savaged by the German army in the town. British newspapers were filled with lurid, exaggerated accounts, which in turn helped galvanize support for war amongst the British public. And so Belgium's war quickly became Britain's.

The first time Joseph Raskin was arrested as a spy by the Germans he was entirely innocent. Priests and primary school teachers had been mobilized as stretcher-bearers and ambulance men for the Belgian army. Raskin was put to work at Beverlo ferrying wounded soldiers around. As word reached him of events in Aarschot, he became desperate for news of his family. At 6 a.m. one Sunday he put on civilian clothes and got on his bike. A German patrol stopped him. A young man cycling in civilian clothes was highly suspicious at a time when the Germans thought every Belgian was a spy. Worse, Raskin did not have his Red Cross papers. The case seemed open and shut. He must be a spy. The sentence was death.

Raskin was taken to a fort that was being used a prison. In a car on the way he noticed that the papers regarding his case were lying on the seat next to him. He slowly edged them underneath him and then to the other side. As the car hit a particularly violent bump, he pushed them out of the side without the Germans noticing. Upon his arrival at the fort, the authorities were lost without the paperwork. In the chaos of the early days of the war, there was nothing that could be done. He would just have to be kept there.

In December 1914, he made his escape from the fort. The family story was that he hid under the hay in a wagon on the return journey of a farmer who had come to deliver food. The reality may have been somewhat more prosaic. German papers indicate that they had been unsure what to do with him, and because he had made himself useful as a cook he was allowed to travel to Stevoort in early December. It was from there that he may then have made his escape, perhaps indeed in a hay cart. Whatever the real story, he was out. He then went to the front lines, again as a stretcher-bearer. This was dangerous work, sometimes involving making one's way right to the front to load up the battered and broken bodies of soldiers and then suddenly having to drop into the mud as German bullets whistled overhead.

He enjoyed a ten-day break in London – not knowing that a quarter of a century later the course of his life would be shaped by his attempts to reach out to that city once again. During that brief visit, there were visits to churches and museums, but Raskin had one problem. With his lively blue-grey eyes, rippled dark hair and infectious laugh, he was handsome, and he wondered how to explain to the local girls who seemed interested in him that he was actually a chaste priest.

When he returned to the front, Raskin's peculiar skills opened the way for him to become something else – an artist-spy. Since his youth, he had been good with his hands as well as his head. He would repair clocks and generally tinker with things. He was particularly talented as an artist. So now, he began to go to the front line, initially of his own volition, to draw what he saw in front of him. The result were beautiful drawings of the trenches and German positions.

When his superiors in the Army saw the drawings, they immediately recognized their military value and they were passed up the chain of command to the highest levels. Raskin was dismissed as a stretcher-bearer and turned into an *observateur* – a kind of intelligence gatherer. He worked across the Belgian front, just north of Ypres where the British were fighting. It was a bleak, apocalyptic landscape. The Germans had initially advanced over the River Yser but the Belgians flooded the land to halt their advance. The Germans then partially retreated back over to one bank. The land in between was laid waste by a mix of water and war. Sometimes the two sides were close – at a place called the 'trenches of the dead' they were little more than twenty metres apart. But in other places, no man's land was far wider and less clear-cut. Shredded trees stood amongst pools of muddy water with the remnants of farm life surrounding them. The Germans had established advanced observation points and positioned snipers in farmhouses across the desolate flooded plain.

Raskin would travel out at night. He would give a password to a sentry and then sleep for a while in a shell hole. At first light, as the birdsong began, he would begin to observe and sketch. Two men would accompany him and provide covering fire if needed. At night, when he had seen enough, he would return. Back in his bureau he would take the rough drawings he had made and turn them into something approaching art. There are beautiful pencil drawings and watercolours of the view from the Belgian side facing the Germans, with each German position carefully marked out. The largest, most dramatic panoramas he made are two feet long, works of art crafted from the art of warfare.

It could be dangerous. In mid–May 1916, he spent three days and nights without food or water trapped in an abandoned flour mill, full of rats, surrounded by Germans. Another time, a bullet shattered the lens of the periscope he was using.

Sometimes in the picture is what appears to be an abandoned building. Look closely and you can just see the eyes of a German soldier hiding in a gap ready to shoot. A caption notes that this was a permanent German observation point. There were also bird's-eye views of the same front lines, again marked out in precise detail with map coordinates and distances. One map has arrows indicating not just the direction in which the Germans shot from each trench but how regularly they fired; for instance, whether they only fired in response to Belgian fire or just at night. At one farmhouse, it is noted that every time the Belgian artillery began firing, a German periscope popped up. At another point it is remarked that the Germans at night sent out patrols so close they would throw grenades into Belgian trenches.

Senior officers were impressed. One went so far as to put his signature on one of Raskin's pictures, which led the priest to realize he needed to sign them himself to prevent others taking credit. In spare moments, the priest's humanity shone through – he would make small pencil drawings of an exhausted fellow soldier having a cigarette or devouring a chunk of bread. And so, without knowing it, the first stage of his preparation for the English pigeon scheme was complete. Raskin had learnt the fine art of military intelligence – which information was of value, and how to present it.

When the war ended, Raskin became, as he had always intended, a missionary-priest. After celebrating his first mass, he boarded a white steamboat for the long journey to China. Pictures show the young man lounging on a bunk with fellow priests in second class and out on deck with a mixed group of priests and nuns, all smiling as they head out on their adventure. On the long voyage, Raskin would play the piano in the evening or draw pictures of fellow passengers. They made their way via Port Said and the Suez Canal, Singapore and Hong Kong before finally reaching China. A photograph shows Raskin in Shanghai, dressed in local clothes, learning how to write the local language. And here was the second phase of his preparation for the pigeon operation – the ability to write beautifully and precisely as he learnt how to trace Chinese characters. The quality of his handwriting would win him a prize in Shanghai and would later be useful in condensing information into a tiny space.

His training complete, Raskin made his way to the heights of Mongolia. There he worked at a school training Chinese priests. He became the closest thing to a local doctor, dealing with ulcers in particular. 'I have more consultations than confessions. That is not good,' he would joke. The part of Mongolia he lived in was the Chinese equivalent of the Wild West. Local warlords would rampage from village to village, looting and killing. Raskin organized the villages so that a signal fire could be lit from a hilltop which could be seen by watchers in other villages to warn them of attack.

After the best part of a decade in China, he was summoned back to Brussels by the chief of the Scheut mission house. His varied skills meant he was needed as what was called a 'propagandist' – a travelling preacher who would go from town to town spreading the word about the missions to raise funds and persuade people to support the organization or become missionaries themselves. In his diary in Mongolia, he wrote of his disappointment at the order to return. 'My soul is sad as if it has died.' But then, in Latin, he adds: 'Your will be done.' Back in Belgium, he would criss-cross the country giving talks about China. Here was another stage in his preparation – building up a wide-ranging network of friends, supporters and contacts.

As the years passed, Raskin became rounder and seemingly smaller, the lines on his face deeper. But still he could attract people round him with his laugh and his story-telling.

And then war came again. Another invasion of neutral Belgium. But this war was not like the one before. This time there were no trenches or static front lines. German tanks, accompanied by the terrifying air power of the Luftwaffe, ripped through Belgium in a matter of days. Raskin acted as a chaplain to soldiers in Torhout during the dark days of May 1940, visiting the nearby Debaillie familiy in Lichtervelde wearing the uniform of a captain. Within eighteen days, Belgium was occupied by the Nazis. Initially, the Germans promised that if there was compliance there would be no need for brutality. But for many Belgians that did not quell the desire to do something. Unlike France, it was a country that had been occupied and invaded many times before. There was almost an ingrained sense in many Belgians of how to find ways to live under occupation while also getting the better of the occupying power. For some that meant small acts of defiance, for others something more risky. Resistance would emerge faster and with greater strength in Belgium than in many other countries, including France. But it would still take time to recover from the shock of defeat and for resistance to become organized. For the first few months, the urge lay largely dormant and barely visible, like a flower bulb beneath the hard earth. By the summer of 1941, it was ready to push through into the open.

This was how resistance often emerged in occupied Europe. Not as the result of activity from London on the part of British spies or exiles, but as groups of friends spontaneously coming together because they hated the German occupation and were desperate to do something about it. People would hang out in cafés, conspiring, starting to collect what they knew might be useful information about the enemy they could see around them, but often with no way of transmitting it to Britain. Now, suddenly, Columba presented some people with an opportunity. Could it act as a link to the nascent resistance?

And so, after a year of occupation, Raskin received the phone call from Arseen Debaillie. The next day he was there in the corner shop, in front of him the pigeon and the two sheets of rice paper, along with a patriotic appeal from Britain for help. He never had any doubts about what to do. Raskin, Hector Joye and the Debaillies made their decision. They would answer the call. They agreed amongst themselves that they would split up over the coming days to maximize the amount of information they could collect.

Arseen, the youngest of the brothers at the age of 27, nevertheless looked the oldest with his broad chubby face and glasses. He was the chief enthusiast and spy amongst the three brothers, although the family would work together as a team, its members supporting each other. Arseen spent the next few days driving along the coast and through the neighbourhoods around Bruges taking notes. Gabriel, thirty years old and the most anxious of the three brothers, would maintain the cover of working the family's growing business – supplying animal feed at Roeselare. But he also went with his brother on a car trip to the coast, ostensibly for business but also to see what information they could gather.

Michel, the gangly pigeon fancier, tended to stay at home. The pigeon had arrived just a fortnight before his thirty-second birthday. As a child he had suffered from rheumatic heart fever, a condition which had left his heart damaged and required him to see a doctor every few weeks. His comfort, like those in Britain who had supported Columba, were his pigeons. Sundays were the days he liked to spend with his birds, often racing them at Lille. He kept them in a large, sideboard-sized coop on the ground floor of the building.

Hiding the British bird carried risks. Immediately after occupying Denmark, Norway, the Netherlands, Belgium and France, the Germans imposed controls on pigeon owners that were progressively tightened. In Belgium, the country's Fédération des Colombophiles had to keep a register of every pigeon, and the Germans checked this regularly. Pigeon keeping would later be forbidden entirely in a number of districts in Belgium and northern France, matching closely the places where the Columba birds were dropped. Sometimes messages brought back by Columba pigeons revealed the pain this brought to those who loved their birds. One message reported a plea to British owners: 'Rear a couple of young pigeons for me. I have to kill all mine.' But Michel and the family were willing to take the risk. It was not too hard for him to hide one special bird that was different from the others.

Marie and Margaret, the two sisters, had their role. They would maintain the appearance that everything was normal at the shop, chatting away with customers while looking out for any signs of trouble. Raskin would go back to Brussels and gather material from there. He would also ask friends whom he trusted for any information they had.

Hector Joye had the time – and the cover – to travel. He had been a soldier in the First World War but while in the trenches he had been gassed by the Germans and was now invalided. During that war he had met Louise Legros, who worked for the Red Cross. Her well-to-do family had been opposed to their relationship, but one person who had encouraged them was Raskin. Theirs had been the first marriage he had conducted as a priest. Louise's career had taken off and she had been appointed the director of a girls' school in Bruges. The family lived in comfort in a house that was part of the grand, Gothic school complex. A family picture shows Raskin enjoying a lunch in comfortable surroundings with the Joye family all around – his visits were always the occasion for a party, events that the Joye children enjoyed.

Handsome, with swept-back fine dark hair, round glasses and a trim moustache, Joye was another tinkerer with similar hobbies to

Raskin. He had once been a carpenter, had designed a heating system for some nuns and had built incubators for the eggs of the pheasants he kept. His finest invention, his son would remember, was a special Christmas tree mobile containing a mechanism that enabled the angels to fly around. As a former military engineer, he was fascinated by maps and fortifications. Like the others, he was a devout Catholic for whom serving God, king and country were as one. Because of his health, Joye had permission to travel up to the coast to get fresh air. With little to do (not least in comparison to his wife), Joye was enthusiastic at the opportunity to turn his hand to espionage.

The amateur spies needed to work fast. The pigeon could not be kept too long. But they were determined to make the most of their opportunity. The amount they collected was astonishing. They fanned out to discover what they could on their travels. Joye was the busiest. There was a particularly interesting chateau near Bruges occupied by German troops, he knew, and airports, and ammunition warehouses and factories producing material for the Wehrmacht. He would see what he could find. Arseen knew about the Bruges–Ghent railway line and a local aerodrome near their house, and could give details about the local population. Marie and Gabriel provided specific information about a nearby chateau. Raskin meanwhile seemed to have a stack of information ready to go. Some of this came from the network of contacts he had built up in Brussels, many of whom were women he knew through the church, and who were beginning, if haphazardly, to gather details of what they observed. Raskin tapped these friends for information. One letter to 'my good Father' from those days provides information about a German storage building in Brussels, and includes a drawing as well as details of munitions.

After days of frantic gathering, all the precious intelligence had to be squeezed into the two tiny sheets of rice paper the British had supplied with the pigeon. Raskin's experience as a cartographer in the First World War and from China as a calligrapher meant he would be the one to write it all up. The Debaillies had just the place for him to work. Their corner shop was the public face of the business, where customers could come in and out. But the building was more of a mini-complex. There was an adjoining house where the family lived. And then, round the back of the shop, past a small, closed interior courtyard, was a structure used as a warehouse to store all the goods. At the beginning of the war, fearing German bombs, the family had built a windowless concrete room towards the back. Relatives would send their children out to Lichtervelde because it was thought less dangerous, and this room was their hiding place. The room had a bed in it where the children could sleep at times of danger, and a strong lock. It was what you might today call a safe room. It was perfect for spy-work.

A niece called Rosa, the daughter of another sister, was only eleven but was staying with the family. She was fond of Raskin. He wrote a rhyme, 'Doosje van Roosje' (little Rosa's little box), on her sewing box and taught her to play the accordion the family had given him as a gift. She remembers Raskin was there more than normal during those days of July 1941. Something different was happening, she knew, but no one told her what it was. That would be too risky, in case she talked. She does remember one of her aunts – Marie, she thinks – heading into the safe room more often than she normally did.

At a table underneath a light in the safe room, Raskin pored over the drawings and details that came in, the spider at the centre of a web of espionage. The drafts of the maps and notes have miraculously survived, pages and pages of them, different types of notepaper and different handwriting reflecting the many hands that contributed to the work. Space was tight. Everything had to fit on two pages, and that meant decisions. Like a ruthless sub-editor at a newspaper, Raskin scribbled out lines with black pen where he thought the detail was superfluous. A line about the Germans taking too many potatoes from people is crossed out, as are general complaints about poverty and life being expensive. That was not hard intelligence, he knew. The next line of a draft, though, stayed in for the moment – how the Germans went from carriage to carriage on trains taking food from people, sometimes even slurping raw eggs. Also retained was a line about how people were taking the copper of phone cables between Bruges and Ghent. A line about how people longed for the English and would point out the black-shirts was scribbled out. Raskin was careful to stick to the exam question – answering the specific queries that the pigeon had carried to them and not inserting extraneous information.

The pigeon sat just round the corner at the ready. For Raskin, it may have represented something more than just a messenger. The pigeon – referred to by its proper name, the dove – has a powerful symbolic role in Christianity. When Jesus was baptized by John the Baptist, 'the Holy Spirit descended on him in bodily form like a dove. And a voice came from heaven: "You are my Son, whom I love; with you I am well pleased."' This dove had come to Belgium from Britain; but perhaps, for Raskin, it had come spiritually as well as literally from above. Faith, duty and spying were all intertwined in the priest's mind.

Material was still coming in as he wrote. The Germans were strengthening their positions on the coast, fearing an English attack. A new division had been installed and there was extensive activity from planes as well as lorries bringing in fuel. Advice was offered as well – if the British were planning to invade then they should avoid delay in moving through the country or the Germans would take all the able-bodied men to Germany. No one had any idea that it would take three long years for the British to arrive.

Finally, he was ready. Raskin took his pen and began the final draft, working through the night of 11 July. He sat at the desk with a magnifying glass to ensure he could cram in as much detail as possible on the tiny sheets of paper. The quill of his pen was precise. Every space would be put to use. A last-minute item of intelligence came in on the morning of 12 July at five minutes to eight. Joye had come through Bruges railway station and had seen a ground air defence post moved. That detail was added in the corner.

Raskin finished with a flourish and a special touch. 'Our seal!' he wrote in the bottom corner, adding a symbol which he intended to be a unique identifier of the group and its future messages. It was a circle with a curly L sitting in a V, one side of the V becoming either a cross or a sword, depending on how you interpreted it. Their name was Leopold Vindictive.

There was no more space. The message was ready to fly. The two pieces of rice paper were carefully folded up and placed inside the green cylinder that had come with the pigeon. The cylinder was slotted into the ring around the pigeon's feet and twisted to secure it.

The group then did something extraordinary, an act contrary to every rule of spycraft. They picked up their family camera and took pictures of the pigeon, and of the message being pushed into the green cylinder. But then, even more extraordinarily, the three brothers and two sisters stood for a family portrait in the inner courtyard. Marie and Margaret are in their aprons, Michel and Gabriel in working shirts with braces. Arseen looks somewhat smarter. At first sight, it could be any other family picture, but look more closely and you can see that Marie, the elder sister, is holding a resistance newspaper, Margaret is holding what looks like a white sheet – the parachute. Arseen holds a pencil, Gabriel the British intelligence questionnaire, and Michel proudly clutches the pigeon. And in front of them, propped against a table with a white tablecloth, is a chalkboard – probably the board that they would normally use to display the latest fruit and vegetable prices for shoppers. But this time, on the board are written the dates of the bird's arrival and departure, its ring number and the phrase 'Via Engeland' to mark its destination. And at the top are three capital V's – the symbol of Victory, which earlier that year the BBC had called on people to daub on walls as a symbol of defiance.

Taking the photos was a mad, risky and amateurish thing to do, and yet it spoke of something that is impossible to criticize – a deep pride in their work of resistance. Raskin is not in the picture, most likely because he was on the other side of the camera taking it.

There was one final picture to be taken. Michel climbed up onto the roof, where there was an oat-attic. This was the place from which he normally released his pigeons, and so it may have looked less suspicious than it sounds to anyone watching him. Up there he opened his cupped hands and released the bird; a picture captures the precise moment. At 8.15 a.m. the bird rose high into the sky and circled for a few moments to get its bearings. Then it made for the Channel and for England. In seven hours' time it would have escaped Nazi-occupied Europe and be home in suburban Ipswich.

CHAPTER FOUR

Arrival

It took thirty-six hours from Michel's release of the pigeon on the roof in Lichtervelde for Raskin's elegant message to reach the hands of British intelligence. The pigeon, which had left Britain on 5 July and was released from Belgium at 8.15 a.m. on 12 July, flew over the English Channel and was back at its loft in suburban Ipswich – about ten miles from the coast – by 3.30 that afternoon. All it knew was that it was home.

Loft owners had been ordered to keep a sharp eye out for the return of a bird, even though they were told nothing of its mission. As soon as a pigeon arrived, they were to take off the Bakelite cylinder, which was about the size of a pen top, attached to its legs. Well-to-do owners might have their own phone and be able to call the special number. But otherwise a child might be sent on a bike with the cylinder to the local pigeon supply officer, who would call in the delivery. Then they would wait. In some cases the roar of a motorcycle dispatch rider could be heard outside in just twenty minutes. The cylinder would be handed over and rushed to London. The orders were strict – cylinders were never to be opened by anyone until they arrived at the War Office. This was partly because the contents were secret, but more so because they were often written in pencil and folded up so tight that they had to be carefully extracted without being ripped or smudged. If that happened, someone would have risked his or her life for nothing.

On the morning of 13 July, the message arrived in London at Room 25 of the War Office. Sanderson and Melland were both on duty that day and early in the war they opened the messages themselves. 'I well remember the fascination of opening these little tubes and unwinding the thin slips of paper which they contained,' Melland later said. When the pigeon service first began, it was feared that the tiny cylinders might be booby-trapped. And so Melland and Sanderson would open them with a sheet of protective glass in front of their faces in order to guard against any 'tricks'. Fortunately, they never had a cylinder explode in their face (although Bert Woodman in Plymouth said he heard that at least one cylinder had been found with explosives). Once a cylinder was open, they would translate the message into English, enter its details in a log book and then distribute the information round other departments.

Both men would always remember that day in July. There was nothing to suggest that message number 37 would be anything different from the other thirty-six they had opened in the previous three months. Melland pulled the first thin sheet of paper, nine inches square, out of the canister. The writing on it was tiny. But the closer he looked, the more astonished he was. Decades later, when Sanderson reflected on the intelligence that he had seen, he would remember this as the 'most exciting and romantic' of all the reports that passed through his hands.

Melland and Sanderson realized instantly that this was something different, something special. The writing spread across the two pages was small but perfectly formed, the accompanying maps expertly drawn. It felt as if every single millimetre of the two sheets had been used to cram in as many words as possible.

The author of the message had helpfully recommended placing the sheets against a dark paper and using a magnifying glass after cutting it up and reassembling it so that it was all in the right order. As the team set about typing out a report, they found that the transcription came to 5,000 words and took up twelve pages. And what was in those pages was gold dust.

'This message is from Leopold Vindictive 200', it began in English, although the bulk was in French. It was the specificity that was so remarkable, comprising precisely the type of intelligence the team had dreamed of when they started Columba. The text referred to maps and specific symbols employed to indicate hidden German emplacements and munitions depots. An old submarine base was now being used to repair boats and was carefully concealed by shrubs and buildings. Bombs would need to fall over an area of 200 by 300 metres to destroy it, Leopold Vindictive noted. The writers had explained when to attack to avoid civilian casualties. The Shell depot near Neder-over-Heembeek should be bombed 'without delay' – a map indicated exactly where the key parts of the oil facility lay. Another important fuel dump was protected by concrete and so would need larger bombs. 'At any price spare the town of Bruges,' they had written with a care for the architectural beauty of the city.

There were also precise battle damage assessments of recent British raids in Brussels. 'Our congratulations to the airmen who carried out the bombardment in the Rue de Birmingham on Thursday 26th June and the Rue de l'Intendant on Thursday 10th July. They were marvellous hits which filled the whole city with admiration.' The first bomb had wiped out a building where parachutes were made while hardly damaging neighbouring houses. Nine Germans were killed, while fifteen civilians had been only slightly wounded. The second had taken out a crucial German factory. More targets were suggested – a palace inhabited by hundreds of Germans, the location of an officers' club, another building 'swarming' with Germans day and night, a garage which only worked on German vehicles, other barracks. The location of a wireless jammer opposite a hotel was also given. Brussels aerodrome should be targeted, but the writers warned that most of the structures around it were actually dummies. Nearly a dozen other factories in the region were also named as playing a role in the German war effort.

In the case of one telephone exchange, the team revealed it was guarded night and day with a machine-gun post in fear of a British attack by parachutists. The Germans were supposed to call the local Civil Guard for help in the event of an attack, but Leopold Vindictive revealed that the guards were in fact quite hostile, suggesting they might take their time to arrive. 'I have this from a man on the spot,' they wrote.

There were also assorted items of intelligence about daily life. Dropping propaganda leaflets was fine, but little packets of chocolate should be dropped with them to show there was no lack of food in England, they recommended. The impact of British bombers and the recent German attack on Russia had worried many of the local 'black-shirt nationalists' who supported the Nazis, and many had begun deserting. The blackshirts trained every Sunday morning between ten and twelve at one set of barracks. Bombing them, it was suggested, would discourage any more would-be recruits, and there was no anti-aircraft gun for several kilometres around the site. The Germans had been trying to recruit locals to fight the Russians, claiming it was a crusade of Christianity; leaflets should be dropped to say that those who joined would be held accountable.

Sanderson in particular found message 37 invaluable. The most significant section of the message answered the question that haunted his waking hours – what were the invasion plans? Belgium was seen as a launching point, with barges potentially heading out from Ostend, Antwerp and other ports. Britain had its own plan to carry out a sabotage mission (codenamed Claribel) to sink barges, damage rail lines and cut power and communications once the first signs of invasion were spotted, although the department tasked with carrying this out had to acknowledge in the spring of 1941 that it had no contact with or knowledge of any Belgian resistance organization and its attempts to send in a radio operator to make contact had failed.

Leopold Vindictive had real information. A map showed the chateau of Tillegem near Bruges and revealed that it was the central communications installation for German High Command in the whole sector. The picturesque medieval chateau, surrounded by a moat, had been undergoing work for four months and Leopold Vindictive were sure it was to be used by an admiral as a base for the invasion of England. It was nearly – but not quite – ready, they reported. One hundred and fifty special technical staff used the latest radio apparatus from Siemens. *Nobody* (the word was underlined by the writer) was admitted to the chateau except for the chiefs and the specialists. Anybody approaching would be shot without challenge.

The site's true purpose and importance had been unknown to anyone in Britain. If an invasion appeared imminent, it could now be targeted by bombers or even by commandos; equally, it would need to be dealt with if Britain wanted to launch its own attack on the Belgian coast. With that in mind, Leopold Vindictive described how the crucial junction for the communication cables was outside the building in concrete shelters nine metres underground, protected with reinforced steel bars. An 11,000-volt current was provided by a cable lying along the road. Further specific details were supplied of the cables and of the antennae, which sat fifty metres back. In order to identify this from the air, the writer explained, a photograph could be taken between eight and ten in the morning from a particular direction he marked on the map. This would make the complex easier to spot. Usefully, it was pointed out which anti-aircraft positions had not yet had their guns installed. In all, fifty separate locations used by the Nazis were detailed; in some cases the paper gave more than a dozen items of note about an individual position.

The professionalism of whoever sent the message was obvious. It asked for a response that would indicate, by referring to letters ascribed to different sections, what in the enclosed information was unknown to the British, and in which areas more information was still wanted. The information, the author promised, was 'thoroughly reliable'.

But who could have produced such treasures? And could they really be trusted? There was no name other than the codename, and nothing else was known except that the team consisted of a staff of three principals and several secondary agents. But to establish his bona fides, the author did offer an unusual means of verification. 'Identify me as follows – I am the bearded military chaplain who shook hands with Admiral Keyes on the morning of May 27th 1940 at 7.30 a.m. Ask the Admiral please where he was exactly at that moment with my most respectful greetings.'

Admiral Roger Keyes was quickly approached by Military Intelligence. He would have remembered the meeting with the chaplain well. It was a day he would never forget. Keyes was close to King Leopold of Belgium, a friendship forged in the First World War when the sailor had led the Dover Patrol and the Belgian royal family frequently crossed the Channel. Leopold, then a boy, had attended Eton during term time, occasionally lunching with Britain's royal family, but returning to serve on the front line during vacations. His father had stayed in Belgium as king during the war, a decision popular in the country.

Leopold had come to the throne in 1934 when his father died in a mountaineering accident. His reign would prove troubled and started darkly. A year after coming to the throne, Leopold was driving in Switzerland when he lost control of his car and it crashed, killing his wife Queen Astrid. By that time, his old friend Keyes had retired as an admiral and been elected to Parliament in Britain. A buccaneering character, although not necessarily of the highest intellect, Keyes had long been a close friend of Churchill, one of his allies who warned of the dangers of appeasing Nazi Germany.

On 7 May 1940, Keyes played a leading role in the unseating of Neville Chamberlain as Prime Minister when he stood up in the House of Commons, wearing his uniform with six rows of medals, and launched a passionate denunciation of the government's ineptitude. Three days later, on 10 May, Belgium was attacked without warning at dawn. The country had desperately clung to its neutrality in the hope it might offer protection. But this proved a false hope. Its armies were poorly prepared for the onslaught of the formidable German war machine. That morning Keyes received a telephone message summoning him to see Churchill. At that moment Churchill was still First Lord of the Admiralty, but by the end of the day, with Neville Chamberlain ousted from Downing Street, he would be Prime Minister.

Churchill told Keyes to put on his uniform and fly to Belgium to act as his special representative to the King. Keyes had already made a number of visits in recent months on behalf of the government to take advantage of his friendship with Leopold (who was also commander in chief of the Belgian army). By 3.30 that afternoon Keyes was flying out of Hendon to Amiens, escorted by three RAF Hurricanes. That night he drove to a blacked-out Brussels, passing lorries and buses full of troops from the British Expeditionary Force, who were suddenly in a precarious position as the German military tore through the country at frightening speed.

Keyes saw the King the next morning at an old moated fort twenty miles outside the capital. Leopold was not yet forty, with a gentle face and curly hair. Nothing had prepared him for what his country was now going through and his ability to lead his nation would be sorely tested. The shell-shocked King told Keyes that as the invasion began a hundred German troops had landed atop a fort and placed bombs down ventilators, putting it out of action, whilst all but seven Belgian aircraft had been destroyed by German attacks on the country's aerodromes. Much to Britain's annoyance, the King had clung too long to the false hope of neutrality; now he pleaded for British air support to avoid what he called 'an absolute debacle'. But Britain's military leadership was also in chaos and coordination with the French and Belgian armies was abysmal.

Initially, the British Expeditionary Force advanced. The *Times* correspondent in Belgium travelling with the BEF (a certain Kim Philby) told a colleague 'it went too damn well'. The reason was that Hitler was trying to draw the British army into a trap.

Over the next two weeks, Keyes's telegrams back to Churchill, who was by now Prime Minister, carried increasingly dire news. The Germans were moving fast – so fast that the MI6 station in Brussels lurched from complacency to panic and had to burn its papers in a furnace and hurl its teleprinter out of the window to ensure nothing was captured, while MI6 officers took turns to guard the office with a long-barrelled Luger pistol. The Germans strafed military and civilians alike as they fled the cities by road and rail. Suddenly, the British force realized they risked being trapped and began to make a desperate retreat under pressure; London was initially less than honest with the Belgians after the decision was made for the BEF to abandon the country, using the Belgian army as cover while they headed towards the coast. They made their way, amidst scenes of chaos and confusion, for Dunkirk where hundreds of boats, including the 'little ships', a flotilla of fishing vessels, pleasure craft and lifeboats, waited to ferry them back over the Channel.

But where did the mysterious chaplain come in? Raskin's royal connection dated back to the First World War. He had played music in a convent whose services were attended by Queen Elizabeth and had been introduced to her. After the Queen's husband, King Albert, died in 1934, she became Queen Mother to King Leopold. She had arrived with the King at the castle of Wijnendale on 24 May. She asked her chamberlain, Comte de Grunne, to organize mass to be celebrated in the private chapel.

Raskin was acting as chaplain to soldiers in nearby Torhout and was asked to come to the royal court as personal chaplain to the royal family. For the next few days, he would be picked up by car and taken to see them. The journey for Raskin on Sunday, 26 May had been perilous as the Germans bombed the roads from the air, leaving craters and burning vehicles. Raskin took confession from the royal family and held a heavy, solemn mass at 10 a.m. by the Baroque altar under the domed vault of the chapel, which was located in the castle's highest tower. His words and the singing of the congregation must have been spirited to overcome the sound of enemy aircraft flying overhead. Afterwards, Raskin spoke to the King at length, one to one. Leopold looked and sounded like a man not quite able to cope with the huge burden that lay upon his shoulders. He asked for the priest's prayers as he agonized over the decision of whether to stay in a country that was collapsing or flee to Britain.

Raskin was a decade older than the monarch, and sought to stiffen the resolve of a man who seemed to struggle with the burden of kingship. He stressed to Leopold the tight bond between faith, the nation and the monarchy, in which the priest himself fervently believed. Raskin said he was sure the nation would support the King. The monarch should face the plans God had for him with patience and confidence. As he finished speaking, the King, trembling slightly, clasped Raskin's two hands. 'Chaplain, I understand. I understand,' he said.

The day Admiral Keyes had met Raskin was the darkest. Everyone knew the end for Belgium was nigh. Churchill was desperate for the King to flee to Britain and not make any kind of deal with Hitler. The question for Leopold was whether he should lead an army in exile or stay with his people. He wanted to emulate his father, who had won support by remaining. But he did not understand this was a different war. His ministers either fled or wanted to leave, and were angry as he indicated he would stay. They were to arrive in London in dribs and drabs, but the bad blood from those days in May and the legacy of the choices each individual made would bedevil Belgium for years to come.

At 6 a.m. on 27 May, Keyes received a telegram from King George VI of England to pass on to his fellow monarch, asking him to reconsider his plans to stay. 'I do not feel that Your Majesty is called upon to make the sacrifice which you contemplate,' one king wrote to another. It went on to argue that the risk of being taken prisoner by the Germans and depriving his people of a leader was too great. Keyes gave the message to Leopold, who took it to his bedroom to read with Elizabeth. Leopold's view was that he had no choice. 'I feel my duty impels me to share the fate of my army and to remain with my people. To act otherwise would amount to desertion,' he replied.

A photograph – taken by the Comte de Grunne – shows the scene on the morning of 27 May. Outside the castle among the trees stand four figures in military uniforms, talking in two pairs. On one side is Keyes, standing with the King's aide-de-camp. On the other side King Leopold is talking to his chaplain, Joseph Raskin. The dark looks on all their faces make clear that they all know the end is at hand. This was the moment referred to by Raskin in the Leopold Vindictive message. He knew Keyes would remember it.

Keyes telephoned Churchill that day to give him the news of the King's decision, adding that the Belgians would not last much longer. At five that afternoon, the King told Keyes his army had collapsed and he was surrendering. Churchill made clear that a new Belgian government would be formed in exile to disassociate itself from the King and his decision to make peace.

By 8 p.m. Keyes knew he had to move fast to avoid his own capture. As his convoy crossed the country, German parachutists landed around them and opened fire. Keyes made one last plea for the King to leave with him. His decision to stay would prove to be a fateful one for the monarch and for his country. Leopold would now never be a unifying figure. At 10 p.m., Keyes left on a road crowded with refugees. By 1 a.m., he was at the coast and found a fishing boat with two sleeping men on board. With some persuasion (which involved rifles and the promise of money on arrival) he was soon sailing back to England, where by the following morning he was at 10 Downing Street to report the King's decision to an 'indignant' Churchill.

Churchill later claimed wrongly in Parliament that the surrender had exposed the British flank, when in fact the Belgian army's resistance had protected the British Expeditionary Force as it was evacuated from Dunkirk. But the public needed a scapegoat for the disaster and the Belgian king served the purpose. The British press poured vitriol on the King for what they said was a surrender without warning. Keyes himself sued the *Daily Mirror* for saying he had been 'bowing on Brussels carpets in a rat king's palace'.

The day Keyes had met the chaplain was the day Belgium was lost. In their short time together, a bond may have been forged between the Belgian priest and the British admiral – perhaps over the fact both had spent time in China before war. Raskin the following day had taken a bike from Lichtervelde and ridden in turn to Torhout and then to Bruges. In Bruges he went to the school house of Hector Joye's wife, which had become a field hospital, and met with the wounded. 'German troops in the city, sad rainy day,' he wrote.

The link to Keyes also explains the mystery of the codename taken by the spy network. Leopold was clearly a reference to King Leopold of Belgium. But Vindictive? It was a tribute to Keyes himself. In 1918, as commander of the Dover Patrol, Keyes had been given the mission of blocking the ports of Zeebrugge and Ostend. Ostend proved a challenge until Keyes sent an ageing cruiser with orders for its crew to sink the ship in the harbour entrance. That ship was the *Vindictive*. Now Raskin had named his spy network in honour of his own king and a British admiral.

For MI14(d), the link to Keyes served to emphasize their new-found source's credibility. 'Confirmation of the value and accuracy of message No 37 has been obtained from the GOC [General Officer Commanding] Belgian Army in the UK and Admiral Keyes has assisted in assessing the sender's bona fides,' the team recorded.

There is one odd fact though. Nowhere is the name Joseph Raskin recorded. Had Keyes recalled meeting the chaplain but not remembered his name? Or did MI14 want to keep the name of their new agent secret? Either way, it was by the name Leopold Vindictive that the spy network would be known in London.

When Rex Pearson saw the original message 37, he marvelled at the way in which the author had crammed so much into such a small space. For a man who had fought to create Columba, it must have been a moment of validation against all those who had been sceptical of using pigeons. The intelligence from Leopold Vindictive rapidly made its way around Whitehall. In July, 174 pigeons had been released in five operations, but the information they gathered had revealed only limited details of troop movements and concentrations and confirmed one or two weapons dumps previously reported by human sources. Without Leopold Vindictive it would have been a pretty poor return. But its report was of a different class, as was clear even to the sceptics of Columba.

Naval Intelligence had been pretty dismissive of Columba until it saw Leopold Vindictive's message. The Admiralty said it was a 'particularly good report' for its 'wealth of detail'. Two MI6 reports had suggested the possibility that the Germans might have a naval headquarters, but there had been no confirmation until Leopold Vindictive drew attention to the chateau near Bruges and for the first time revealed its role in invasion plans. 'Having seen such a detailed report as No. 37 it is clear that action should be taken' in the event of an invasion, Naval Intelligence noted. Further photographic reconnaissance was ordered on the sites mentioned in the report.

There had been questions about Columba and its value. Was the bizarre scheme really going to work? Message 37 put those concerns to bed. Keep it going, but under regular review, was the order from the top of Military Intelligence. Columba offered speed and relevance. It is not hard to imagine that for Claude Dansey at MI6, whose service had been one of the sceptics, there was a touch of jealousy that this strange sideshow had suddenly delivered results that gained the appreciation of the rest of Whitehall whilst he still struggled to rebuild his European networks. One of the many secrets that Dansey was keeping was just how little real intelligence his own agents had so far delivered.

Something else happened to message 37. It was shown to Churchill himself. Why? Churchill loved intelligence and asked to see fresh Enigma decrypts from Bletchley every day to help him guide the war. Significant as the specific details of the intelligence in message 37 were, though, there was no reason he needed to know the exact location of a particular ammunition dump, or even a naval headquarters. The real reason was different. The message from Leopold Vindictive represented much more than just a collection of useful facts. It represented the spirit of resistance, confirming to Britain's spies and leaders in that troubled hour, when they still feared invasion and when defeat seemed possible – perhaps even likely – that some of those living under the tyranny of Nazi occupation in Europe were willing to risk their lives to help. It was a sign of a spirit that Churchill hoped to inspire in the British people should the disaster of invasion ever befall them; a sign that out there in Europe were people who wanted to work with Britain and who stood ready should Britain be able to return to the continent to drive the Nazis back. All that was required now was for the two sides who needed each other so much to be able to communicate. A humble Ipswich pigeon had made that possible. Both sides were determined that this should be just the beginning. So now the question was, could they manage to get back in touch with the bearded chaplain?

CHAPTER FIVE

Listening

After the pigeon was released, Margaret and Marie sat by the radio in Lichtervelde listening intently. Every night at the assigned time they clutched pencil and paper, determined not to miss a word as they tuned their radio to try to pick up the erratic crackle of a signal. The elder sister, Marie, may have been more cautious but both were now committed. Their father, who had passed away, had been ambitious for all his children, including his daughters, and had ensured they had private lessons in French in addition to their native Flemish. That meant they could scan broadcasts in different languages for some sign that distant London knew they were there.

That the two sisters pressed their ears to the radio to make out the words was itself an act of resistance. The BBC's broadcasts provided a reassurance to those living in occupied Europe that they were not alone. The broadcasts encouraged them to defy the invaders and parodied the propaganda spouted by the Germans. For that reason, the Nazis hated the BBC for its subversive influence. Almost every member of the population listened. A German officer given the accurate time by a little girl on the street asked how it was possible she knew it was a quarter past seven when she had no watch. She replied, 'Don't you see? There is no one on the street. They are all listening to the English radio.'

When the Nazis raided a house in Belgium, one of first things they would do was check what frequency the radio was tuned to. The penalties for being caught were severe, especially if the Germans wanted to make an example of someone. The headmistress of an Antwerp girls' school was sentenced to five and a half years for permitting her pupils to listen to the BBC.

The Germans also did their best to jam the signal, which was why one of the items in the Columba questionnaire was about audibility. Responses saying which wavelength provided the best listening quality were hugely useful for the BBC's technical staff. The broadcaster's European Intelligence Director told MI14 that Columba was of 'the utmost value' thanks to the immediacy of its messages – often they provided feedback within a day or two of a programme's broadcast, faster than a letter might arrive today. 'Everything interests us but speak clearly and loud,' wrote one person in a Columba message, echoing the kind of encouragement BBC broadcasters continue to receive.

There was audience feedback not just in terms of reception but also of editorial content. 'My wife would like to kiss the well-known speakers, as they are so patriotic,' one writer from Pas-de-Calais in France said enthusiastically. A pigeon message from Brittany said a wife was cheered up by hearing her husband speaking from London and they wanted him to know. Sometimes there was frustration married with the enthusiasm. The V for Victory campaign started by the BBC in its broadcasts to Belgium caught on like wildfire. It led to the daubing on walls of a flurry of signs in what seemed like every village, as well as on the chalkboard held up by the Debaillie family in their picture with the pigeon. Churchill himself joined the act with his trademark two-finger V for Victory sign. The campaign encouraged ordinary people to feel they could resist, even if only in a small way.

The downside was that it created an expectation amongst many that victory and a British return to Europe must be imminent. 'You have announced your coming too long now. It would have been better to have done it and said nothing,' one person wrote in frustration. But the BBC did not only support the war effort by broadcasting news and information. It had a direct operational role in the clandestine world of espionage.

The greatest prize for those brave enough to send a message via Columba was the possibility that for a brief few seconds they would become the stars of the BBC broadcast by receiving an acknowledgement on the *messages personnels*. When this was required, a British intelligence officer would ring up the BBC and identify himself with a codename – rather bizarrely, for Belgium this was Napoleon Bonaparte and for the Netherlands Bing Crosby. He would then ask for a specific phrase to be broadcast, such as 'here is a message for Adolphe – the wine is warm' – which was meaningless to everyone else but acted as a coded signal for a particular group. The messages could be used to signal an upcoming drop by parachute, to establish the bona fides of an agent by proving they were in contact with London or to signal that a person – or information – had arrived in London. It was the last function that Columba used – offering the chance for an acknowledgement that a pigeon had arrived to be broadcast using a code provided by the writer.

For all those listening, the messages were a sign that somewhere out there were people taking risks who were in touch with Britain. For Columba message writers there would have been a real but clandestine thrill in knowing that a code-phrase they had scrawled on rice paper and attached to a pigeon was suddenly being read out from London.

Leopold Vindictive's message had asked for a response on the Dutch and Belgian BBC radio news as soon as possible. They did not have to wait long. The stunning intelligence haul had left the Columba team in London knowing they had something special on their hands. On 15 July – only three days after Michel had set the bird free – Marie and Margaret heard the answer to their prayer.

'Leopold Vindictive 200, the key fits the lock and the bird is in the lion's cage.' The acknowledgement was sent that day on the Dutch, Belgian and French BBC news services – all three to make sure. Now, in Lichtervelde, the band of friends knew that the crazy plan had worked. The pigeon tended by Michel had successfully crossed the Channel with their treasure.

The relief, joy and excitement were overwhelming. But the family may also have understood there was a cost. Their codename had just been broadcast across northern Europe. Thousands in Belgium would have heard it, and among the listeners would be the German secret police, hunting for resisters. The chase to identify a new band of spies had begun.

There was, though, another sign that their pigeon had got through. Towards the end of the message, they had mentioned a German radio station at Ichtegem, near Wijnendale, which consisted of a camouflaged wooden shed and two aerials. This was bombed by the British, creating what was described as a magnificent fireworks display. Not only had the intelligence got through but it was making a difference. From being powerless, it must have almost seemed as if the RAF were at the Belgians' beck and call, and that the Belgians were forward air controllers calling in air strikes to the targets they selected.

The BBC acknowledgement raised hopes that a fresh consignment of pigeons might already be on their way. The first part of the BBC message had consisted not of intelligence but of details for the next drop. That was because the group of friends were convinced that this bird had just been the start. They had so much more to offer and all they needed was the means to communicate it back to

London. The instructions to British intelligence were clear and precise. Leopold Vindictive needed more pigeons.

Raskin had written that he heard that up to ten other pigeons, in addition to the one they were setting free, had landed in the area on the same July morning. But all the rest had been handed in. Not because people disliked England, he explained, but because they feared Germany. So future birds would need to be dropped carefully. He was reluctant to put the exact location of the drop in the text in case the pigeon was captured and the Germans used it to trap him. So he told British intelligence to get a 1:40,000 military map of Belgium and find the point where Keyes would say he had met the bearded chaplain. They were then to place a ruler south-east from there along the axis of the main road. At the extreme east the ruler would meet the letter 'e' on the map, which was the last letter of the name of a village. The second letter of the name on the map lay over a field 300 yards by 300 yards square which was full of crops. That was where the new supply of pigeons were to be dropped. Planes were to avoid spending too much time in the air or else they would wake people, who would get out of bed to see what was happening. Nor should birds be dropped on Saturday night or Sunday morning, as people would be heading to church and it would be harder to hide them. The men had asked for a drop of three birds on 15, 16 or 17 July. 'We will do our best but failure is not impossible,' Raskin had written. 'We suppose also that you know that such relations are rewarded by death.'

Raskin had stayed in the Debaillie house in Lichtervelde the night after the pigeon's release and had taken the train the next morning. The pages of his small pocket diary from 7 to 13 July are all cut out as he tried to cover his tracks (he would also sometimes write in Chinese for the same reason). That left it to the Debaillie family to wait for the birds.

From sunrise on the first of the designated days, the Debaillies waited for the hoped-for delivery. Arseen had originally thought about using lamps to highlight the drop zone from the air. Gabriel and Michel talked him out of it. It was too risky. But when the brothers went for a walk in the early morning, doing their best to look natural, as if they were just ambling around, there was no sign of another container anywhere in the field. Their message had specified a three-day window and they waited nervously and walked the fields on each of the three days. But each time there was nothing. A disappointment. The first, but not the last.

The friends were moving too fast for Columba. Raskin had no idea about the logistics required in organizing a pigeon drop – why should he? The message had only arrived in Ipswich on 12 July. For MI14(d) to analyse it, verify it with Keyes and others and decide to respond by radio in two days was extraordinarily fast – a tribute to the importance of the message. But dropping fresh pigeons in a hurry required a level of coordination and cooperation that was a challenge for Columba. The delivery of pigeons was far less flexible than the Belgians imagined. They were dropped incidentally, as an adjunct to existing RAF Special Duties missions for the intelligence services, rather than on commission. Pigeons were low down the pecking order of intelligence requirements, way behind MI6. A flight needed to be carrying an agent over the right part of Belgium to allow for a drop of pigeons in Lichtervelde. That would be at best perhaps one in every half dozen flights of those that made it over the Channel. And the planes only flew during the full-moon period. In July, the last successful flight had been on the 12th, the day the message arrived in London. A flight on the 15th crashed, with eight of those on board ending up in hospital. After that the moon promised no light until August.

Here was Columba's weakness. Columba excelled at gathering ad hoc intelligence from villagers in Europe. But it was harder to use as a reliable, regular tool of communication in the way Raskin imagined.

MI14(d) were nevertheless determined to contact their new prize asset. One item of evidence in Sanderson's personal papers reveals the effort that went into following up the message. A photograph dated 21 July, and taken by an RAF plane, shows an aerial view of a patchwork of fields of different colours intersected by paths and roads. A scattering of fluffy clouds hang lazily above the fields. Sanderson's notes indicate that the RAF aerial reconnaissance team had been tasked to photograph the exact location suggested by Leopold Vindictive for the second drop of pigeons. They had found the field. The message from Leopold Vindictive said that if weather made the first drop time impossible, then the next occasion should be 30 or 31 July, or 1 August.

Raskin and his friends were not going to wait passively for the next pigeon, whose arrival they were sure was imminent. And so they simply got on with the business of spying. Drafts and notes of their work survive in a box kept by the Debaillie family: handwritten notes, maps and coordinates, details of factories in Brussels, of movements on the Belgian railways. As well as the information the group collected themselves, Raskin's many contacts in Brussels and elsewhere had been picking more up. All of it would be ready to go.

Raskin also needed to pass on an important item of news. He wanted to do away with Leopold Vindictive; not the group but the name. Raskin had gone to the royal court at Laken to speak to his friend and contact there, Comte de Grunne, the Queen's chamberlain. De Grunne knew about the espionage network and perhaps may even have aided it quietly. The name Leopold had been a tribute to the King, but when Raskin told the count he was horrified. Having stayed in his own country, the King was in a precarious position – a virtual prisoner under house arrest – and the use of his name for the purposes of espionage by a person associated with the court risked the assumption that this was a spy network with – quite literally – a royal seal of approval. 'It is as if the King himself is now a spy!' exclaimed the count.

And so a chastened Raskin decided he should change the name of his group. He wanted to call it 'John Victoire'. Raskin wrote out a message, stating that it was from Leopold Vindictive and requesting that in future, in a BBC acknowledgement at 19.00 in Dutch or 19.15 in French, Britain should respond to John Victoire, and that they were waiting for the next pigeons as stated in the original message. But how was he to get this urgent message back to London?

Raskin had always been a man in a hurry, and his impatience grew after the first window for a pigeon drop closed in mid-July. He needed to send the news about the name change to London. Pigeons were the best way of passing on maps and long, detailed intelligence reports, but radio was better for short, urgent messages. He was now desperate to find a working clandestine radio transmitter, both to announce the new name and also to try to hasten the arrival of the next pigeon. But radio sets were rare and dangerous. They got you killed. If the Nazis came through your door, you might be able to explain away a pigeon, but not a radio transmitter. The Germans were on the hunt for those using them. Especially in the early months of the war, a reliable, trusted radio transmitter was almost a mythical creature for those involved in espionage; to find such a rare prize would require a long tortuous path of whispered conversations and dangerous meetings, always with the risk of being betrayed by a double agent. But Raskin thought he knew someone. So he passed his message of the name change through his Brussels contacts to try to ensure it reached London.

Raskin's circle of contacts in Brussels, largely female, had been involved in sheltering airmen and had also supplied intelligence to the priest. The central figure was a woman known to everyone as

'Madame Roberts'. She had been born Anna de Bruycker, but had married a British man called Jesse Roberts from Blackpool. As soon as the occupation began, Madame Roberts had involved herself in helping Belgians who wanted to go to England. She helped hide two British servicemen for months, providing them with lodging, food, clothes and money. Raskin himself, it seems, was involved in helping hide people from the Nazis, these often being British servicemen who had not made it out at Dunkirk, or Belgian servicemen who wanted to leave for Britain. The details of Raskin's work on escape and evasion are hazy, although one note in the Belgian Security Service Archives from a woman says she and Raskin took food and clothes to the Forêt de Soignes for evaders who were hiding there, and that four evaders were tended for three months by 'Père Raskin and his group' in the forest and in cellars.

Madame Roberts was a friend of Raskin through his Catholic missionary network (which would increasingly become a spy network). As the war started Raskin had confessed to her that he had an ardent desire to help his country but was not sure how to do so. To think of Roberts and her friends as a formal resistance network would be a mistake. They were less organized than that name implies. By the middle of 1941, resistance was just beginning to build and establish itself in Belgium. Britain had not yet been defeated as some had expected. There was still hope. Food shortages and the conscription of workers were taking their toll. There were occasional strikes and small acts of sabotage. People who wanted to do things were starting to work together, but they were not yet organized into coherent networks. Rather they consisted of over-lapping groups of friends and contacts, who often lacked much understanding of the kind of security they needed to protect themselves.

As the second drop period approached at the end of July, Raskin, Joye and the Debaillie family waited anxiously, their prized notes ready to be transferred onto rice paper, the priest ready with his calligrapher's pen and magnifying glass. But on the morning of 31 July, the field again failed to yield a pigeon. Marie and Margaret listened out anxiously for an update on the BBC.

The sisters heard what they were listening for on two consecutive nights – 31 July and 1 August. The message was relayed on the French, Dutch and Flemish news services again. That was the good news. The bad news was that it still began with the old call sign and not the new name – confirmation that the radio message Raskin had passed on had not gone through. 'Leopold Vindictive 200 Allo Allo' it began. It said there was much appreciation for the bravery and volume of their efforts. But there was news of a delay, given in a coded phrase, 'The key is turning in the lock.' But when it came to the 300 square metres – a reference to the field indicated by Raskin – they would have to wait some days. Regarding the information, it said that the details marked 'A' – in other words information from the original message relating to the invasion plans and the chateau – were of the greatest importance. It also asked what was happening 3 km south-south-east of location B2. But there was a strange ending: 'Long live the courageous V of Lille and Nieuport.' This was a riddle to Leopold Vindictive. They were not in Lille or Nieuport. Was there some kind of confusion as to who they were? Had another group somehow adopted their name or their pigeons? Or were the British trying to divert any listening Germans from the group's identity?

In London, they were finally ready. 'With the help of photographic recce, it is hoped to check the information still further; in the meantime it has been possible to locate the exact site recommended by source for a further release of birds and this operation is taking place tonight weather permitting,' a note from Columba of 3 August reads.

At 3.35 a.m. the following day, 4 August, Ron Hockey took off with the RAF for Belgium on Operation Periwig. His flight plan took him on a path over the field mapped out by MI14(d). Searchlights lit up the plane and heavy flak headed his way as he reached the coast. The pigeons were released and he flew back above the clouds. But when they looked the next morning, the friends in Belgium could find no sign of a pigeon.

CHAPTER SIX

Battle of the Skies

I n the occupied Channel Islands a poster went up on 3 August 1941. It announced that Frenchman Louis Berrier, from the town of Ernes just south of Caen, had been shot by a firing squad the previous day. The poster stated that the punishment had been for a crime the Germans were already starting to worry about – the sending of intelligence by pigeon.

Above the skies, in the fields of France, the Netherlands and Belgium, and even on the cliff-tops of Britain, a battle was being fought that might be deadly both for Columba's pigeons and those who tried to use them. Only one in ten of the birds sent on Columba missions made it back alive. The frustration experienced by Leopold Vindictive in trying to obtain fresh pigeons was a mark not only of the inherent challenges of Columba but also of how much effort the Germans put into stopping it. Even though the operation had just started in the summer that Leopold Vindictive waited for its fresh pigeons, the Germans were already working to counter it. The challenges to ensure that the British birds first reached the hands of sympathizers and then found their way home with a message were immense.

Just one month after the beginning of Columba in 1941, reports had come from Courtrai, close to Lichtervelde, of birds falling into the hands of Germans rather than local sympathizers. Columba was in many ways an oddly un-secret operation. It was designed to elicit sensitive information, and yet its workings were anything but clandestine. From the start, the Germans could see the pigeons with their parachutes and questionnaires. The team at MI14(d) had a phrase for this level of awareness on the part of the enemy: 'The Germans are fully pigeon-minded and our continued activities can hardly make them more so,' it warned. It did not take long for Germany to develop counter-Columba tactics and become still more 'pigeon-minded'.

As with their defences against British bombers, the Germans developed a multi-layered defence against pigeons in this further battle of the skies. 'Our defence against the carrier pigeons was vast,' one German counter-pigeon expert boasted. Rewards were offered. An MI6 agent reported that a notice displayed in one Belgian town offered 625 francs to anyone who delivered to the authorities any pigeon dropped by the enemy; in other places, a sliding scale of rewards was on offer, the largest sums being available for a pigeon carrying a message.

As well as the carrot there was also the stick. The point of the Channel Islands poster was to issue a warning. Others too paid the price, and the penalties were always made public. A Belgian called Julien Ferrant was executed for trying to send messages by pigeon, while in Antwerp two Frenchmen were shot for the same reason. 'In future, the Courts-Martial will impose the death penalty inexorably in all cases of this nature,' a local newspaper reported. Fear had its effect on the local population. 'An Italian found one of your pigeons and killed it. The coward!' a message from Florennes in Belgium read. The Germans sometimes planted a parachute and watched it from a hiding place nearby, waiting to arrest those who picked it up; occasionally they even placed a booby trap underneath. Rumours began to emerge that the Germans were planting false pigeons to trap people. 'I do not sign because the Germans also drop carrier pigeons, which you must understand, take the messages to the kommandatur. Various patriots who wrote their names and addresses have been arrested,' read another Columba message.

The Germans actively hunted the birds. A Columba report from Loudun in France's Loire Valley said that many pigeons had fallen into enemy hands after a German observation post spotted the RAF flight passing overhead. An hour later 150 Germans arrived in motor cars, searched gardens, paddocks and roofs and went door-to-door asking for pigeons. Amidst arrests, four birds were found. News was brought back by one of the pigeons they did not catch.

The Germans targeted the birds directly in flight. A Columba report from northern France reported that there were 'marksmen on the coast endeavouring to shoot down pigeons from time to time'. The Germans had used snipers in both the Siege of Paris in 1870–1 and the First World War to try and take down birds in flight suspected of carrying messages, and similar orders were given again.

Just as in the past, the sight of a pigeon and the knowledge that it might have been carrying messages seems to have rattled the Germans. 'Considering the wide area covered, the dropping of our pigeons may contribute in a small way to a kind of a German-invented nerve war,' it was noted in London. A seed had been planted whereby the British began thinking what could be done to make use of this German fear of the pigeon; it would bear fruit later in the war thanks to British deception specialists.

Pigeons had many enemies, German snipers and hungry locals among them. But their most deadly foe was natural. Radar might have been arriving and the Spitfire fighting the Luftwaffe in the Battle of Britain. But in the battle of the birds it was the pigeon against the hawk. Hawks, and especially the peregrine falcon with its wingspan of three feet, were the pigeon's nemesis.

In action the falcon was a fast, vicious, carnivorous predator of the skies – part Spitfire, part dive bomber. If a pigeon crossed its path, the falcon would swoop down vertically at a staggering two hundred miles per hour and then at the last moment pull up to strike with its rear talons, sometimes with such force it cut the pigeon's head clean off. If it missed, the avian equivalent of an aerial dogfight would still take place between the two. In this engagement, the poor pigeon usually came off worse.

The Germans were swift to weaponize the hawk. Before the war, a British falconer on holiday in Germany had come across what he described as a set of 'princely mews' – the buildings used to house hawks – which was controlled by the state. The countless birds were, he said, looked after by a team of uniformed men who were exempted from regular military service. Hermann Goering, the man in charge of the German air force, was also the guiding hand of its hawks. An amateur falconer, he adored the imagery of being seen with the powerful predator on his wrist more than the actual work of training one. German hawks were bred, and were flown along the coast from Belgium, France and the Netherlands to catch and kill Columba birds as they headed for Britain.

British agents undercover in Europe using pigeons sometimes even witnessed first hand the power of the hawk. One British officer took two pigeons with him on a commando raid upon the coast of France. Radio silence was required for the operation, so the pigeons would be used to signal his arrival. He released them at 6.30 a.m., but as he watched them swirl above him in order to orient themselves, he saw a terrible sight. Hawks descended from the cliffs and swooped on his only means of communication with home. Both pigeons were dead within seconds. How many pigeons perished this way, and how many valuable messages were lost, is unknown.

A few brave pigeons did escape the talons of the falcon. Fanciers supplying Columba complained that their birds were returning with gashes. But the dangers from hawks sometimes lay closer to home, on British shores. One pigeon carrying a message from Pontivy with useful details of troops in the area was found by Pembrokeshire police after having been killed by a local falcon. A messenger pigeon called Mary, released with a message for the Army, came back after four days, ripped open on her neck and on the right of her breast by a British hawk. Her owner cleaned her up and tenderly put seven stitches in her. All this meant that Columba offered a new card for pigeon owners to play in their long-standing war on British hawks.

Pigeon owners had been complaining for years about the carnage wreaked by falcons. The falcons had protected status but pigeon owners were desperate to persuade government to license their destruction in order to protect their precious pigeons. With its new-found role as part of the war effort, the fancy seized its chance. In February 1940, a Plymouth fancier wrote to officials that one of his pigeons on NPS duty in a training flight along the English coast had returned 'distressed and scared' after an encounter with a hawk. The local pigeon officer confirmed that there were peregrine falcons in the hills surrounding Plymouth, and that losses during training flights were running at 40 per cent. That month the secretary of the NPS forwarded to the Air Ministry a grisly package of five pairs of feet and rings collected from a nest of hawks on the Cumbrian coast to make his point. Stories even surfaced of mysterious hawks spotted in Dorset, owned by suspicious characters who had links to Germany before the war. MI5, perhaps knowing pigeon owners were on the warpath and might be behind such tales, decided it was probably not worth an exhaustive investigation.

A very British civil war broke out, one that pitted two sets of bird lovers against each other. Pigeon lovers wanted the peregrines dead. But there were those who preferred the elegant hawk to the humble pigeon. The Scottish Society for the Protection of Wild Birds complained about the way in which 'the homing pigeon fraternity in the past have indulged in the wildest and most extravagant assertions', blaming falcons for every failure of a pigeon to return. Some suggested that the number of pigeons lost to falcons was small compared to fog and ice. This might be true, an official replied, but there was not much that could be done about such impediments. 'We find it difficult to deal with ice and fog unless the Treasury means to suggest that we fit de-icing apparatus to pigeons,' he wrote sarcastically.

The fancy won an early victory. In order to avoid fortune-seekers there would be no 'price on the head' of falcons but Defence Regulation 9, issued in July 1940, designated a series of counties where a strip ten miles deep would be purged of falcons. About 100 people, usually ornithologists but sometimes gamekeepers, were given permits to destroy them. One individual covered 2,400 miles and killed seventeen peregrines in one month, but the process was haphazard and there were questions as to whether some were taking advantage of the petrol allowance. So instead a mobile unit was established to replace the ornithologists. This special crack team was called the Falcon Destruction Unit, and could be sent to a particular area at the request of any government service. The 007 of the bird world, it had a licence to kill. It also had the wheels to go with the mission. The group of five men drove round in an open touring car, an American Packard generally agreed to be an absolute beauty by those who saw it – including Bert Woodman of the Plymouth Group of fanciers as the unit worked along the north Devon cliffs. Attached to the car was a caravan in which the men could sleep. Around a fire in the evening, the oldest of the group, a retired Irish colonel and champion shot, would regale the others with stories of his freebooter and marauder ancestors. By day, the men would scour the cliff-tops for a nest, using ropes to climb down to it. Then they would lay spring traps among the debris at the bottom.

When a falcon landed, its talons would become trapped. The men, wearing a thick leather gauntlet, would then go down in a sling to retrieve it. The Irish colonel would be ready with a shotgun if it escaped. Tragically, one of the men fell off a two-hundred-foot cliff and was killed during their work.

The unit was soon in heavy demand as requests flooded in from a variety of sources, including the Army Pigeon Service as it tried to protect the Columba birds. For Columba's team – and especially the volunteer pigeon fanciers who supplied the birds – it was clear the hawks were a menace that had to be dealt with. But in the battle of the skies between hawk and dove, the worlds of intelligence and counter-intelligence would collide. Columba's work gathering intelligence was not the only pigeon game in town.

Using pigeons as spies cut both ways. If Britain and Columba could use pigeons to communicate with agents undercover and gather intelligence, could the Nazis do the same? Were Nazi pigeons stealing British secrets? Enter MI5, Britain's spy – and pigeon – catching service.

Spy fever had gripped Britain as the war began, and pigeons inhabited the nightmares of some MI5 officers. In the First World War, even regular everyday pigeons on the streets of British cities had been eyed with suspicion. 'It was positively dangerous to be seen in conversation with a pigeon; it was not always safe to be seen in its vicinity,' wrote one official. One foreigner was even arrested after a pigeon was seen flying from where he had been standing in a park; it was assumed he had liberated it. The same spy hysteria, whipped up by the media but also based on a sliver of truth, resurfaced at the beginning of the Second World War. This was one reason for the registration of all pigeons at the start of the war and the wholesale slaughter of any foreign birds whose background could not be accounted for. Pigeons were under 'very strict surveillance, and a deadly weapon of espionage was rendered useless from the start', Bert Woodman claimed. But the anxieties persisted despite the strict controls.

On 29 August 1940, Guy Liddell, head of counter-espionage at MI5, was rung by the Admiralty. Invasion fears were still at fever pitch and there was concern that German spies were either already in Britain or on their way. The Admiralty said a carrier pigeon had been captured by the Portland signal office. It carried a message: 'Beach Hotel. The barmaid's drawers are pink. Sutton on Sea from Rogues Roost Louth.' Was this evidence of German espionage, preparing for invasion using some bizarre code? 'There was no other means of identification on the bird,' Liddell noted in his diary. Two days later the mystery was solved when Liddell had dinner with David Boyle, a senior MI6 officer. 'He has, I think, solved the mystery of the message about the barmaid's drawers. The pigeon was probably one of his, as he has communication not only by wireless but by pigeon to a loft at Willesden.' Quite what the code about the barmaid's drawers actually meant was not revealed.

Not all the fears were misguided. Germany had launched Operation Lena to penetrate Britain by sending in undercover agents – sometimes by parachute, sometimes hiding among refugees from the continent. Most were of low quality and were relatively easy to find, especially after Bletchley Park broke the codes of German intelligence. But there were signs that someone in Britain was secretly using pigeons. A cylinder was found with a message in numerical code with a preamble in German. It was suspected that the pigeon had arrived via a German U-boat and a neutral freighter. It referred to Army, naval and air matters and had apparently become detached from a bird in flight which had been released from London. This was not the only time during the war that fears of Nazi pigeon-spies would surface.

In October and November 1941, a loftman in the Army pigeon loft on the Scilly Isles saw something suspicious. Pigeons were flying low from the north-west and heading south towards the French coast. A number of pigeoneers made eleven sightings in all in the following months. These were men who prided themselves on being able to tell the difference between a wild and a homing pigeon. They were sure the birds they saw were homing pigeons, and they were not from the local Army or RAF lofts. Each time they crossed between midday and 2 p.m.

MI5 sprang into action with its counter-pigeon team – Section B3c – led by the dedicated Richard Melville Walker, the security service's counter-pigeon expert. His job was to be 'pigeon-minded' when it came to Germany's activities.

A special pigeon security meeting was called. Major Frost from MI5 said that it had previously been thought that the danger of the enemy using pigeons in the UK was remote. But now there had been a change of mind. It was considered that the danger of the enemy dropping pigeons by parachute with sufficient accuracy to be used by agents hiding in Britain had to be 'seriously considered', he told the assembled group. The Director of Signals for the Army suggested that all pigeons not used for national service could be banned, something MI5 also favoured. But the civilian representative of the NPS explained to him that there were 50,000 fanciers outside the NPS and only 11,000 inside. In the event of invasion, the police would be responsible for the dramatic move of destroying all pigeons so that they would not fall into German hands. Bert Woodman and other NPS officers would receive a coded instruction which would require them to go about the task. But it was considered too disruptive to destroy all non-NPS birds now.

The Germans were better prepared than the British for the use of pigeons in war. They had seen the French use pigeons in the 1870 siege of Paris and had begun their own military research soon after – and, unlike Britain, they had not abandoned it after the First

World War. At the beginning of the Second World War, they quickly conscripted birds, as well as some of the 57,000 fanciers who were too old to fight. Where Britain had to scramble to create the NPS, the Germans already had tight control of their birds under the state-run German Pigeon Union. To own pigeons you needed a certificate of morality and political behaviour. This meant being '100 per cent German' – Jews and foreigners were banned. Heinrich Himmler himself was a keen fancier and both the Army and SS had their own birds. A secret pigeon base operated out of Spandau, where over 2,000 pigeons were being bred and trained at any one time. At the peak of activity there were at least 50,000 birds in German service, with 600 to 800 men looking after them.

A pigeon section was attached to most Abwehr military intelligence units across Europe, but they were used most frequently in the west and the Balkans rather than on the eastern front. Before the war, the Germans had also organized races from England back to Germany – one such, including 1,400 birds, went from Lympne in Kent in 1937 and another from Croydon – and MI5 realized only later that this was highly suspicious.

The occupation of Belgium had allowed the Germans to requisition the best pigeons and lofts. Pigeons were one of the spoils of war. The German in charge of Belgian lofts, Hauptman Zimmerman, may even have flown over England in 1940 or 1941 to release pigeons on practice flights. One German pigeoneer later claimed that a bird had been flown from Harwich and another from Dover all the way back to their home in Freilassing, taking twelve or thirteen hours.

One advantage Britain did have in the pigeon wars was that the Germans could not copy Columba. If they had dropped pigeons into England, it is hard to believe many people would have chosen to fill in questionnaires; if they had, one can begin to imagine the choice phrases and epithets that might have been used.

In response to the spy-pigeon fears, MI5 instigated a watch by all coastguards and Observer Corps posts on the southern and south-eastern coasts to spot any birds flying out to sea. Walker worried that messages could be concealed on the birds. Small holes could be burnt in the feathers with a fine nail, a trick he was shown by a retired British intelligence officer who had studied the use of this method by the Germans in the First World War. Another method was to insert a small roll of rice paper into the hollow part of a feather after it was cut in two. Few would notice anything suspicious about such a bird.

A series of mysterious finds on the east coast in 1942–3 would heighten pigeon-spy fears. Two birds were found on a British vessel seven miles off Orford Ness, not far from Ipswich. One carried a message in German. A bird whose wings were stamped 'Wehrmacht' came aboard a motor launch off Lowestoft in early December. More with German army stamps were found in the following days. It seemed to Guy Liddell at MI5 as if the enemy were experimenting to find out if they could train birds to fly across the North Sea for German agents. Indeed, at the end of the war, a captured German who worked at a Dutch loft confirmed he had taken pigeons out onto the North Sea to train them on that line of flight for agents who were to be dropped to spot invasion preparations. One bird with a German practice message that had landed exhausted on a British ship was nursed back to full strength and dropped over the Netherlands with a 'plant'. 'Reaction, if any, will be awaited,' it was noted. Two others were adopted and given an English loft as home. 'Both birds are now prisoners of war working hard breeding English pigeons,' Walker noted.

Britain did have one possible defence against German birds. But it was the same one that threatened Columba. The Columba team and the fancy had been worried about wild hawks killing British pigeons. But what about the growing risk of German pigeons flying out of Britain with secrets? Having created a Falcon Destruction Unit, MI5 decided that it now also needed its own hawks and falcons in order to intercept and kill German pigeons. In a strange reverse, that meant creating their own elite, trained unit of killer falcons.

Falcons have been trained to hunt for sport for thousands of years in the Middle East and China. In England the sport was introduced before the Norman Conquest but had almost died out by the end of the seventeenth century and was kept alive by just a few enthusiasts. These were the small band that now MI5 needed. The director general of MI5 approved the creation of a falconry unit at what some thought the rather high cost of £200.

The Army Pigeon Service said they had a hawk expert who they were about to use to trap the wild hawks which were playing havoc with Columba. MI5 approached him and asked if he would like instead to help use hawks to hunt enemy pigeons. He was enthusiastic. In June 1942, he headed out to the scenic coast of Pembrokeshire to find some young hawks. A picture in the MI5 archives shows him in a rather dashing tweed jacket retrieving a wild hawk that had been trapped in a net after it had pursued a decoy pigeon. In all he caught half a dozen on that trip.

The best method of training was to take young falcons, feed them pigeon meat and then fly them out towards live pigeons, training them to recognize that the pigeons represented food (the Americans even looked at training hawks to associate parachutes with food, to see if they could be used to take out enemy parachutists). A falconer could carry a falcon on their wrist with a leather hood, which would be whipped off when a suspicious pigeon was seen. More effectively, the birds could be trained over a period of three weeks to remain in the air and patrol a certain spot employing their remarkable vision. Ideally, hawks could learn to bring a dead pigeon back rather than eat it, so that any message it was carrying could be examined.

After five weeks' training in Pembrokeshire, the hawks were ready for aerial combat, and the falconry expert and his two assistants went down to the Scilly Isles in late August. By then, reports of enemy birds had died down and the spy scare was already passing, but the team still took their task seriously. They were based at the local golf club. One would stand at the highest point of the course, another across the island, on the coast – hardly the worst job in summer – looking out for enemy pigeons, their falcons ready on their wrists to let slip. The Air Ministry supplied them with some pigeons to practise on. Some hawks patrolled quite well, but one preferred to perch on a mast in the middle of the golf course. Soon the trainers let them fly out on patrol for a couple of hours on beautiful summer days to watch over the whole group of islands. The diary of MI5's head of counter-espionage records the results. 'The ones in the Scilly Isles caught several pigeons but they were found to be our own,' Guy Liddell wrote. Hawks knew no nationality. No 'Friend or Foe' identification system had been invented, as would be done for aircraft. The only pigeons killed were seven British birds, two of whom were carrying messages. Two of the hawks were also shot by local children: 'Some boys will be little devils,' one of the trainers commented. But despite the lack of any evidence of Nazi pigeons, the case of the suspicious Scilly birds remained open and 'unproved', the ever-watchful Walker declared.

By the end of October 1942, the weather was turning and there were new reports of suspicious pigeons, this time near Swanage on the south coast. The Falconry Unit had its next mission. The three-man team kept surveillance along the cliffs, falcons at the ready. Unlike their time on Scilly Isles, now it was cold. On 15 December came a sighting – a pigeon flying fast overhead. But the trainer was caught off guard. His hand was so frozen by the cold that he fumbled and released his falcon too late. The pigeon disappeared south over the sea.

Next they let loose the falcons on patrol where they would circle an area hunting anything that came in their path. Three pigeons were brought down in the following months. A lighthouse keeper called to explain that a hawk was eating a pigeon in her garden but, like others, this turned out to be a British rather than a Nazi pigeon. Soon after that, two of the falcons simply gave up – perhaps annoyed at the lack of food – and flew off on their own. The teams were left convinced there had been some kind of suspicious activity – the pigeons that had been spotted flew straight as if they were homing to a possible German loft in Cherbourg. The unit was then dispatched to Wales by the Air Ministry to catch some peregrines that were disrupting their pigeons.

Overall the results were not exactly an overwhelming success. 'We were sent out to catch pigeons,' said one member of the team. 'If they were not "spy" pigeons it was not our fault.' An MI5 report at the end of the war notes that the hawks never actually brought down a single enemy bird – 'probably because there never were any'.

CHAPTER SEVEN

Reaching Out

With so many enemies, it may seem a miracle that any pigeon dropped as part of Columba survived to reach home. But in Belgium, all Leopold Vindictive knew was that Britain had managed to drop the birds once and that the one they found had then made it back home. The communications channel had worked, so why should it not work again? As the days passed, however, the frustration began to grow. The birds dropped on a flight on 3 August were never found. There was an attempt to drop more birds from another RAF flight in early September, but as a result of bad weather it returned to base with its pigeons still in their containers.

On 27 September 1941 Marie and Margaret heard a deeply discouraging message on the BBC: 'Here is a special message for our correspondent Leopold Vindictive. We regret the absence of anything new from you, despite our best efforts. But – as before – have courage.' Did the reference to 'our best efforts' mean another pigeon had been dropped? If so, it had not been received. And nor had the message yet reached London about the change of name, since they still used the original designation (no doubt annoying the royal court). The two sides were like star-crossed lovers whose messages constantly missed each other. Sitting on a huge stash of intelligence was both frustrating and dangerous.

On the night of 3 October, a few days after the BBC message was broadcast, pigeons were dropped again. Another RAF Special Duties flight crossed the Channel with specific coordinates to drop pigeons near Lichtervelde. It was again a secondary mission to an agent drop. Britain was still struggling to work out how to make contact with nascent intelligence networks. Belgium might have been small, but it was strategically important and a vital target for British intelligence services. It was littered with airfields and ports that might be used to attack Britain, and criss-crossed with main railway lines that ferried material from Germany into France. But how could you establish a link to the people there? Sending agents in and out to contact the networks was the ideal, but Belgium posed unique challenges. The coast was too well guarded for agents to be landed by sea. It was also the most densely populated country in Western Europe, which meant that – unlike France – it was near impossible to land agents or pick them up by aircraft without being spotted.

That night saw a rare success. Jean Cassart – a captain in the Belgian army codenamed Hireling – floated to earth by parachute south-east of Liège along with his radio operator. It was the third attempt to get them into the country, a sign of just how difficult these drops were. The two men hid in the woods until morning and then headed to a hotel to meet their contact. Cassart was there to coordinate sabotage – 'he will organize small groups to kidnap and kill individual Germans,' read his instructions.

The agent made it in, but what was the fate of the pigeons designated for Leopold Vindictive? Pilots were improving their dropping skills and on one occasion, the containers were dropped with neat precision in a row of back gardens from a height of fifty feet, almost as if Santa Claus on his sleigh were dropping off presents house by house. But this time the pilots seem to have dropped the birds five to seven miles to the west of their target. Navigating at night was a challenge. Columba worked if the intention was to hit a general area but was less effective when a specific spot was aimed at. Another opportunity had been missed.

Raskin continued to travel across the country giving religious talks. In his letters to his brother Albert he made no mention of his clandestine work. He stayed regularly at Lichtervelde with the Debaillie family. Whilst there he heard a rumour that pigeons had been dropped somewhere nearby but had fallen into German hands.

With no pigeons, the hunt for a radio transmitter or a way of getting a message to London gathered intensity as every day passed. Hector Joye had an idea. He would talk to his friend Clément Macq in Brussels. Macq had built his first radio in 1923 and had set up a business to sell wireless sets. Joye had been one of his clients and knew he was a patriot, having worked out Macq's sympathies when they had a coded discussion about whether a new radio might be good enough to receive the BBC; discussing such a possibility was a signal of where one's allegiances lay.

Joye first paid Macq a visit in July and asked if there was a way to construct a radio to send a message to England. Macq, a thin, angular middle-aged man, said he was unable to do so. That was not true: Macq was already secretly involved in a resistance network. But you had to be careful what you told people.

Joye was persistent. On a second visit, he went further in his pleas for help, asking Macq if he had heard the name 'Leopold Vindictive' on the radio. Of course he had, Macq said, an interesting sign of how the fame of the group was beginning to spread. Joye confessed – perhaps with a touch of pride – that he was one of its members. 'We had a pigeon,' he explained, 'the English received the information and want more.'

Joye showed Macq some of the information they were now collecting, and Macq was astonished at the level of detail. Joye explained that they had no means of getting it to London since they had not received any more pigeons. Could Macq help establish a line to London in order to ask for more pigeons? Perhaps there was a way. Macq relented, realizing that this was a serious, if not necessarily experienced, group of amateur spies. He knew a man in Brussels who might be able to get a message through. He would speak to him.

Joye introduced Raskin to Macq, who would say that Father Raskin was 'toujours bouillant' – always on the boil, eager for action. But such enthusiasm was also a risk. Raskin said he wanted a radio transmitter to be ready the next day. Macq had to explain it was impossible. Could Macq perhaps build some kind of short-range transmitter which could send a message to a passing RAF plane, Raskin asked. Not possible, Macq explained. He could sense Raskin's impatience.

Macq did say he might have one way to get a message to England. But it would not provide direct contact; rather it would be transmitted via a route using couriers carrying messages by hand. Nevertheless Joye gave him the message. 'Leopold Vindictive 200 requests a bird without delay,' read the text. 'A message of the highest importance is ready to be sent. In the first message give instructions for dropping of the pigeons (ie 300 is ok). If you cannot, please give us a different route for sending maps. For information: our key position is in the castle of Wijnendale. We change our name to A.M.20. Use this for radio communication.'

As this note makes clear, there had already been another name change, this time to Ave Maria, a short prayer for help. Raskin told Macq during their meetings that the plan for his network had been submitted to someone close to the King, who had approved. That was the reason that they now needed the change of name – in order to protect any link. The urgency of their requests for pigeons also reflected the men's knowledge that they had achieved something special.

When Macq paid a visit to Raskin at the missionary house of Scheut in Brussels in order to discuss installing film projection machinery, the priest showed him something that left him speechless. The frustration for Leopold Vindictive was that their efforts had now far eclipsed the work on the original message which had so stunned the British. The group's appetite for espionage had been whetted. The first pigeon might have been the starter; now they were ready to deliver the main course.

After the fall of Belgium, the Nazis had begun building a set of defences along the Channel, including the coast of Belgium. This was initially to protect their forces as they were marshalled for a potential invasion of Britain. But from March 1941 the emphasis shifted to protecting the continent from British commando raids. A directive that month established a new unified command and ordered an increased pace of construction. In 1942 Hitler would order the extension of the coastal defences all the way from Norway through to the border with Spain; it would become known as the Atlantic Wall, designed to ward off an Allied attack or invasion. Belgium, along with Norway, was the forerunner in 1941 because it was considered the most likely target for enemy action. In May 1941, there had been two attempts to make some kind of landing on the coast but they had been unsuccessful. Belgium had the most heavily defended coastline in the world.

These defences were the grand project the three friends had been working on – an astonishing feat of intelligence gathering. They had travelled along the coast and mapped out the entire Belgian coastal defence system from De Panne near Dunkirk on the French border to Knokke on the Dutch border – a distance of 67 km, precisely drawn out in the same meticulous manner displayed in the first message.

Raskin travelled to give religious lectures on China, often appearing at schools where he would write out the children's names in Chinese characters. He had permission from the Germans to travel, and there were bicycles he could use littered across the country. On the trips he would also scan for birds through a pair of binoculars, whilst at the same time noting down the defences he observed. He would also talk to his extensive network of contacts.

Arseen meanwhile did his spying while going about his business, the buying and selling of animal feed (which also bankrolled the operation). He drove a large American 1939 Pontiac and owned a set of binoculars and a Leica camera – all the tools needed for spying.

Hector Joye was free to make the most of his spare time, and he seems to have carried out the bulk of the reconnaissance work. The permission he had been given to visit the coast because of his need for fresh sea air gave him the perfect excuse to head out in his large Minerva car, touring Bruges, Ostend, Zeebrugge and other coastal spots. His two teenage sons came along on some of the trips and may perhaps even have been directly involved in the espionage work themselves.

The men first used a military map on which they would add the information they discovered. Next they made their own detailed, coloured drawings. Slowly, visit by visit, they updated these and added specifics. Barbed wire here. German emplacements behind some dunes. Roads to barracks and aerodromes. Munitions depots. A detailed legend was included to help the reader interpret all the details. German military buildings were depicted from different vantage points and angles. Arseen Debaillie travelled along the coast in August and September to spot machine-gun installations. His brother Michel told him about the existence of an ammunition depot in a forest. Sometimes the brothers travelled together, some-times with Joye.

The Joye family still possess drafts of their coastal defence and Atlantic Wall map. The plans are breathtakingly beautiful and delicate, written out on near translucent tracing paper which could be folded tight to fit into a pigeon cylinder. Each consecutive draft from the early summer of 1941 onwards reveals more detail and – strikingly – more colour. By the end there are reds, yellows, greens, blues, oranges and browns. Red ink for bunkers, military installations, machine-gun posts, airports; black ink for railway lines; green ink for forests and woodlands; brown ink for roads and paths. The drafts were put together over months and were far more detailed than the message they had already sent by pigeon to London. Later versions are packed with tiny writing, noting updates such as when German troops took part in maritime exercises and what time guards were on duty on the coast, and which places were mined. Huge amounts of tiny text accompany the maps. The places where bombs might do most damage were marked out. The writing is illegible without a magnifying glass.

Across each significant section is drawn the symbol for Leopold Vindictive – a curly L in a sharp V. The final versions had the group's seal. The result was Joye and Raskin's masterpiece – as much a work of art as the watercolours and panoramas Raskin had drawn in the First World War.

If Belgium and the continent were ever to be liberated, everyone knew that there would have to be a landing on the coast, and that for it to work it would have to penetrate layer after layer of bunkers and hidden firing positions, barbed wire and large guns installed by the Germans. But it was not just for the longer-term eventuality of a full invasion that details of the defences were invaluable. Churchill was determined in the meantime not to adopt a passive mentality. 'The completely defensive habit of mind, which has ruined the French, must not be allowed to ruin all our initiative,' he wrote just after Dunkirk. 'We should immediately set to work to organizing raiding forces on these coasts.' This would be a task for newly created 'Commandos'. Churchill was keen to target the coast, and Leopold Vindictive was collecting precisely the information needed to do so successfully. If the British wanted to launch a raid (as they did in Dieppe in August 1942, although with serious losses), let alone a full invasion, few things could have been of greater use than the maps that showed where each camouflaged *Blockhaus* with German guns lay in wait.

The maps were so detailed that when they were shown to Clément Macq he initially thought he was looking at the original German defence plans, and wondered how the priest had managed to steal them. The amount of work involved in both collecting the intelligence for the maps and then drawing them is astonishing. Only by understanding that can one appreciate the frustration of those who had produced such masterpieces but had no way to ensure they were seen by their intended audience in London.

The maps had to be carefully hidden. Joye concealed his own set of drawings in his house, placing them in the frame of the kitchen door. Inside the large complex of Scheutist missionaries where Raskin lived, there were plenty of rooms, basements and gardens which offered up hiding places. Raskin took his set of maps and drawings and placed them in a stainless steel briefcase, which he buried in the peaceful gardens. He told one person what he had done – Father Remi Verhaeghe, an assistant to the head of the organization and the one person there to whom he entrusted the secret of his resistance work. Raskin had made colour microfilms of the maps, and it was these that he hoped to send to Britain on the next pigeon. On the first floor of the mission house Raskin had his own room, hung with ornaments from China and containing his own books, papers and drawings. A two-foot plaster statue of the Virgin Mary stood on his writing table. The statue was hollow. Inside he hid the films.

The plans were incredibly precious, their possession dangerous. How to get them to London remained the challenge. Raskin did not want to risk passing them through networks of couriers – the chance that they would be intercepted or lost on the long, tortuous journey, which could take months, was too great given the work that had been put into them. There was still no doubt that the safest and fastest way to get them to London was by pigeon. They just needed to get a message to London to ask for pigeons. Macq said he would try his contacts.

Macq's initial contact in Brussels was a former gendarmerie commandant, René Dufrasne, who had asked Macq for help with radios for resistance work in 1940. Dufrasne passed Raskin's message on to the next link in the chain, an engineer who lived a couple of streets away called Maurice Muylaert. But then something odd happened. Muylaert surprised Dufrasne by telling him that he already knew all about Leopold Vindictive. More than that, Muylaert boasted that he played a key role in it.

The news went back though Macq to Joye, who then spoke to Raskin. It was time for the priest to make his own confession. Raskin sheepishly explained that he had been trying so many routes to send messages to London that Muylaert had been passed a radio message in July which he would try and get out to London. Muylaert had first met Raskin in February 1941 after being introduced by Madame Roberts. Muylaert had not, as he boasted, helped found the group, but he had known about it. He was part of Raskin's circle of Brussels contacts, the secondary agents who supplied the priest with material.

Hector Joye was only now realizing that the pigeon which had landed was not, after all, the beginning of his friend's espionage work. Rather it had been a gift from above, providing a route out for information collected by someone who had already been trying to spy for some time. Even before the arrival of the first pigeon, Raskin seemed to have been stockpiling intelligence from his contacts.

Raskin's restless determination was both his strength and his flaw. It led him to try every avenue, and that was dangerous. Muylaert had been showing off by claiming to have founded the group. He had a reputation for boasting about his intelligence work, especially to his numerous girlfriends – in one case telling a girl in a cinema that he had a secret message in his pocket. He was proud of what he was doing. But pride could be dangerous if it was not tightly contained. Word about Leopold Vindictive was spreading. Radio broadcasts from the BBC – the only means of contact – did not help, but nor did the ever broader circles the group were moving in as they tried to find a way to reach London.

The Germans were already on the hunt for Allied airmen and those sheltering them. Now, as resistance began slowly to organize, it found itself facing a formidable adversary. Belgium was effectively under military administration and Section IIIF of the Abwehr, Military Intelligence, had the task of hunting for spies and disrupting enemy intelligence activity both in Germany and the territories it occupied. In Brussels the work was led by Major Mohring. But the key investigator was Georg Bodicker (also spelt Boedecker), originally from Hamburg. Bodicker was in his late thirties, slim with blond hair and glasses, his teeth artificial after his real ones had been knocked out in a car accident. He had the scholarly appearance of a teacher and spoke English and French.

Bodicker was no thug. He understood that rooting out spy networks required running your own spies. That was Abwehr IIIF's speciality. It realized that the challenge of occupation required the active penetration of resistance cells and escape networks, after which as much intelligence as possible should be carefully gathered. Playing a long game in this way allowed you to try to understand every contact and connection before you eventually pounced, enabling you to arrest a wider network rather than simply the first people you had spotted. Abwehr IIIF was characterized by an effective combination of patience and boldness, MI5 in London reckoned.

Muylaert had passed Raskin's messages to a police inspector named Joseph Dehennin. At the start of the war, Dehennin had fled to France and developed contacts with French intelligence. He returned to Brussels and promised to work loyally with the Germans, but instead sought to use his contacts to work against them. Dehennin and his group were in the early stages of building a network, passing political information to a French officer who would visit Brussels throughout 1941 and using a courier who could move across the border carrying material about German military movements and facilities.

Dehennin in turn had passed on Raskin's messages to try to get them to London through one of the various routes his network employed, but this relied primarily on trusting the French to carry them out by hand through the Iberian peninsula. Documents – and eventually people, whether airmen or resistance fighters whose identity had been blown to the Nazis – would slowly follow the network's path of contacts, first into France, then down to Spain and usually to Lisbon, from where they could eventually make it to Britain. Every step carried risk, and there was never a guarantee a person or a message would get through.

In April 1941, Bodicker had begun an investigation into Dehennin. His great success came from inserting an agent into Dehennin's network itself. The Germans often did not speak the local language and so delegated much power to local agents, tasking them with the infiltration of enemy networks. Bodicker was careful to keep the identity of this new informer secret. In a cruel twist, the culprit was Dehennin's own brother-in-law – a portly, 35-year-old fellow policeman called Eric Pieren who was being used as a courier for the messages. No one had any suspicions about him. But somehow this man, who had been seen as a patriot, was quite the opposite. By the summer, he was passing all the messages he received from Dehennin on to Bodicker, who would copy them before allowing them to move on so he could trace the network.

In early October, Dehennin passed to Pieren a long letter for the Belgian government-in-exile in London, who had also established contact, asking for a link to be set up to a group codenamed 'Zero' which could supply regular intelligence. Bodicker decided it was time to swoop. The next morning, Dehennin was picked up. In quick succession, Muylaert and two other members of his group were arrested by the Germans.

The Germans were careful to protect Pieren's identity as the source of the intelligence. No one knew he had betrayed the group and he continued to inform for the Abwehr, collecting 4,000 Belgian francs a month for much of the war.

Everyone who knew the arrested men held their breath. Would they be next? Some of Raskin's contacts in Brussels who helped on escape lines had already been arrested. How close were the Germans? Had the message from Raskin passed to Muylaert given him away? And would the prisoners talk about their contacts once they were interrogated? Raskin and his friends held their breath and waited. At any moment, the door might be kicked in. But slowly they were able to exhale. It seemed, after a while, as if they may have survived.

But there had still been no pigeons for Raskin and his friends. Their first alternative route to London had been cut off, and the Germans were now on his trail. Raskin did not know it, but the traitor Pieren had heard something in August to pique Bodicker's interest – he had heard there was a priest in Brussels who was sending messages to England via pigeons dropped by parachute. But Pieren did not know his name.

CHAPTER EIGHT

Resistance

B y October 1941, Raskin and his friends were becoming increasingly desperate for a means of contact. The hunt for a way of getting in touch with London became more desperate and dangerous by the day. But Arseen Debaillie now had another potential route. He was in touch with an insurance agent named Fritz Devos, who lived in Roeselare, and whom he knew through business. Devos was a patriot who might know a way to get a letter to England. It had to be worth a try. With no sign of a pigeon, they were forced to reach out ever further to try to find some route to Britain. But each new contact exponentially increased the risk as the circle of knowledge widened beyond a small group of friends. All it took was for one part to be penetrated and the whole web could be rolled up. That was why small self-contained groups were often the best. If Leopold Vindictive had received its pigeons it might just have stayed that way. But that was not to be.

The other option would have been to simply give up – to decide it was too difficult and too risky to try to get the intelligence material back to London and instead to go back to ordinary life as a priest, a farmer or a pigeon keeper. But that was not the nature of these men and women.

On 9 October, Raskin and the Debaillies gave Devos a message to get to England. A draft the priest wrote the previous day survives. 'To the Commander in Chief of all British Forces', it begins grandly. 'We have important information.' It asks for multiple pigeons to be dropped in the hope that at least one would get through. Raskin believed that pigeons had been dropped on the right day for him but at the wrong place and had fallen into German hands. He also explained that his group had tried to send a message by radio but assumed that this had not worked. New pigeons were needed and could be dropped at the same place on a date London should indicate. He asked for acknowledgement that the letter had been received through a reference to AM 20 on the BBC. Never use Leopold Vindictive, he stressed.

'We are neither from Nieuport nor Lille, but a self-built self-standing group of just three men,' he added, still trying to correct the confusing British message of a few months earlier. They had heard that pigeons had been dropped near Nieuport but explained they were not able to get hold of them. They thought the British had wrongly dropped them there for them, although it may have been that they were just another regular Columba drop.

'Some try to steal our name and reputation,' Raskin wrote, offering a fascinating insight into how jealously he guarded that reputation. 'Never believe messages that do not bear our seal,' he continued, explaining that this seal consisted of the curly initials used in the first July message. No one else would know what that looked like or be able to copy it. He said nothing would be spared to help – including their lives. The message promised that the group had new information 'of the utmost importance', referring to plans of the Belgian coastal defences. After an Allied victory, his group would reveal their identity and congratulate the British, he went on. But before that, they wanted it to be impossible for the Germans to discover them. The message ended: 'Long live England! God save the King and us with Him! Leopold Vindictive 200.'

The message was given to Devos to pass into his network during a visit to Lichtervelde on Raskin's travels between two lectures. But would it reach London?

In London, the Columba team were themselves becoming increasingly desperate at the lack of news from Leopold Vindictive. In December 1941, Rex Pearson, running the drop operations from Army Signals, wrote to a commander in Naval Intelligence who received the material from the Columba team, saying that they had repeatedly tried to get in touch with Leopold Vindictive but with no response. 'Whether it is the fault of the RAF or just bad luck, I cannot say,' Pearson wrote. 'The matter is of such extraordinary importance however that I am wondering whether you could consider inspanning the Fleet Air Arm,' he pleaded. It is clear from this note that the team were sufficiently worried about their failure to reach the Belgians that they were casting around desperately for help. Pearson seems to have feared that the pigeons were just too low in priority for the RAF team and that other departments might be enlisted to drop birds especially for them.

'If you would consider this, I would be glad to meet you and talk things over,' Pearson ended his plea. But in the files of Naval Intelligence, those sentences are met with a large black cross, and 'NO' is written in the margin. There would be no help from the Admiralty. Columba was simply not a priority for the military and MI14(d) lacked the heft of other intelligence agencies to demand resources.

The winter of 1941 was a low moment for the Columba team. The performance of the pigeons had begun to dip through the autumn. In September, ninety-nine birds had been sent but only seven returned, just three of those bearing a message. The team were sufficiently worried that Brian Melland suggested keeping back the figures until they could be combined with those of October to improve their appearance. But October produced a mere six reports. It was a bleak winter for those sending and receiving the pigeons alike. 'One hears many people say "what are the English waiting for before they come"', a Frenchman wrote. 'We Frenchmen wait impatiently for your help to get us out of this misery,' said another.

Pearson wrote to Brian Melland of MI14(d) in mid-January 1942 proposing to pause operations. The awful winter meant that the pigeons' white parachutes would barely be spotted. Few people were likely to be in the fields anyway. Most of the birds would freeze to death when they were not discovered fast enough. The aim was to go slow and build up a stock of good birds to be used in spring when, as the team put it, the 'invasion season' started and they needed to watch for signs of renewed German activity.

The subsequent three-month break was the only time during the war when Columba would halt its operations. These were precisely the three months when Raskin and Leopold Vindictive continued to wait, hoping for a delivery.

The planes dropping Columba pigeons and secret agents, like those of RAF Bomber Command, travelled a perilous path. As they crossed the Channel, German anti-aircraft guns and the Luftwaffe's night fighters lay in wait. Belgium – lying on the main air route to Germany – was the scene of some of the most concentrated defences. Searchlights were controlled by radar and when they found a plane, it was lit up so brightly that the crew were near blinded. 'When they got a fix on the aircraft you immediately became illuminated, isolated and vulnerable – and by God, do you feel naked,' one pilot recalled. 'You are up there weaving about trying to get out before you are spotted by the night-fighters.'

As pigeons and agents were dropped, German searchlights and night fighters picked out British planes with uncanny accuracy. The initial Battle of the Beams had been a response to German bombers' success in striking Britain. Next, R. V. Jones wanted to know why German defences were so good at spotting British planes heading over Europe, whether on bombing missions or to drop agents and pigeons.

Germany had been shocked when its bombing of London was reciprocated by RAF strikes on Berlin, and it invested hugely in defending its homeland with the most advanced technology. From autumn 1940, Jones had begun glimpsing a new set of advanced defences – a belt of searchlights which sought out British bombers as they flew over France and the Low Countries heading for Germany. Alongside the searchlights, the German night fighters seemed inexplicably accurate at finding British planes. At the lowest point, the RAF was losing two hundred bombers a month, 80 per cent of these due to night fighters. Why were the German defences so effective, asked Jones. The answer had to be that they were guided by some kind of radar. But where were the stations, what did they look like? And how did they work?

Mysterious pictures taken by Americans in Berlin pointed to some kind of new tower, while Enigma decrypts talked of something called Freya. The problem for Jones was how to get intelligence from the ground, especially in places where MI6 had no coverage.

Jones realized Columba offered something new. Columba was already helping find targets for the RAF. A message signed 'Bernard Franklin' from Courtrai provided a readout on recent bombings and specific map coordinates for ammo dumps and aerodromes, including the location of dummy wooden aerodromes and aeroplanes, installed by the Germans in the hope they would be hit. The difference between these and real aerodromes could not be discerned from aerial reconnaissance. This was one of many ways in which Columba offered something inaccessible to eyes in the sky.

(Sometimes it provided glimpses of the dark events that were unfolding – one message in Dutch from Assen in the Netherlands on 24 September 1942 ended not with a signature but a single plea: 'Help our Jews.')

Now, Jones was realizing the operation could be used for something more than random drops; it could be more closely targeted in its intelligence collection. He asked the Columba team to drop pigeon containers with questionnaires in precisely the spots where he suspected radar stations might be, and where there was limited agent or aerial reconnaissance coverage. 'As with every other kind of source, it was essential to ask questions that the finder could answer. The chances were that the finder would be an agricultural labourer; so the questions had to be such that this kind of man could usefully answer them,' Jones wrote. So the questionnaires were deliberately written in a way that required no technical knowledge. 'Are there any German radio stations in your neighbourhood with aerials which rotate?' the questionnaire asked, since this was something so distinctive and unusual that people could not but be curious. 'Even unskilled observers could hardly fail to identify these, and to give fairly accurate pinpoints,' Jones said. 'So we had the pigeons dropped in areas where agent cover was bad, near where we thought radar stations ought to be.' The birds were dropped. Now he just had to wait to see what came back.

As the year ended, Raskin kept himself busy giving lectures, carrying two heavy suitcases as he tried to travel around the country, the trains now irregular thanks to occupation. His only relief, he wrote to his brother, was being able to play the accordion for half an hour on the one or two nights a week when he was at home in Brussels.

Following the arrests of the Dehennin group in October, the channel via Devos was now Leopold Vindictive's best – perhaps their only – hope of establishing contact with London. And, eventually, this channel would offer Raskin the first chance since the pigeon to make some such contact. The channel relied on a growing network engaged in smuggling people over the border.

After the arrests in October, Madame Roberts introduced Raskin to the man at the centre of the channel. Henri Michelli was emerging as a major player in resistance work in Brussels and was Devos's key contact, the man behind the much-hoped-for link to London. Michelli looked like the forty-something accountant he had been, rather boring, old-fashioned and upright. Like many others, he was a middle-aged man who had fought in the First World War but had been denied – either by age or by the sheer speed of Belgium's collapse – the opportunity to fight second time round, and so had sought to express his patriotism by getting involved in resistance work. By September of 1940, he was helping stranded British servicemen and Belgian pilots escape to London and distributing clandestine literature; the following year he would become involved in sabotage. He had his finger in many pies. One of those was the most important escape network of the war, which offered a way to get people and information through France, into Spain and out of occupied Europe.

In August 1941, the strikingly elegant 24-year-old Andrée ('Dedee') de Jonge turned up unannounced at the British consulate in Bilbao in neutral Spain. She explained to officials that she had singlehandedly smuggled a group of escaped Belgian prisoners and British servicemen through France and over the Pyrenees.

At first, British officials were incredulous that this well-spoken young woman could have achieved such a feat. Was it a Gestapo plot? Back in London, the organization tasked with helping Britons escape was MI9. But Claude Dansey at MI6 – as ever – pulled the strings. He was interested in escape and evasion work largely as a source of intelligence, but kept a close watch on it since he disliked the idea of anything happening without his knowledge. 'My job,

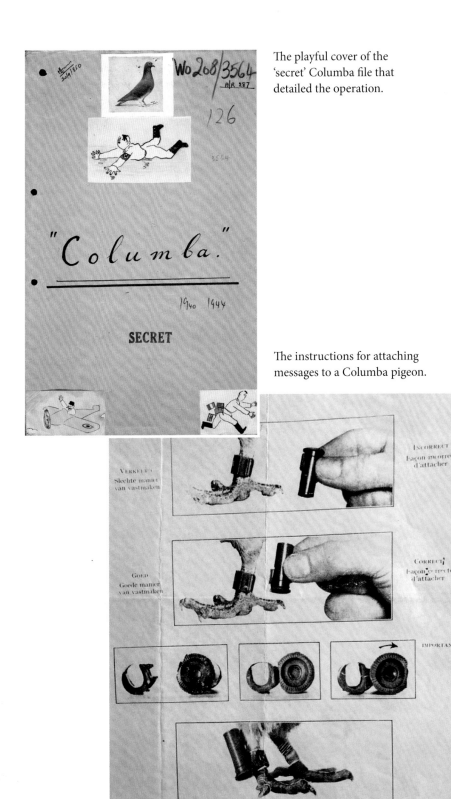

The playful cover of the 'secret' Columba file that detailed the operation.

The instructions for attaching messages to a Columba pigeon.

Columba message 37 from Leopold Vindictive.
This image is roughly the same size as the original.

The message covered both sides of the rice paper and required a magnifying glass to read.

Michel Debaillie clutches the pigeon destined for Britain.

The message about to placed in the container.

The pigeon with a sign detailing its arrival and departure date.

The pigeon that carried Columba message 37.

The message being placed in the container.

The pigeon with the Debaillie family (from left to right: Marie Debaillie, Michel Debaillie, Arseen Debaillie, Gabriel Debaillie, and Margaret Debaillie) and the details of its arrival and departure date.

Michel Debaillie releases the pigeon from the roof.

Brian Melland – the leading figure behind Columba in MI14(d) – strikes a theatrical pose.

Joseph Raskin, the leader of the Leopold Vindictive network.

Joseph Raskin while serving as a missionary in China.

Hector Joye (looking at the camera) and family entertaining or being entertained by Joseph Raskin (with his back to the camera).

The RAF reconnaissance photo of the field Leopold Vindictive requested for the second pigeon drop.

and that of my agents, is to collect information about the Germans' intentions and activities, not to act as nursemaids to people who seem totally incapable of doing much to get back on their own,' he explained to Jimmy Langley, the man he installed at MI9 as his liaison. Dansey told Langley he was to keep him informed about everything that went on at MI9, even above his own nominal boss inside the organization. Dansey, never a great believer in the ability of women to take part in clandestine work, was suspicious about de Jonge's feat. But despite his scepticism, after ten days officials on the ground were won over and realized de Jonge was something special. She would become known as 'Little Cyclone' and the evasion network that grew out of her visit would be code-named as Comet, passing on escapees from safe house to safe house while false papers were prepared and then from guide to guide along the route, with schoolchildren often couriering messages. By the end of the war, Comet would become a legend, helping eight hundred Allied airmen and seventy-five intelligence agents escape from under the Nazis' noses. It sacrificed the lives of more than a hundred and fifty of its own members in the process.

The network was initially run by Andrée's father, and Henri Michelli had become his trusted lieutenant after they had met earlier in 1941. Like other Belgian intelligence and escape networks in the early years of the war, the people involved in Comet over-lapped and interconnected with the intelligence networks called Marc, Luc and Zero, as well as with the smaller Leopold Vindictive. It was inevitable that the networks' personnel should intersect in the early stages of occupation, but it took time and hard lessons for those involved to understand just how dangerous this was.

Raskin's message 'for the Commander of British forces' in early October 1941 had been passed from Devos through to a man whom Michelli was sending out of the country on the Comet line. This was a Belgian aviator in his late thirties called Jean Vandael. Michelli was helping Vandael move in and out of the country as the airman tried to establish his own intelligence network in Brussels, Antwerp and Liège. He had made at least three journeys between Vichy France and Belgium that year, and every time he had taken messages with him which he would pass on to people in the hope they would make their way to England. It was a slow, difficult process with many possible points of risk and failure.

Raskin's message slowly made its way out with Vandael in October. It eventually found its way to the crossroads of Lisbon. The capital of neutral Portugal was a place where people trying to get in and out of occupied Europe congregated – some trying to reach Britain, others South America. It was also crawling with German spies. People frequently turned up at the British embassy claiming to be secret agents or escapers. Sometimes it was true: they were just trying to get out. Sometimes, though, they were working for the Gestapo.

The British presence was a mess, replicating the rivalries that soured relations in London. As well as the regular embassy staff, there were representatives of three separate British intelligence teams – MI6, the Special Operations Executive and the escape and evasion service, MI9. If there was any cooperation it was on a personal level, because two people got on with each other, and despite – not because of – orders from London. MI6 in particular looked down on SOE. 'Our recently constituted junior half-sister was rash and untrustworthy, lacking in security,' was how one MI6 officer in Lisbon had been taught to see his partner agency.

After his October trip, Vandael returned to Belgium, but now the Germans were on his trail. He was 'burnt' and realized he needed to leave. Jean Cassart, the agent who had been dropped in October, knew Vandael as they were both air force officers, and he gave Vandael 10,000 francs to pay Michelli to take him out again through the Comet line.

But Cassart himself now needed to flee, and his story reveals just how difficult it was for London to maintain contacts and get people in and out. His life was in danger and London was desperate to extract him, both for his own sake and in case he was caught and compromised their networks. In early December, Flight Lieutenant Alan Murphy (known as 'Sticky') flew out to pick up Cassart on an RAF Special Duties mission. It was a snowy night and Sticky arrived after midnight, looking as he approached the field for the reception committee to flash the letter L, for Leopold, in Morse code as a recognition signal. But he saw the wrong letter.

Sticky was supposed to head home if that happened, but he circled whilst deciding what to do. Could they simply have made a mistake? He decided to land a short distance from the flares. As the aircraft landed he pulled out his revolver. He flashed his torch towards the flares. Then he heard a bang.

On the ground, Cassart and his wireless operator had been delayed by ice on the roads and arrived just before the pick-up time. As they went to lay out the torches, Cassart heard voices. Were they locals or Germans? The five dark shapes were wearing helmets. Cassart cocked his revolver. At that moment a bullet hit him in the arm and he slid down a slope. He jumped over a stream and lost his gun as he slipped on the ice and raced into the woods. Two more rifle shots followed him, and there were five soldiers on his tail. At this moment, Cassart was watching as Sticky's Lysander flew overhead. He prayed it would not land but watched in horror as it did. The Germans came out firing and he watched the Lysander plane turn and take off again. One German bullet went through Sticky's neck. Fortunately, he carried one of his wife's silk stockings as a lucky charm and wound it round to reduce his bleeding. By the time he made it back to Britain he was barely conscious from the loss of blood. Colleagues at the RAF base told him dirty limericks over the radio to keep him awake as he approached. When he landed, they found thirty bullet holes in his Lysander.

Cassart himself was captured within a few days. One of his contacts on the ground had been a double agent. After this mission, British intelligence and the RAF decided after that it was simply too dangerous to land in Belgium to pick people up or drop them off.

Over Christmas, Andrée de Jonge took Vandael on a week-long trek over the Pyrenees. On 19 January 1942 he arrived in Lisbon. Here he was questioned by British intelligence, keen to talk to him because something strange had happened. Officials in London had begun an investigation to find out what had happened to the October message from Leopold Vindictive brought by Vandael to Lisbon. He was questioned as to what it contained and what he had done with it. He recounted the details as best he could – for instance, Leopold Vindictive's desire to change their name and to be sent more pigeons – although he also got some details wrong. He explained that he had given the message to a man called Harper in Lisbon, although there was another intermediary called Eric.

The investigation suggests London had never received the message from Raskin and Leopold Vindictive, and that it was now trying to work out why and reconstruct its contents. A note from February 1942 details the report of an agent investigating the message's route in Lisbon, and explaining that it was proving very difficult to talk to people. At the Passport Control Office (which was cover for the MI6 station), someone said they thought Vandael had sent a message from Leopold Vindictive about pigeons, but they also said that there seemed to be a lot of boasting and that there was some kind of confusion – probably between different Belgian and British intelligence services, which proliferated in the city and did not always talk to each other – as to whom the message had been delivered to. It may simply have fallen into the hands of someone who did not understand its significance. Lisbon was yet another place where the attempt to reach out failed.

After five days' debriefing by a Belgian intelligence officer including investigation of the route of the Raskin message, Vandael went to Gibraltar, and on 11 March he reached Scotland. He carried with him another message for British Intelligence, this time hidden in the epaulettes of his jacket. The message consisted of one sentence and three words in code, so that if he had been caught it would not have made sense. He told British intelligence that Michelli had offered his services to help any agents they could drop into Belgium. When an agent was dropped, a message was to be broadcast with the codewords 'Expect a visit'. The agent was then to make contact using a recognition phrase which included the words *Michelli*, *Marcel* and *Malaga*. Michelli's message also said he was in touch with a resistance network that urgently needed a radio set – Leopold Vindictive.

The arrival of Vandael in person with this new message had immediate effects. Events were gathering pace. British intelligence realized now that Leopold Vindictive were still in existence and eager to cooperate. The pigeons had not got through, but there might after all be a way to reach them. Urgent action was needed. This time the contact would be more direct – as soon as possible they would parachute in an agent who could act as a radio operator.

But who in British intelligence had received the message and was now running the show? This was not MI14 and Columba – they dealt with pigeons and German military intelligence, not with people coming through escape lines or agents being parachuted in. Intelligence from that route went straight to Claude Dansey and MI6. Dansey would have known who Leopold Vindictive were after their startling intelligence had been circulated around London, and even to Churchill himself, the previous summer. Now there was a chance for MI6 to muscle in on the group that, in his mind, the amateurs at MI14(d) had stumbled across. This would now be an MI6 operation, a chance for his service to deliver the goods. And that would prove to be a problem.

What no one knew was that Bodicker in the Brussels office of Abwehr IIIF had begun a number of parallel investigations. One was into reports of British airmen being sheltered in Brussels. Another was into the mysterious priest who had been using pigeons. A third was into the group calling itself Leopold Vindictive, to which the BBC had been broadcasting messages. Bodicker wanted to know the identity of this mysterious group. The King himself had at some point been questioned as to whether there was any royal link to this apparent new intelligence network, since it at least partly bore his name. Bodicker and the Abwehr pressed on with their investigations. They had no idea that all three lines of investigation were leading them towards the same place.

CHAPTER NINE

Secret Agents

Jef Van Hooff felt afraid. Even his MI6 minder looked tearful, he thought. He and Marcel Thonus climbed aboard Whitley aircraft 'B' 4166 and the engines started up noisily. It was a cold night but their flying suits kept the two Belgians warm as they set off on their mission.

The pilots did not know the real names of those they were taking to Europe. But they knew this was an MI6 job. Those were even more secret than the missions organized by SOE. MI6 usually insisted that its agents must never share an aircraft with agents of any other service, and that nothing be put in writing about them in operational log books. MI6 liked to keep things tight. That was going to be a problem for Raskin and Leopold Vindictive – that, and the petty rivalries among spy services in London, in which men like Jef Van Hooff were pawns. MI6 had decided that Van Hooff and his companion Thonus would be dropped with instructions to establish contact with a number of groups and individuals. Among those groups – added late after Vandael's arrival just a few weeks earlier – would be Leopold Vindictive.

Van Hooff looked down at the floor of the cabin, where he saw two containers and two small baskets of pigeons. They were for the resistance, it was explained. But not for Leopold Vindictive. Van

Hooff and Thonus swigged rum to keep warm as the plane made its way towards the Channel just after ten at night. Thonus seemed a world away. Van Hooff was having dark visions of what might lie ahead. After a while he drifted into a deep sleep.

He was woken with a start. The sound was different. Enemy fire? The jump door was opened. Just in case they needed to make a sharp exit, the sergeant flying with them explained. Thonus and Van Hooff sat with their legs dangling. Suddenly there were bright streaks across the aircraft. 'What's that?' Van Hooff asked the sergeant. 'It's the engine,' the sergeant replied, not very reassuringly. Van Hooff was convinced it was tracer fire coming from all sides. The men pulled their legs back in quickly. But it was just the port engine causing problems. Sitting in the containers, the pigeons seemed as scared as he did, thought Van Hooff.

After an hour or two, they approached the drop point in a wood near Valenciennes. It was just after midnight.

They looked at the light which told them the correct moment to jump. A red light meant get ready; green meant go. Red came on. The men tensed, and the plane began to descend. But the light did not change. Van Hooff's eyes began to hurt as he stared at it without blinking, desperate not to mistime his jump and miss the right landing spot. But it stayed red.

The seconds ticked by. The sergeant emerged from the cockpit to explain that the pilot could not locate the right point for the drop. There was too much ground haze.

'What now?' Van Hooff asked.

'Back to England,' he said.

Van Hooff tried to quell his anger by gulping the last swig of his rum, and sat behind a container cursing. The pigeons sat next to him in their baskets, oblivious.

Just after half past three in the morning, the plane was home. Exhausted, Van Hooff fell into a sleep so deep there were no dreams or nightmares. For Jef Van Hooff, the irony was that after the crazy things he had done to get out of Belgium, the planned parachute jump to go back in as an undercover agent working with the resistance seemed almost straightforward.

The 30-year-old had left Belgium nearly a year earlier. He had been a footballer with FC Mechelen and then a sports journalist. A picture of him in his football kit before the war shows him as an apparently carefree, well-built young man with a broad, easy smile and dark hair. After the occupation, he first made his way into France and then hid on a boat from Marseilles that crossed the Mediterranean to Algiers. From Algiers he headed to the border with Morocco. Then he clung for twelve hours to the underside of a wagon which crossed the hot desert. From there he made it – perhaps inevitably – to the crossroads for those trying to hide or escape: Casablanca. On a dark night, Van Hooff stripped off and swam naked with thirty others to clamber aboard a boat that would take them to the British outpost of Gibraltar. The boat had not gone far when the motor gave out.

After six days and nights packed in like sardines, they landed in Algeciras. Eventually a British destroyer picked them up and took them to Gibraltar. A month later Van Hooff made the dangerous crossing on a transport ship and eventually arrived in Liverpool.

For Van Hooff, like all the other refugees arriving from Europe, his treatment at his first experience of Britain was not dissimilar to that meted out to their children by the British elite. He found himself cooped up in a place that was ostensibly a school but actually more like a prison. The Royal Victoria Patriotic School in Wandsworth, south London was a vast neo-Gothic castle that acted as the processing centre for arrivals from Nazi-occupied Europe. Beneath its battlements laced with barbed wire, the guards were ready to shoot. The security was tight thanks to the fear that the Nazis were sending in agents posing as refugees.

After a cup of soup and a tiny scrap of meat, arrivals were interviewed carefully about the smallest details of their previous lives and their journeys to Britain. Interrogators were looking for inconsistencies. Not only the answers they gave, but the clothes they wore and the documents they carried were scrutinized for evidence of deception. The discovery of some sticks, cotton wool and white powder in a wallet of one Belgian who arrived in the spring of 1942 was the beginning of the end for him since they were telltale signs that he had been trained to use invisible ink. For him and other spies who were discovered, the hangman's noose lay ready at Wandsworth prison across the road.

But as well as looking for enemy spies, the sifting was also a means whereby British intelligence could find their own recruits. Van Hooff told people he had left Belgium pretending he was going on holiday to France but instead had come to the UK to join the Belgian section of the RAF. But in October 1941, he was marked out as a man with the independence of spirit and will to survive that would make for a good secret agent. The job of a recruiter is to understand the character of the man in front of him. Over whisky and cigarettes, one recruiter regaled Van Hooff with the risks and the romance of clandestine work. By the end of the conversation, Van Hooff was intoxicated with the idea of parachuting back into his homeland. He saw himself arriving as a hero to the rescue of his friends and family.

Two different British intelligence services were sending in agents undercover into occupied Europe. There was MI6, the well-established and rather sniffily superior Secret Intelligence Service, which gathered intelligence, and then the noisy new kid on the block, the Special Operations Executive, SOE, tasked by Churchill with setting Europe ablaze with acts of sabotage. It was the latter service which reached Van Hooff first. On 21 October 1941, SO2 – a unit of SOE involved in using agents to spread black propaganda and stir up resistance – sent a request to MI5 for a trace on Van Hooff because they were considering employing him as an agent. On 14 November, an MI5 officer wrote back saying 'Nothing Recording Against', meaning there was no indication of anything negative about the man, adding that 'he made a good impression at his interrogation'.

The leading figure of the SOE section dealing with Belgium for much of the war was a colourful character even by the eccentric standards of the secret world. Hardy Amies joined the beehive-busy SOE HQ at Baker Street in 1941 aged 32 and the Belgian section that November. A fresh-faced, good-looking young man, his civilian occupation was noted as 'dress designer'; after the war, he would gain renown as the Queen's dressmaker, and a fashion label still bears his name. His colleagues in British intelligence soon realized that the fact he was gay (in both senses of the word) did not disqualify him from work specializing in violence. 'He is far tougher both physically and mentally than his rather precious appearance would suggest,' noted one instructor. Amies played by his own rules and could be ruthless. During the war he planned the Belgian end of 'Rat Week', in which collaborators who had sold out members of the resistance were shot or beaten to death.

Amies's willingness to undertake such actions likely reflected his frustration at the failures SOE had endured in Belgium and the heavy losses it had suffered. The year 1941 had been bad for the team he joined. 'None of the officers on the staff of the Belgian section had any practical previous knowledge of clandestine work. They gained it by experience which can only be described as bitter,' read an official evaluation.

Recruits were often of poor quality. A mechanic they trained was deemed 'absolutely appalling' by the security team thanks to his fondness for drink and for picking up 'the most awful women'. Amies overruled the warnings and sent him into the field, where he picked up a peroxide blonde and took her to the Palace Hotel in Brussels, which was packed full of Gestapo. He was arrested and eighteen people were shot as a result. Amies had been the man who had to identify the mutilated body of the agent whose parachute caught when he jumped over Belgium in July 1941, at the time Leopold Vindictive's pigeon was dropped. It was a sight he never forgot.

Belgium suffered in comparison to the resources devoted to France. 'We were very much the poor child of northern Europe,' Amies reflected. 'We had low priority. If there was a moonlit night – weather-wise correct for parachuting – and there was only a certain number of planes that were available for taking off agents and parachutes, France got priority over us. There would be a lot of frustration. A great deal of my energy was taken up in assuaging the distress and the anger and the nerves of the parachutists that were delayed. There's nothing like getting teed up for going off and then it is delayed.'

SOE needed unsentimental agents, hard men with little to lose, willing to obey orders to carry out sometimes morally as well as practically challenging tasks. At interview, they decided to see what Van Hooff was made of. 'A train is occupied by hundreds of Germans and war material of the highest importance,' an SOE recruiter asked him. 'But it also carries a member of your family. Could you blow it up?' Van Hooff's answer was honest. No. Then he was not right for them, it was explained. SOE only wanted those who would answer yes to that question.

The next afternoon someone else came to interview Van Hooff. The Royal Victoria Patriotic School was the site of fierce competition between spy services. This time, the man said he was called Page. He was in his mid-forties and English in character but Latin in look, Van Hooff thought, with his olive complexion and curly jet black hair. He could also speak French like a native. The interview this time was more like a conversation than an interrogation, cordial as if the two men were exchanging pleasantries in a park.

As he spoke of the work of his agents, Van Hooff thought the mysterious Page talked with respect and affection, almost paternally, of his charges. He did not gloss over the hard truth of the torture they had endured after their capture by the Gestapo. By the end of the long conversation, Van Hooff was sold. Page had worked his magic and reeled him in by care rather than bludgeon. The Belgian wanted to be worthy of Page's respect – even if that meant taking a gamble with his life. Page had just recruited Van Hooff for MI6.

The Belgians knew the man as 'Major Page' but his real name was Frederick John Jempson (after the war he changed his name to Page-Jempson). He joined the police in 1914 and then Special Branch, but after twenty-five years he left as war began and joined first the military and then MI6. He would be the officer in charge of Belgium at MI6 HQ for much of the war. He had a sometimes flamboyant manner but was an effective operator, and was spoken of with high regard by those who worked with him – apart from SOE, whom he fought to keep off his patch.

Page served directly under Claude Dansey, the all-powerful, almost spectral presence whose hidden hand guided MI6 operations all over Europe. Dansey's job title was assistant chief but many thought him the real power behind 'C', the Chief. Dansey was battling to rebuild MI6's work in Europe, and his wily character meant no one was to stand in his way, no one else was to know what he was doing. SOE was supposed to stir up resistance through sabotage and by setting up secret armies. In contrast, the task of MI6 was to gather intelligence. There was an inherent tension between the two types of work. Sabotage was loud and noisy and drew attention. Espionage was designed to be stealthy, to keep a low profile so that it could endure.

Dansey did his best to control SOE in the early days – insisting that all SOE radio traffic from the field went through his hands at MI6 – but control was wrested from him. The month that Van Hooff and Thonus were to be sent was the lowest point of relations between SOE and MI6 in the whole war. Dansey thought SOE were amateurs, crashing around, but he also recognized that what Churchill wanted was someone to make a lot of noise and carry forward the spirit of subversion and resistance, as much to boost morale at home and in occupied Europe as for the actual impact of its activities. The perception was that at least SOE was doing something, which was not always the view of MI6's work. MI6 even feared being swallowed up if a new figure was appointed to run both organizations. At one point, SOE paraded a letter from the Air Staff saying it had carried out the finest piece of intelligence gathering during the war. R. V. Jones was summoned to a meeting with Dansey, who wanted to find out who had written the letter. Jones was forced to reveal that it was he. He explained that SOE had produced a report from one of their agents – a member of the French resistance – who had infiltrated a German control hut which operated its latest navigational beam for night fighters, and whose report of his findings showed remarkable bravery combined with technical understanding. When Jones finished, Dansey began walking round the room shouting 'The cheats, the cheats, the cheats!' before claiming that the agent was actually from MI6.

There was competition to recruit the best agents, for RAF slots to drop their men into enemy territory, even to prioritize which messages were sent out on the BBC. The Royal Victoria Patriotic School was itself a flashpoint. Amies had furious rows because he believed that the best men were always being funnelled to MI6 and not to him. In the case of Van Hooff, SOE let him slip through their hands and into those of MI6.

Van Hooff was next introduced to the Belgian intelligence service in London. This drew him into a vicious, murky realm of refugees and spies. British intelligence operations in Belgium were a poisonous brew of vitriolic rivalries and in the spring of 1942 they too had reached their lowest point. MI6 and SOE were not just feuding with each other but also with the Belgians in exile. London was home to a myriad of exiles from each country, all manoeuvring for influence in the hope of perhaps running their country if the Nazis were ever driven out (as de Gaulle managed on the French side). The Belgians were no exception. Layered on top of political ideology and personal ambition were the linguistic divides that addled the country, and also the question of how loyal to be to a king who had remained under occupation. There were two intelligence outfits linked to the exiled government. The Sûreté (tasked with protecting the state) was focused like MI6 on intelligence gathering. Around the corner in Belgravia was the Deuxième Bureau, which like SOE was more interested in military intelligence and sabotage. The resultant infighting was savage and spilled over into relations with the two British services, each of the four trying to play off the other side against their competition. 'It is many years ago since I first had to deal with the Belgians and their intrigues. They have not altered one bit in twenty-five years,' Dansey, a man who distrusted the security of exiles, noted bitterly, whilst understating his own role in fuelling the various intrigues and the fact that his service drew much of the intelligence it presented as its own in London from the Belgians and other foreign services.

The Sûreté was led by Fernand Lepage, a 35-year-old magistrate who had escaped to London and started to set up the intelligence agency virtually from scratch. Lepage had been in Britain as a child during the First World War when his family fled the conflict, and had been educated at English schools. That meant he could speak the language fluently as well as navigate its politics. Within a few weeks of returning to London in 1940, he had been contacted by a mysterious Englishman – Page again. The MI6 officer took Lepage to a flat in St James's Street where he was confronted by Dansey, who gave him a lecture on starting a freelance spy service. 'Do you realize, Lepage, that you are endangering the security of the realm?' he was told.

Lepage confessed that he knew little about intelligence work but wanted to learn. Dansey softened, and eventually the two men concluded a written agreement which would be the basis of close cooperation. Lepage preferred MI6's intelligence work to SOE's sabotage, which led to bitter, vicious rows. He did not want to blow up his own country's factories and potentially kill civilians, even if the Nazis might be using them. Lepage feared that the SOE's supply of weapons to militia groups risked arming groups who would fight each other to take over the state after the war. That was the kind of thing the rival Deuxième Bureau wanted to do, but Lepage warned MI6 that they wanted to build a 'crypto-fascist regime around the monarch'. The Deuxième Bureau meanwhile said it would only cooperate with SOE if it promised to have nothing to do with the Sûreté. It was an unholy mess which had real consequences for the lives of agents operating in Belgium.

On 11 March 1942, just before Van Hooff made his flight back to Belgium, Lepage and Amies's boss at SOE had a screaming match in which each called the other a 'bloody liar'. Lepage was convinced SOE had been sending agents into Belgium without telling him. He was right. SOE had not told the Belgians, as they believed their own sabotage operations were being sabotaged. They thought the Sûreté was carrying out surveillance at SOE training schools and then getting hold of any SOE agents before they left for Belgium and warning them not to engage in sabotage. One of Lepage's aides had been caught by Hardy Amies frightening off nine potential recruits for SOE who withdrew at the last moment. Each side withheld messages they were supposed to pass on, and Lepage was left 'hopping mad' when he discovered that SOE had sent a message to an agent in Belgium asking for details about his own background.

SOE thought the problem stemmed in part from Lepage's personal ambition. 'To achieve his ends and safeguard his own position he can be proved to "double-cross" to an unlimited extent,' went one SOE memo, highlighting the personal vitriol that bled into relations and even led to the darkest possible accusation as part of an attempt to oust him. 'This "double-crossing" gives rise to the strongest suspicions of treachery.' Another SOE official said the leader of the Belgian government-in-exile was using Lepage 'as a head of a Gestapo service to brow-beat and terrorize all Belgians in this country and watch their every movement to prevent by all means in his power anything which might jeopardize his apparently dominating position'.

But Lepage had the full backing of the Belgian government-in-exile – and of MI6, who saw him as their man. Lepage was particularly close to Page (leading Lepage's own staff to mutter occasionally that he was in the pay of England rather than Belgium). SOE considered Page a 'very cagey individual' who might even be happy to see the rift grow deeper. The mansions of Belgravia made for a bitter, distrustful backdrop for the agents who risked their lives. This could have real consequences for resistance networks like Leopold Vindictive operating on the ground.

For Van Hooff, after his recruitment by MI6, the following months were a mix of hard training and hard carousing. Soho and Piccadilly were the playgrounds for men preparing to risk their lives and desperate for one more night on the town. Londoners carrying their gas masks often looked on disapprovingly, unaware of why he and others were drinking and dining at the best restaurants. Agents wanted to party; but this meant word often got around the small exile communities about who was about to head back home.

Van Hooff's training took place in a large house in Hans Place, just south of Harrods department store in Knightsbridge. There were no uniforms, no names for the recruits – just a serial number and nickname. Guards watched them during the day. The fear was that German spies might identify or turn agents before they even landed back in their own country. They were also tested. Could a recruit's tongue be loosened by too many drinks? Or by a conversation with a pretty girl (who was, unknown to the agents, working for British intelligence)? Many failed the tests. By the end of two months, half the original entrants had been weeded out. Van Hooff learnt to look on everyone with suspicion. He would need to do so when he got back to Belgium.

The school for spies included training on radio sets – how to transmit and receive, how to take a set apart and put it together again, how to encode a message. There were also lessons on enemy weapons and uniforms. Van Hooff paid attention. He knew his life might depend on his ability to remember each answer. He was quickly singled out and promoted to lieutenant.

After classroom education, there was physical education in Manchester with a former officer of the Lancers of Bengal, and finally parachute training. What would you do if your parachute did not open? Put on another, the instructor joked to a group of Poles, Czechs and Belgians. When it was Van Hooff's turn to do his first training jump he preferred to close his eyes.

Finally, Van Hooff was given his instructions, stamped TOP SECRET – details of his cover and his mission, his codes and contacts. There was a week in a fancy hotel to read and learn his file by heart with orders to make no contact with anyone except Page and a man assigned to mind him. But on the fourth day, something strange happened. Van Hooff's minder had gone off for a chat with some women when the hotel front desk called up on the internal phone and said there was a guest to see him – a captain. This did not sound right, he thought. He knew he was not supposed to have visitors. He said the man should wait a few minutes before coming up. Van Hooff called Page, who said he had not sent anyone and told Van Hooff to hold the man there for ten minutes if at all possible while Page tried to organize a response.

The visitor made his way up to Van Hooff's room a few minutes later. He was dressed in British uniform. He knew Van Hooff's codename – Lieutenant Press. Without any niceties but in a well-spoken accent, he asked the Belgian how he was getting on with his instructions and his codes. He said he wanted to see them. Van Hooff's suspicions – already strong – were now sky-high as the man became more insistent.

'Who sent you?' Van Hooff asked.

'Major Page,' he replied.

Van Hooff knew this was false since he had spoken to Page. He tried to play for time – talking about this and that but handing nothing over. Eventually, after a final refusal to show him the file, the man left.

Outside the hotel was a parked car. As the mysterious captain walked past, he was pushed inside the car. Later, when Van Hooff tried to ask Page about what had happened, he just smiled. 'Lieutenant Press, you have done a good job,' was all the MI6 officer said. 'Don't worry.'

Don't worry? thought Van Hooff. It seemed to him that a German spy might have tracked him down, which meant he was not safe in London, let alone Belgium. Was that really what happened? A strange reference in an SOE file a few months later refers to Page having a 'stooge' who had now been removed to a 'cooler'. 'This man, you may know, has been a source of great trouble to us and to the Belgians themselves,' SOE wrote. Was this stooge linked to the hotel incident? Page was a man who liked to play games. It is possible the hotel guest had been sent by Page as one final test for recruits; perhaps it was the same person as this stooge, perhaps not. But there is no record of a German spy infiltrating British intelligence in this way, or of any investigation by MI5.

By March, Van Hooff was ready to go. When he arrived at the airfield, he met his partner for the mission, Marcel Thonus. The two men knew each other from training school but it would be going too far to say they were friends. Van Hooff was the smarter and more professional of the two. He knew Thonus was a hard-boiled veteran of the Foreign Legion, and he was not entirely sure about him, not least because of his fondness for a drink.

Thonus had been recruited by MI6 in September 1941, aged 32. 'Was recruited at a time when agents were extremely scarce,' reads the opening line of his MI6 service file, almost apologetically, perhaps aware that he was not one of the best. He had a square chin and short, slicked-back hair. No father was named on his birth certificate from Liège and he had taken the name of his mother. At the end of 1941, MI6 had informed the Belgian intelligence service in exile that they wanted to employ Thonus. One of Lepage's aides had met Thonus, who told MI6 that he had been with the Foreign Legion and participated in various operations before coming to Britain to join the Belgian forces. But the man from the Sûreté discovered from the records that Thonus had actually deserted from the Belgian army. He explained to MI6 that it was impossible to use a deserter as an agent. The British were insistent and eventually Lepage gave in, agreeing he could be sent on a mission 'so that he could redeem himself'. 'The Belgians were good enough to arrange this matter for us. He was sent as a mutual agent,' his MI6 file noted.

That last line was telling. These agents did not owe their loyalty of service to MI6 alone but also to the Belgian Sûreté. That was what was meant by 'mutual agents'. Thonus's MI6 service record notes that financial responsibility for him – in other words his salary and costs – was undertaken by the Belgian government. One thing the Belgians in exile did have was money, thanks to a steady income from their colony in the Congo.

With their training over, the only thing left for the Belgians to do was to take the leap into the unknown. On 25 March, Van Hooff's MI6-assigned bodyguard-cum-watcher, already edgy after previous events at the hotel, took a phone call. They were told to head for Tempsford airfield. Their flight was to be one of the first since the RAF Special Duties squadron had moved there a few days earlier. Tempsford, in Bedfordshire, was built on a swamp and said to be foggy and boggy, especially if you were a pilot and veered off the runway.

After the disaster of Cassart's pick-up in December 1941, land-ings in Belgium had been ruled out. Parachuting agents in was the only option. Dropping agents from planes had been tried in the First World War but was hampered by the agents' regular failure to jump at the right moment over the targeted drop zone. A cruel solution to this had been found. The poor agent would sit in the passenger seat of the RAF plane, which had been modified so that at the right moment the pilot could pull a lever (probably shouting 'Tally-ho!') and the passenger's seat would give way – just like one of those movie scenes in which the arch-villain disposes of a poorly performing subordinate. The agent would be dropped into the sky below and, it was hoped, would gracefully parachute to the ground.

By the Second World War, things had moved on. When a mission was to be run the RAF team would get a call from SOE or MI6. That evening the BBC might broadcast a *message personnel*, including a phrase meaningless to everyone except the reception committee, who would now know a landing was coming. They would wait at the designated field for the sound of an engine. With torches at the ready they would flash in Morse the right code letter for that day and then light up an 'L' shape for the plane to land on, guns at the ready in case of ambush. Sometimes agents would be dropped 'blind' with no one waiting for them, and have to make their own way to a rendezvous point with contacts.

Pigeons were a part of life at the RAF Special Duties airfield. Four mobile pigeon lofts were looked after by a staff of three who lived on site, always on standby to pack and dispatch birds for a flight. As well as Columba, pigeons were given personally to some agents sent behind enemy lines. When the war started, portable radio transmitters were in their infancy, unreliable and dangerous to be caught with. Sending an 'innocent letter' using an agreed code took its time. But a pigeon could fly back immediately and inform London of a safe arrival or of any problems. The first success had come in early October 1940 when Philip Schneidau – Agent 'Felix' – was parachuted into France carrying with him a pair of pigeons supplied by a fancier vetted by MI5. William Dex Lea Rayner of the Air Ministry advised Schneidau to cut off the toes of a pair of socks and stuff the pigeons into them so that their heads peeped out. On the sixth attempt, Schneidau finally parachuted into France. But ten days later the Lysander that was supposed to pick him up did not appear. He was unaware of it, but the weather had been too bad back in Britain. Schneidau encoded a message and attached it to the leg of one of the pigeons, releasing the bird from Fontainebleau at 8.20 a.m. on Sunday. By 3 p.m. the same day, the pigeon arrived in Kenley, just south of London. Fifteen minutes later a dispatch rider arrived and raced the cylinder to the Air Ministry. But in true bureaucratic style, it took another thirteen hours before anyone with the right authority actually read the message. A Lysander had already been dispatched. As Schneidau climbed into the plane, a bullet shattered its compass. The pilot became lost en route home and Schneidau was still trying to change into civilian clothes in case they were over enemy territory when they eventually ran out of fuel and crashed. Jumping naked out of the wreck, he and the pilot were relieved to find they were in Scotland.

This use of pigeons to acknowledge the arrival of agents and send brief messages soon found favour primarily not in MI6 but in SOE. The leadership of SOE first heard reports of Columba and of MI14(d)'s successful pigeon service in November 1941. It was keen to get hold of the intelligence it had gleaned, while agents with the French and Belgian sections were also using pigeons. Much to the annoyance of Rayner, who felt cut out, SOE ran some tests and decided it preferred MI14's civilian birds to those of the Air Ministry. In November 1941, Rex Pearson told SOE they were welcome to use Columba birds. Radio transmitters might be the future but SOE found pigeons had some advantages. Many agents preferred pigeons, because once released they left nothing incriminating and required little specialist training, although there was the disadvantage that pigeons were a means of one-way communication only and a message might not get through. If they were to be released immediately on arrival simply to tell London that the agent had landed successfully, pigeons were sometimes carried around the neck of parachuting agents. They could also be carried in a rucksack (although there was the danger of an agent falling back and crushing them) or strapped to the stomach.

SOE agents were soon given up to six pigeons from the Columba lofts selected for their stamina and experience. Agents were given written instructions on how to look after their pigeons. They should not hold on to a pigeon long – after a day or two in a confined space the birds would get wing stiffness, but a bird could be kept for up to ten days if there was somewhere it could exercise, like a shed, attic or outbuilding (but you had to beware of cats and rats). The agent had to be careful because if a pigeon could see out of the shed or attic it might get used to its surroundings and refuse to leave. The birds should be given 30–35 grams of food a day – not more, or they might prove unwilling to leave their comfortable surroundings. Agents were also told to check the birds' droppings. 'Colour provides guidance. If showing Green and Watery pigeon is out of sorts and not reliable for flying. Cause of above generally flight or rough handling on the journey. Remedy – quiet and normal feeding.' Light brown poo tinged with white meant they were ready to fly.

Agents were advised to liberate pigeons clear of buildings, high trees and wires. Fog meant they might lose their way, headwinds would slow them down. In darkness they would stop flying, which meant they travelled further in summer. The best time to liberate them was early morning, so they could home the same day.

One place to which agent messages returned was Bletchley Park, home of the code-breakers. Thirty to forty pigeons lived in a loft around the back of the main mansion house above a garage. A landing board with an electric bell would alert staff if a pigeon returned in the night. Messages would then be taken to the local police station, where a dispatch rider would pick them up. SOE's messages were delivered to Room 055a at the War Office, who then took them to HQ at Baker Street.

Columba itself could be used to drop pigeons for agents who were waiting at specific points, rather than, as more usual, dropping them over a wider area for whoever found them. Often the pigeons were dropped at the same time as arms, ammunition and other equipment. In these cases, four or six pigeons were dropped in a special container on one parachute. One RAF team was shot down on the way home, killing all on board. The return of a pigeon from the reception committee with valuable intelligence was the only way the RAF knew the plane had arrived at the drop site. But among British intelligence services, there was a sharp division over the use of pigeons – and it would be one that cost Leopold Vindictive dear.

Van Hooff himself, ironically, was a fan of using pigeons to send messages back from the field, preferring them to radio. The Belgian Sûreté at the same time he was sent was beginning to examine their use (contacting some fanciers in Folkestone). But the Belgians only started properly in May 1943 and the problem was that MI6 – who had sent Van Hooff and were now trying to reach out to Leopold Vindictive – was never as keen. Rex Pearson's concern, when SOE started using his birds, was that MI6, having previously cold-shouldered the idea, might wake up and try to take over pigeon operations now they were producing results. He did not need to worry. The intelligence they brought back made R. V. Jones pretty much the only backer of pigeons within MI6. At one point, he persuaded an air commodore posted to MI6 that the pigeons on the windowsill at the service's Broadway HQ were the primary means of communication with the French resistance. 'For days, at our instigation he solicitously provided them with saucers of water!'

MI6 were sniffy about the whole Columba 'racket', SOE noted, and 'have got no belief in it'. MI6 seem to have initially been dismissive of both Columba and the use of pigeons by their own agents. The use of birds was 'spasmodic and only ancillary to our normal communications with agents in the Field', a report noted.

Pigeons were perhaps not what the macho spies at MI6 thought should be at the heart of the spying game. This perhaps explains why Thonus and Van Hooff – agents of MI6 rather than SOE – were sent in with radios but no pigeons for Leopold Vindictive when they left in March 1942. The tragedy was that there were pigeons next to them in the planes as part of a regular Columba drop. But they were not intended for Raskin and Leopold Vindictive. It seems a terrible oversight from MI6, who would have known that

Raskin and his collaborators had originally used pigeons. But why did Melland and Sanderson in MI14 not ensure the pigeons were sent with the agents?

The reason was that MI14 itself was in the dark about the whole mission. This was down to MI6 and secrecy. Melland, Sanderson and the team at MI14(d) may have been the first to contact Leopold Vindictive through Columba. But the subsequent messages from Leopold Vindictive – like that given to Vandael – had been delivered through evasion and intelligence networks, which belonged to Dansey and MI6. And MI6 kept itself to itself. In its mind, this was all about the problem that other agencies were 'leaky' and amateurish. It was an analysis which had some truth: 'The gossip tends to swell,' Amies conceded. But this could also be used as an excuse when secrets meant power. MI6 had seen the intelligence from Columba and knew how good Leopold Vindictive's network was. But now MI6 wanted to contact Leopold Vindictive itself. It had not told MI14 about the message received from the network. Nor had it told MI14 it was now dropping in agents to make contact. And it did not want to use pigeons, even though these were precisely what Raskin had asked for. The rivalries and secrecy of British intelligence came at a terrible price.

Thonus and Van Hooff were primed to go in March. The full-moon period had started on the 23rd, two nights before Van Hooff's first flight ended in the anticlimax of a return to base following sparks and engine failure. It was to be a bad patch. Seventeen operations were attempted and only four completed. Drops into Belgium had failed to find any reception committees. But the following night, 26 March, Van Hooff and Thonus were ready to try again. Agents – known as Joes – were normally driven to Tempsford at the last minute from a country house nearby which acted as a holding place.

Thonus and Van Hooff were first taken to a building known as the barn where they were prepared. Then the two men had their pockets inspected carefully. Their clothes had been made in Belgium so as not to arouse suspicion. They had to be sure there were no receipts or items which might give away the fact they had spent time in London. They were given false papers in their cover names. In one room, their parachutes were prepared and fitted by a dispatcher. In another, the radio sets were handed over. Then on went the flying suits, and each took a weapon, and finally a shovel to bury their parachutes, a bottle of rum and enough food to last them a day. Now they were ready.

They flew with other planes and other agents in a larger operation. Van Hooff and Thonus' plane crossed the coast at the Pas de Calais. Encountering haze, the pilot dropped his height and set course for Cambrai. This time the light went green. The containers of pigeons were dropped on the same flight – but not at the same place as the men – before the plane made its way home just after midnight. The agents were in.

CHAPTER TEN

Undercover

Over Valenciennes, the red light had come on. The sergeant gave the parachutes one last check and opened the door. A blast of cold air hit the two Belgians. Jef Van Hooff's heart was thumping. This time the light switched to green and he jumped out into the dark night.

In training there had been a long drop – a chance to close your eyes and feel the sensation of falling for a few moments. But when it happened for real everything seemed to take place much faster. After fifty metres of free fall, he pulled the cord and felt a jolt. In what seemed no time at all, branches struck his face. He tensed for impact on the ground. But it did not come. He had fallen into a wood and was suspended from a tree like a scarecrow, twenty metres in the air. His radio had fallen next to him. He could just about see the RAF plane still circling above him, a small sliver of light visible from the open hatch door from which he had jumped. Then it was gone. The last few months of freedom were over. Now he was heading back home to fulfil his own romantic ideal of helping free his country. But in reality he was a spy on the run, hanging like a puppet from a tree.

A feeling of abandonment and helplessness washed over him, but survival instincts quickly kicked in. The Germans might have heard the plane and would come looking. By wriggling back and forth, he was able to break a few branches, although with a painfully loud crack that reverberated through the quiet forest. It took him nearly an hour in all to extricate himself from his parachute, an effort which left him sweating from head to toe despite the cold of a March night. He then began to dig with his shovel to bury his parachute and flying suit in the temporary hiding place of a pit. In another hole, he hid his radio. It was too risky to carry everything around at first.

But what about his partner? Thonus should have fallen less than one hundred metres away. They had agreed on the rather unusual signal of making the sounds of a cat on heat to try to find each other, and so Van Hooff started imitating an amorous feline. There was no response to his cries. Van Hooff began to explore the wood, gun in hand. Eventually he found a clearing. There, to his horror, was what looked like a man swinging in the tree, as if hanged. As he came closer, Van Hooff saw with relief that it was just the parachute and flying suit, with no trace of Thonus inside. Thonus had already disobeyed orders by abandoning rather than burying the incriminating items. There was no sign of him. Van Hooff was slowly learning what others would realize. Thonus was sloppy.

Van Hooff headed off, trekking through a field of cows. He glanced at his watch. It was five in the morning. As he came to a farm, a dog began barking. Weapon in hand, he approached the door of the farmhouse. 'What have I done wrong?' the farmer asked when he saw a stranger bearing a gun.

'You haven't done anything wrong, but do what I say,' said Van Hooff gruffly. He ordered the farmer to help retrieve Thonus' parachute. The farmer at first refused. Van Hooff threatened to burn his farm down, at which he complied.

The two parachutists had agreed that if they lost each other they would meet at Valenciennes railway station. When Van Hooff arrived later in the day, the station was packed with German soldiers. One of them asked Van Hooff for a cigarette. 'I don't smoke,' the undercover agent replied, his voice shaking. Around a corner he spotted Thonus reading a newspaper. Despite the seriousness of the situation, Van Hooff crept up and surprised Thonus, making him jump out of his chair.

Thonus apologized for the previous night's carelessness. He said he had been overcome with panic and abandoned his parachute. That night they travelled over the border to Brussels. They were carrying tens of thousands of francs which Van Hooff hid down his trousers. Thonus was so relieved to make it that he knocked back whisky after whisky in a bar on arrival.

At dawn, having had just a couple of hours' sleep in a hotel, Van Hooff and Thonus were up. The two were embarking on a life in which survival depended on acting normally, but in which your nerves were shredded daily. Every time you approached a German control point where soldiers asked for your papers, you would fear they might notice something odd, some incongruous detail. Or would reference be made to something that had happened and which you had missed whilst you were away in London? Survival depended not just on your own wits but also on the network of helpers who would shelter and move you from place to place. All it took was for someone who knew you to be captured and talk – or for there already to be a traitor amidst your ranks. The longer you lived undercover, the more – rather than less – paranoid you became. Capture was not the exception for agents like these. It was the norm. You were living on borrowed time.

On a train journey, one person recognized Van Hooff and said, 'Everyone thought you had gone to England.' It was a reminder that Belgium was a hard country in which to be a secret agent. It was small, and people always wanted to know who someone was or where they were from. Friends and family talked. Sometimes the agents themselves boasted. If a member of the Belgian army disappeared for a few months and then came back, gossip quickly spread that he had probably been to Britain and was back on a 'special mission'. Even when agents were dropped at different locations with instructions not to contact each other, they would end up meeting – sometimes by chance, sometimes by choice. Networks which should have been separate became intertwined and compromised.

Van Hooff and Thonus plunged straight into their work. Like many agents, they had been given multiple tasks by Page and MI6. One of Van Hooff's jobs was to liaise with a network codenamed Beaver. But this network had already begun to collapse following German arrests. He was also supposed to go to Liège and build a network of contacts that connected to Brussels and Mechelen. Thonus would stay in Brussels and act as the radio operator based in the capital.

Among their assigned missions was one that had been added at the last minute. Vandael had arrived in Britain two weeks before the departure of Thonus and Van Hooff, and MI6 had decided that the two parachutists should be given the task of establishing contact and supporting Leopold Vindictive. The primary role was given to Thonus since he would be based in Brussels.

The pair had been told that their contact with Leopold Vindictive was Fritz Devos. Vandael had reported that he seemed to be competent, and had money. They arrived at his house in Roeselare on 29 March and gave him the password – Madeleine.

The next day, 30 March, Devos and Thonus went to the Debaillie house in Lichtervelde, the home of the pigeon nine long months earlier. Raskin and Joye had been phoned, and so the band of friends was together once more. It was a moment which filled them with hope. At last, Britain had received their messages reaching out for further contact. And London had judged them important enough to parachute in agents to help. This surely was the beginning of a new chapter in their work. MI6 with its radio sets had arrived.

Thonus handed over 30,000 francs to the men. In return the parachutist was passed a message to send back to the British. A surviving typed note from Raskin dated 7 April 1942 begins. 'Leopold Vindictive demand a pigeon with great urgency to send back important information.' It asks for an acknowledgement on the BBC of receipt of the message, and requests a drop around midnight; it gives precise coordinates, saying that the site, near a forest in Uccle near Brussels, will be marked out with two white lights and one red light. Three pigeons are to be dropped. It is suggested that other pigeons be dropped at locations 10 km away to try to divert the German search parties.

Behind the sparse instructions lies a deep sense of frustration – and of hope. Why had the pigeon route begun so successfully last July proved so difficult to maintain? Pigeons were the best way of getting the detailed maps of the coastal defences they had toiled over back to London. Van Hooff was impressed at the quality of the map when Raskin showed it to him at their meeting. A map could not be sent by radio. But the pigeons had still not come, even though Van Hooff himself was a fan of the method and they had sat on the plane next to the men as they parachuted in. And every moment that passed increased the danger of the net closing. Raskin said that Michelli's friends would look after the agents in Brussels. And he introduced them to Madame Roberts, whose network of friends and helpers would aid them.

Thonus got to work. Being a radio operator (or 'pianist', as they were sometimes called) involved moving from house to house for security. It took time for an operator to convey a message. First, you had to painstakingly encode it. Next you had to wait for one of the moments agreed with the British to transmit. You then had to hope they could hear you, and that atmospheric interference or a fault on one side or the other did not get in the way. All the time, you would have half an eye on your protection team in case they gave you a warning signal that someone was coming. In his rather vague hand-written testimony, Thonus says he began trying to send messages but there was no contact. When he had landed in the tree, his radio set had taken a battering. Something was not working.

Devos initially put Thonus up and provided him with a new identity card. The first priority was a new transmitter. They began to ask around, hearing that perhaps there was a working set in Tournai. In the time they worked together Thonus and Devos did not get on. Thonus described Devos as 'very imprudent', and said he had to change safe houses because the people he met spoke too freely about who he was and why he was there. One helper demanded 100 francs a day and insisted Thonus should pay at every café. Devos meanwhile blamed Thonus for lax security. He was 'superficial', he said, and 'frequented bars and dangerous women. I warned him that he would expose us all.' Word eventually got back to London that Thonus was 'constantly drunk'. Devos claimed that Thonus ran out of money and so he had to give back the money the parachutist had brought for him. Michelli eventually intervened to place him with another helper. Thonus was moved around from safe house to safe house in the suburbs of Brussels through the network of contacts that Raskin had used to gather intelligence in the city. But wherever they tried, the transmitter would not work.

Meanwhile, Marie and Margaret listened to the radio in Lichtervelde hoping that the radio message given to Thonus would get through and the BBC would respond, confirming a pigeon drop. But by the end of April, they had heard nothing.

In London, too, there was frustration. The agents had gone in but now there was silence. Leopold Vindictive was still out of reach. Had the agents been captured? A note from Page at MI6 says that even though a wireless operator was sent with money and instructions,

'He did not establish wireless communication with us and we do not know what happened to him.'

The Germans were beginning to close in. Bodicker in the Abwehr's IIIF turned to his best man, Willy Plate (also known as Peeters), as his investigations gathered pace. Now in his early fifties, Plate had originally been a civilian German secret policeman in Düsseldorf, and had been attached to the Abwehr's IIIF in Cologne before being sent to work out of its office on Place Rogier in Brussels. He was red-faced, fat and bald with glasses, but was always well dressed and chasing after women. Plate was involved in the Abwehr's *Hauskapelle* network, a small team designed to be kept secret from everyone else, and tasked partly with spotting enemy agents and also with undertaking possible work if the Allies ever invaded. Colleagues noted that he hoarded his archives of papers and never let colleagues see what he was up to (perhaps because he had a sideline in buying and selling paintings). He was given the most difficult and complex cases.

Plate was running multiple agents. One of these, Augustin Leduc (codenamed Laurent, but with so many aliases that one file just ends with 'etc' as the list goes on), was given the task of finding the priest and the pigeon about whom Bodicker had been tipped off. Leduc, in his late thirties, worked only for Plate – no one else either wanted or was able to deal with him. Plate disliked Leduc but also rated his abilities. He was a Belgian who betrayed his compatriots for hard cash – 10,000 francs a month, sometimes more – and even Plate would call him a '*grand bandit*', later saying he had to send him off to France because he was so difficult.

Van Hooff went to Liège to set up his network, having first paid a visit to an old friend. Before he even had a chance to say anything, he could tell from the friend's eyes that something was wrong. Van Hooff's mother had passed away, the friend explained. Anger welled up against the Germans. If it had not been for their occupation he would have been there to see her. Van Hooff's response was to throw himself into his work, trying to find people who might know about the movements of military convoys around Belgium.

On his fourth day in Liège, he tried to radio London for the first time. He found himself wishing he could use a pigeon instead to communicate – not just because it would be easier but because he was jealous of the idea of the pigeon being able to fly away from the danger that encircled him at every moment. But, like Raskin, he was to suffer from MI6's prejudice against the use of birds and their preference for radio. He waited in room five of the Star Hotel for the assigned moment and then went up. Van Hooff was always nervous when he used his transmitter, knowing he had maybe ten minutes at most before the risk of being found began to grow exponentially. German direction-finding teams (known as the *Funkabwehr*) were becoming increasingly efficient at locating agents by triangulating signals with detectors. Sending a message was a race against time. Every extra second that an operator spent tapping out his message increased the chances of the Germans crashing through the door. Being a fast operator was not only efficient; it was the difference between life and death. Van Hooff was particularly nervous, since staying in room six next door was a German officer. Then, with his headphones on he heard the code letters EFD – his call sign. He almost cried with joy. But his nerves got the better of him. Clumsily and hesitantly, he tried to answer, but he could not get his response right and made mistake after mistake. Eventually came back the depressing response from London, 'Repeat Tomorrow'.

The next time he was steadier, and over the coming days he began collecting information and meeting contacts, often transmitting from a cemetery at night.

Van Hooff had another, even more clandestine mission, one that remains shrouded in secrecy. Making contact with Raskin was not merely about securing a route for the intelligence whose value had been shown by the original Columba message. Thonus had been assigned to work with Leopold Vindictive, but Van Hooff was given a specific mission which required Raskin's help. What he describes as his 'political mission' was to find out as much as possible about the inclinations of key political and religious figures. The well-connected Raskin would be his liaison in finding some of these people. It may have helped that Van Hooff's own brother was a Scheutist missionary, and so he was welcomed with open arms.

The most delicate aspect of the mission was the attempt to establish a secret back-channel contact to the King of Belgium. The government-in-exile had a difficult relationship with the monarch, each side being angry with the other for their decisions in those chaotic days of May 1940. In his mind, the King had decided to stay with his people rather than flee, but in many people's minds he had effectively lent his legitimacy and support to Hitler. Could relations be repaired between the two sides? And what were the monarch's real views towards the Nazis now, after nearly two years of virtual house arrest?

Just before Van Hooff arrived, the King's position had taken a turn for the worse, many of his compatriots seeing a further sign of faulty judgement. In late 1941, Leopold had remarried. For many Belgians, it seemed odd that a man who was supposed to be a prisoner should be in a position to marry. An intelligence report from MI14 noted that some wags had chalked a message on the walls of his palace at Laken saying 'Des poules pour nos prisonniers' – 'Tarts for our prisoners'. The refrain was frequently heard that 'King Albert [Leopold's father] would not have done that.'

The British government wanted to know what the King's disposition was now. But he lived in the palace at Laken under the watch of a German colonel. He could not communicate with outsiders or travel without German permission, and he was never seen in

Brussels. There had been an attempt to drop an agent to make contact with the King in May 1941 but the agent had been arrested hours after arriving in Belgium. Now Leopold Vindictive offered a new opportunity.

The testimony of Roger Keyes from the turbulent days of May 1940 would have made British intelligence realize how close 'the bearded chaplain' was to the royal family and that he might offer a way of establishing a clandestine contact. Raskin would regularly visit the Comte de Grunne, chamberlain to the Queen Mother, and even keep him informed about his espionage. Raskin also knew the secretary to the King well. Around New Year 1942, through the Comte de Grunne, the King and Queen Mother had both passed on their greetings to Raskin personally in an exchange of messages. Raskin was an occasional visitor to the palace and it is even possible the King himself knew about Raskin's espionage. But for a man already carrying many secrets, Raskin himself knew this was the most sensitive of his roles, and his relationship with the royal court was close but discreet. It was not something to be talked about. This was especially the case since he took confession from the King; few things could require greater discretion. But one of the Belgians who worked with Van Hooff, moving him from one safe house to another, would later confirm that it was thanks to Raskin that a link was established with the King. This, he said, allowed information of great importance be sent to London. The precise details of those contacts remain in files still classified on both the Belgian side and the British.

Van Hooff's work was complicated by his partner's misfortunes. He received a message from Thonus to say that his radio set was still not working. Thonus explained that he had dismantled it and was trying to put it back together again, but he could not work out where all the pieces were supposed to go. Van Hooff headed to Brussels by train to meet him. The two agents went to the house of

Madame Roberts, where many meetings would take place in the coming days. Here Thonus tried again to transmit, but the fuses in the transformer blew. They seemed cursed. Raskin told them Henri Michelli might be able to help. The two agents were now becoming increasingly enmeshed in the Brussels network featuring Mme Roberts with Michelli at its head.

Thonus was beginning to panic. He was frustrated that his radio was not working and was also hearing of more German arrests. He was sure they were on to him. 'I felt burnt,' he later said. Undercover agents who lost their nerve like this were almost always useless. Agents often had a short shelf life and were extracted when they were in trouble. Over-confidence got you caught, but so did excessive fear. Thonus made clear he wanted to go back to London (in order to be sent on another mission, he said). It was time to get him out. The Comet line was the obvious way to do so. The plan was for Thonus to make his way to Michelli's house on 6 May to organize his departure.

Henri Michelli was a busy man and was moving to the fore of operations in Brussels. At the end of April, the Abwehr was getting too close for comfort in its hunt for Frederick de Jonge, the leader of the Comet line and Andrée's father. With a price of one million francs on his head, de Jonge fled (growing huge sideburns to disguise himself). He ate with Madame Roberts the night before he left, telling her Henri Michelli was now to be in charge of Comet. Michelli's office in Brussels had become a central meeting place for an array of networks. A well-meaning man whose ambition for his clandestine work exceeded his ability and experience, he wanted to be almost a chairman of the board for the underground resistance – the big chief. As well as playing a key role in Comet's work, he was carrying out his own intelligence gathering and trying to set up a sabotage network. He was also in touch with groups like Leopold Vindictive – by some accounts a total of seven or eight different networks. His work overlapped between SOE and MI6. This was too much. His time in charge of Comet would be counted in days.

At Abwehr IIIF's headquarters, word had reached the Nazis, German police files indicate, that someone was hiding British soldiers and airmen in Brussels. Bodicker and Plate turned to another agent in the search for them – a man who was just beginning a career which would haunt Britain and Comet through the war. This agent's name was Prosper de Zitter, described as possibly the single most important traitor in Europe. At the age of 22, in 1915, de Zitter had fled Belgium for Canada to escape a charge of rape. He returned when, thanks to the statute of limitations, he could no longer be prosecuted and became involved in fraud and crime. The arrival of the Nazis offered a man like him an opportunity and soon after May 1940 he offered his services to German intelligence, penetrating escape lines. His time in Canada meant he could speak French and English and pose as a Canadian helper using one of at least thirty-one different false identities (although the fact he was missing part of his right little finger was one potential giveaway). His great skill was his ability to engender trust in people, and this was exactly what Abwehr IIIF was after.

From Plate, the orders came to trace the network which would become known as Comet. As early as June 1941, de Zitter would start to work his way round the edges of the early Comet line, doing what he did best – infiltrating, watching and reporting back. Later he would form his own fake escape network to trap servicemen. Many hundreds were caught and died because of the actions of this one individual, who took millions of francs in payment (as well as abusing some of the women who were captured). Stories and wild rumours about him spread (including that he slept in a coffin), to the point that some wondered if he was a fictional bogeyman. But he was real, and was to be the Comet line's nemesis through much of the war. British agents would be given instructions that if he was ever spotted, he was to be killed instantly.

On 22 April, a message had been sent to another Belgian agent and radio operator, Jacques Van Horen – codenamed Terrier by SOE – a handsome, square-jawed former member of the Belgian army. The message told him to send someone to Michelli saying he was from 'Marcel' and was interested in 'Malaga'. This was the code Vandael had told London could be used to contact Michelli if they needed something – in this case the evacuation of agents via Comet. The message came back to London saying that Michelli had agreed but needed more guidance. At the end of April London kept up the contact, a message on the BBC saying that another agent was arriving who would come to see Michelli. What few knew was that this was part of the Abwehr operation and the net was closing in. Michelli – without being aware of it – was a dangerous man to know.

The early resistance networks had always been messy, overlapping and intertwining. In London each network might have a separate codename but on the ground they consisted of people who knew each other, and who met and talked and helped each other. It was further complicated because the two British agencies sending people over – SOE and MI6 – were feuding at home in London and failing to share information. Yet in Brussels, their respective agents on the ground were intermingling. This was a recipe for disaster.

One of the reasons for the intermingling was the very unreliability of many early radio sets, which meant that when word went round of anyone who might have a working set, everyone wanted to use it. As a result, MI6's intelligence networks would often end up using the same sets as Belgians parachuted in by SOE for sabotage. At times London had no real idea who a message was coming from, and there was confusion in Brussels as well. London was realizing they needed to 'compartmentalize' the networks with much higher walls, so that if one person or group were discovered, the Germans would not be able to roll up many others. SOE had contacted Page at MI6 on 28 April regarding the overlaps. Page had understood things were going wrong. But it was already too late.

The plan was to hold a meeting on 6 May at Michelli's house. Thonus and Van Hooff would be there and could discuss Thonus's departure with the guides for the Comet line. There was also a British airman called Larry Carr who they were due to take out. It would be a chance to work out what messages from the various networks also needed carrying to London. Many paths led to Michelli's door, and on 6 May that would prove a disaster.

CHAPTER ELEVEN

Battle of the Skies II

Larry Carr's parachute had taken him down into Belgium just after midnight on 28 April. But he was no secret agent. Before the war he had been a surveyor from Kent. That night he was part of the crew of an RAF Halifax bomber that had set out from Yorkshire on a bombing raid destined for Cologne. But as it flew over Belgium, the Halifax was attacked by a German night fighter flown by Reinhold Eckardt, one of the Luftwaffe's top pilots and a veteran of the Battle of Britain. Carr bailed out over Hamois and came down about a kilometre from the wreckage of his aircraft. He hid his parachute and headed south using a collar-stud compass.

Half an hour later, as he was crossing a track, two Belgians approached him. One was a commandant of the gendarmerie. It was a moment of tension. Would he be arrested? They asked if he wanted to get back to England. Fortunately, it was no trap. He was taken to a house and given a meal and some civilian clothes. The commandant called the local German HQ and told them that there had been no survivors of the crash.

The next day Carr had been taken by train – changing a few times to be careful – to meet a representative of the Comet line. He would now be moved from house to house around the Brussels suburbs by Michelli's network, learning along the way that the gunner on his plane had been betrayed by a Belgian whom he had called out to in a wood.

For those RAF men who crashed in Europe and were lucky enough to find their way to sympathizers, Columba pigeons offered a way to send news back home. One message from Le Neubourg in northern France came from a 'patriotic organization' formed in 1940 which explained how a local anti-aircraft gun had shot down four bombers. After that came a message in English:

Dear Mum, I am glad to be able to relieve your minds on my whereabouts, and to tell you I am in good hands. It shouldn't be long before I'll be back in good old England. Already, I know of two other members of my crew being safe, Wally Jones and George Henton. They are a few miles from here and are much the same as me. I haven't seen them yet but have received a note from each. There isn't much else to say, only that I am in good health and happy. The chatter of an unfamiliar language gets a bit monotonous. There isn't any more to say, so will stop. Your loving son, Stan

R.197072 Sgt Jinks, S.B.

Next comes a series of one-line messages from allied airmen hiding with Stan. Each just gives their number rather than their name. 'Good luck, feeling pretty cheesed,' says the first RAF man. 'Always smiling. Also cheesed,' writes the second. 'Keep up the good work,' says the third. Then follows a characteristically American-sounding line from a US Air Force officer: 'Doing what we can. God's speed.' Then another RAF man: 'Am okay now injuries healed up. Okay.' And finally one more RAF line: 'Feeling fine, but as the rest, cheesed.' They might have been cheesed but at least, thanks to Columba, their families knew they were safe.

One Columba message had a particularly personal connection for an RAF pilot dropping the pigeons. Guy Lockhart's Spitfire took off from Biggin Hill just after lunchtime on 6 July 1941 to escort six Stirling aircraft to Lille. But less than an hour into the flight, enemy fire shredded one of the wings and he crashed not far from Calais. Lockhart parachuted out but was knocked unconscious on the ground. Fortunately for him, he, like Carr, found help. The 25-year-old was hidden for three weeks before making his way back to Britain. He was then talent-spotted by the RAF Special Duties team responsible for dropping agents and pigeons. Columba message 214 came from a pigeon dropped in preparation for the Dieppe Raid in August 1942. It was from Pas-de-Calais and a group calling themselves LMN Kommando 6, who were a pair of brothers who had sheltered Lockhart. 'He will remember the two brothers,' they wrote, providing the pilot's home address as verification of their bona fides. They offered allegiance to de Gaulle and said they wanted to fight, offering extensive information on local German movements. The authors asked for greetings to be sent to Lockhart and two other aviators. Lockhart would have their address, they explained, and so that would allow more pigeons to be sent to them. Unfortunately, by the time the pigeon made it back home on 3 September, Lockhart was in no position to receive the greetings. Three nights earlier he had flown his Lysander to France to collect an agent. The pickup proved disastrous because the agent (who appeared to be drunk) had laid a flare path across a ditch, with the result that the plane sustained damage as it landed. Lockhart was forced to make a second escape from behind enemy lines through Gibraltar. He then joined Bomber Command. On his forms he had to enter the countries he had visited and for what purpose; his answer was 'France. Twice. Escaping'. The third time was not lucky for Lockhart though. In April 1944, he was shot down and killed by a German night fighter.

★ ★ ★

In the battle of the skies, pigeons saved the lives of some RAF airmen out on their mission. At 11.30 a.m. on 10 October 1940, a pigeon arrived back at the royal family's loft in Sandringham, having been released in the Netherlands at 7.20 that morning. It was the first to carry details of a crew that had made a forced landing on the continent.

Down in Plymouth, Bert Woodman and his group would deliver birds by van to the local RAF station every Wednesday and Saturday to be taken out on flights. Two baskets of pigeons were given to many RAF planes in case their radio failed and they had to make a forced landing. The birds would be carried in the upper half of the plane to reduce the risk of drowning if the plane ditched in water. Inside the lid of a box were instructions on how to use a special indelible pencil to write on the container and then release the birds. The lofts of fanciers in the Plymouth group were fitted with alarm bell traps; when the bell rang they would call Bert's wife, who would then contact the RAF signals officer.

Despite its early royal success, the RAF scheme nearly did not survive. In May 1941, there were complaints that no message had led to a crew's rescue. Often the planes were sinking too fast and the crew, perhaps understandably, had other things to worry about than following the proper pigeon release procedure. The Director of Signals thought that it was time to consider discontinuing the service.

But Bomber Command came out strongly in favour of keeping the pigeons. It was not just about the number of times they had actually saved lives. Morale would be affected by the pigeons' removal, it warned. Officers realized that crews found the pigeons a genuine comfort. In the event of the horror of being ditched at sea, why would a crew not want one more possible means of rescue, however slight? There was also something in the warmth of another creature and the knowledge that it was heading off home; its value was intrinsically more reassuring than the valves and wires of a radio set, whose message – like the bird – disappeared into the vast sky above the sea. Bomber Command had recognized that there was an emotional comfort to carrying the pigeons that exceeded their practical value. Often birds would become mascots. One air gunner would only fly with a black and white chequered bird because the first time he carried one on board he had not been fired upon once. The only crew Bert Woodman and the Plymouth fanciers were not so keen on was a group of Australians, since there had been mysterious losses of pigeons liberated on their training flights. An inquiry found the crew had developed a taste for pigeon pie.

The RAF rescue pigeons received a stay of execution in the middle of the war and were provided with a new watertight container that could be sealed in four seconds. This could be thrown from the aircraft into the water and picked up by crew once they were in their dinghy (the container could even be used by the crew for buoyancy if the dinghy was too far away). Soon afterwards, the pigeons began to show their worth. A bomber crew crash-landed in the Netherlands at 10 a.m. on 21 February 1942, and 11-month-old Billy delivered his message the following day at 13.40 'in a state of complete collapse' after having flown through a gale-driven snowstorm, making a journey of 250 miles back to the RAF station at Waddington.

The real star was a bird called Winkie. That same month a Beaufort ditched into the sea at short notice owing to engine failure. The crew managed an SOS but the aircraft broke up on impact. An open pigeon container fell into the sea. The crew – now in a dinghy – tried to recover the container but in doing so, the door was broken open. The pigeon became wet (which hindered its ability to fly), and it escaped at 16.30 before the crew could get hold of it and attach a message. A second pigeon was recovered but it was too wet to fly, so the crew carefully massaged the bird to dry it by hand and then attached their SOS message before releasing it at 17.00. This second pigeon never made it home. But the first pigeon arrived at 8.20 the following morning. A radio SOS signal had been received, but it was so weak that the resultant fix was extremely vague and the ensuing air search was attempting to cover an area of 70 square miles. On the arrival of the pigeon, an NCO linked it to the missing aircraft; seeing that the bird was wet and smeared with oil, he was able to assess the pigeon's condition, the time of the aircraft's ditching (as established by the faint radio signal) and the weather, and work out that the bird had flown 120–140 miles. He suggested that the search should operate within a much more specific area. The search parties changed their bearings and the aircraft and dinghy were spotted fifteen minutes later, 129 miles from base. Four lives were saved. It was at a subsequent dinner in the pigeon's honour that the name Winkie was bestowed, since in her pen she 'winked' by drooping an eyelid at one of the men she had rescued – although in truth, the slow action of her eyelids was almost certainly a sign she had not recovered from the exhaustion of the flight. Only a handful of pigeons were, like Winkie, responsible for the saving of lives, mainly at sea, but many other RAF men found them a comfort in dangerous times.

For R. V. Jones, the struggle to stop the German night fighters which were inflicting such a terrible cost on Bomber Command was a top priority. His task was to try to understand the nature and location of German defences against the RAF so that they could be countered and men like Larry Carr might avoid being shot down. Jones went to see Page, head of the Belgian section at MI6. 'Tell me what you want,' Page said with a wave of his hand, 'I will get you anything.' Jones suspected it was an idle boast, but Page began to deliver. In February 1942, his Belgian agents produced a report about an object 35 km east of Brussels. Using the information, Jones sent in aerial reconnaissance to get pictures. It was a radar installation codenamed Freya and there was also in the vicinity a large paraboloid about twenty feet in diameter with other structures around it. This was what would be called a 'Giant Wurzburg'. A combination of sources led Jones to understand that the Germans had constructed a vast ground-based interception system. Freyas and Wurzburgs allowed the Germans to fix the position both of enemy aircraft and their own at long and short range. They could help target gunfire and guide a night fighter directly onto the tail of a British bomber.

Mapping these defences was vital. Scattered as they were across north-west Europe, however, finding the sites was a challenge. The one advantage was that the installations looked very unusual if you got close enough. A Giant Wurzburg or a Freya looked distinctive because no one had ever seen a radar dish before. Locals struggled to describe them, often calling them 'inverted umbrellas'. Jones asked resistance agents to pass on information if they saw any buildings that might be searchlight or radar stations so they could be photographed from the air. One Belgian agent managed to steal a map of searchlights. But getting agents' reports out remained problematic. They were sometimes smuggled out on the express train that ran from Lille to Lyon, the fireman hiding them under the coal so that they could be shovelled into the fire and burnt if a search began. But the final leg back to Britain proved harder. Page told Jones that at one point there were fifteen hundredweight of reports waiting in Lisbon to be taken by plane back to England. They needed to get the reports back faster. The answer was pigeons.

Columba would provide Jones with some of the vital intelligence he craved. He had asked locals to spot any large structures with rotating aerials that looked unusual, and soon replies to his questions were starting to arrive at MI14(d). On 5 June 1942 a Columba message came back. The writer said they thought the bird had been meant for Belgium rather than the Netherlands but decided to provide some details anyway, and reported news of a camp at Opperdoes with a great many 'technical installations, listening-in-apparatus, jammers … From this camp, the night fighters get their instructions,' the author wrote, helpfully providing a map that showed the precise location. 'Do come over this way and do not fly so high so we can see that you are British.' Jones and the Air Ministry considered this message 'first class'. It was just the start. 'Pigeons drew first blood on three night-fighter control stations,' Jones recalled.

One of the Columba messages Jones valued came via a strange route. An English racing pigeon bred in Barrow-in-Furness was blown over to the Netherlands in July. It was taken to two Dutch patriots on 21 July. They could see it was a British pigeon and called it 'Tommy'. It was exhausted, and so they tended it carefully until it was ready to return to its home in Lancashire, where it arrived on 9 August. A message was attached in which the authors said friends wanted to send their greetings to Winston Churchill as well as to the queen of the Netherlands, who was in exile in Britain. She should be told the opposition in the country was 'at the highest grade it has ever been owing to the latest German measures against the hostages and the Jews'. But after the salutations came hard military information. The authors explained that near the village of Sondell in Friesland was an enormous installation designed to hear approaching British aircraft. It had a diameter of ten metres and they had learnt that it could hear British planes when they approached the coast. There were enormous cables to carry information from this facility to an aerodrome where German fighters could be launched in response. A British plane had been shot down on the night of 25 July after dealing with two German planes, but the crew had since been arrested. If Tommy the pigeon was found, they asked for a message to be broadcast on the Dutch bulletin of the BBC. 'Long Live Great Britain, Long Live the Allies, Long Live the Queen', they ended before a special greeting to some friends, which was followed by the rather wonderful signoff: 'Cheerio!!!!! Twee Geuzen' (Two Pirates).

The bird had brought details of one of the main radar posts in the Netherlands, one which Jones and London had not been aware of before. And more information was soon to follow. Message number 235 came from a pigeon found at 5 p.m. on 27 September 1942 on an island south of the Hook of Holland, which made its way back to the Isle of Wight three days later. The author gave his name as Smuggler. Perhaps that was why he was so observant about details of coastal defences. The crucial point for Jones came with one line: 'At Oostvorne there are wireless masts made to rotate, situated in the dunes.'

Jones found this detail invaluable. And Britain made use of it. A month later, Rex Pearson at the War Office wrote to Commander Cyril Tower at the Admiralty saying that he understood that the location station 'has since been quite satisfactorily dealt with'. The Admiralty said it wanted the locations of more radar stations on the coast.

By January 1943, Jones said that Columba had located three stations in the Netherlands 'which could not be fixed by any other means'. He specifically asked for the Columba team to be thanked on his behalf. More were found by pigeon that year. It had taken a combination of intelligence sources to understand the German night-fighter system – from captured maps to RAF combat reports, radio intercepts to aerial reconnaissance. But Jones specifically cited pigeons alongside these better-known tools in his reports.

Columba also brought Jones news of the success of the counter-measures he was working on. Jones and others in scientific intelligence had developed a way of confusing German radar by dropping thousands of strips of aluminium foil from a plane. The strips – codenamed 'Window' – reflected back the radio waves and made it impossible to pinpoint a British plane. Jones had to push hard to deploy the technique against resistance from those who feared the Germans might develop their own version against British radar. But finally in the summer of 1943 they received the go-ahead. Columba brought a stunning insight into its effect.

On 13 August 1943, a Frenchman in Ville de Landrecies in northern France shoved a message into one of Columba's green cylinders. Two days later the bird was back at its loft in Mitcham and the message had reached Brian Melland and the Columba team. From them it went straight to R.V. Jones. Message 486 was a cracker, second only to Leopold Vindictive's message 37. Extensive details of infantry movements were given, not at the level of Leopold Vindictive but still amongst the best that would be seen. There were precise coordinates of munitions depots and detailed assessments of recent RAF bombing raids – how two factories and a railway repair shop which had been targeted were now back up and running and needed to be struck again.

The author reported that a German ship had apparently received 600 tons of a gas, and that French prisoners at a particular base had been provided with gas masks to work with it. There were calls for the BBC to name collaborators and warn them of their fate. Columba writers frequently asked for such broadcasts, for the BBC offered one of the few ways of exerting any power over those who betrayed their communities. A tutor at Prisches worked for the Gestapo. An insurance agent, a fruit merchant and collector's clerk were also named. Then there was the husband of a teacher who was a 'keen collaborator' and a police spy. The writer warned that the Germans dropped their own agents disguised as British airmen to trap potential helpers. He suggested perhaps providing passwords and recognition signals which could change every fortnight or every month, and which only the chiefs of the French resistance organisation would know, in order to vouch for airmen's identity. This would 'also enable us to do away with a few agents of the Gestapo', noted the writer.

But then came the real prize. There were details of what the author called a 'Radio listening-in and guiding post for night fighters'. It was located at Croix-Caluyau and the author provided a precise description and location for the two hemispheric and one rectangular apparatus. Twenty English bombers had been shot down in a radius of around 25 km from it, the author noted.

And finally came the detail that made Jones fall in love with the message. There was a remarkable description of events a few days earlier, on the night of 9–10 August. The writer described how the British aircraft had dropped 'a multitude of black bits of paper metallized by contact with a piece of tin'. The writer would not have known that this was the British countermeasure 'Window'. But the writer managed to describe the reaction it inspired amongst the Germans at the base. A German operator said he detected seven hundred signals in the sky but could not localize a single one to respond. 'The officer commanding the post was mad with rage and declared that he would prefer to be bombed by a 100 aircraft rather than submit to that flood of papers.' The writer added that a fairly large number of the bundles of paper did not scatter properly during the descent. The message ended with a request for a signal on the BBC to acknowledge receipt with the words '*deux pigeons s'aimaient d'amour tendre*'.

'I have never seen a pigeon carrying such a profuse message,' said Jones.

Who had sent the message on what Jones called a 'heavily-laden and very gallant pigeon'? Whoever it was, they must have been inside the control room of the night-fighter station to hear the exact words spoken by the German, Jones thought, believing at one point it may have been a cleaner, although also wondering at another if it was an agent since the message as a whole read as if its originator was someone who knew about resistance work.

Within two days of the message's arrival by pigeon, Jones had shown it to the Secretary of State for Air, the Deputy Chief of the Air Staff and the Chief of Bomber Command. The revelation of the frustrations that their German opponents were facing was an enormous morale boost (and of course a vindication for the scientists who had developed 'Window'). There was another advantage to the message. It was considered less secret than the Enigma decrypts and so could be shared more widely. 'This information coming so soon after the raid, was of extreme value in that it could be told at once to all our bomber crews, to their satisfaction, whereas information arriving through more secret channels could not have received so wide a distribution,' Jones said.

Columba was proving its worth. 'From my point of view, the Pigeon Service produces occasional extremely valuable reports and this is one of them,' he wrote to the Columba team. The combination of the mapping of night-fighter defences and the use of Window proved a turning point in the air war. From that summer, RAF losses began to dip. This Battle of the Skies was being won, thanks in part to the pigeons of Columba. But for MI14's most important agent on the ground, the net had closed.

CHAPTER TWELVE

Capture

The morning of 6 May 1942 in Brussels promised a beautiful spring day, one which Henri Michelli expected to prove busy. He had three meetings. In the morning, Michelli took Van Hooff to see the president of the local football club, FC Mechelen. For Van Hooff, this was not a chance for a kick-around. The president was a well-connected clergyman named Dessain. He and Van Hooff had clashed before the war over the journalist's criticism of his leadership of the club, but now Van Hooff was welcomed and they began to chat eagerly, Van Hooff about England and Dessain about the club. Van Hooff gave Dessain a long questionnaire about relationships between the church and the Nazi occupiers that had been drawn up by British intelligence. Dessain took the list and said he would fill it in later. He also promised to lay flowers on Van Hooff's mother's grave and say a mass in her memory. If things went wrong, Van Hooff asked Dessain to ask for forgiveness from his father for abandoning his family for his mission.

The next day in Mechelen Van Hooff was due to see Cardinal van Roey, a strong royalist, in the hope of forging a link to the government-in-exile. Raskin had arranged the meeting. A crazy plan was hatched in which Van Hooff was to go to the cardinal's palace in disguise, dressed as a priest wearing a cassock. It was an

absurd disguise. He was well known in the town from his football-
ing days. But before that meeting could take place, events took a
dramatic turn.

At four in the afternoon, Madame Roberts came round to see
Michelli at his office. She brought along a dark-haired woman in
her thirties whom she had only recently got to know. The new
friend had won Madame Roberts' trust thanks to the help she had
provided in supplying clothing, papers and coupons for the resistance. The two women and Michelli talked. Michelli mentioned that
there was going to be something of a party later that evening.
Madame Roberts' friend left just after half past six.

Van Hooff and Marcel Thonus arrived at Michelli's soon after in
order to discuss their route back to England. The meeting was also
a social get-together. That evening Michelli's place would be filled
with members of the secret world. Also present was another agent,
Gérard Wauquez, along with Charles Morelle, who acted as a guide
on the Comet line. Michelli's secretary and girlfriend were there
too. Members of a handful of networks were gathering to meet. The
plan they discussed was for Morelle to meet Thonus and two English
airmen – Larry Carr and Ron Shoebridge – the next day at a square
in Brussels. He would then take them out on the Comet line along
with messages from the various networks.

The gathering was unusually – dangerously – large, something
of a farewell party for those planning to depart. The food spread
out on the table was mouth-wateringly extravagant for people
who were used to rations. Each person was to get two boiled
eggs, and there was asparagus and bottles of fine wine brought up
from the cellar. For those living under the heavy burden of
resistance, this was a moment to relax and be with those you
trusted and who shared the secrets for which you risked your
life. The pace was wonderfully slow as they talked before sitting
down to eat.

Sitting by an open window, Van Hooff heard the sound of children playing. As he closed the window, he saw a large grey car on the other side of the street. He caught a glimpse of a woman tipping her hat. Next he heard the bell ring. Then everything became a blur. Five, then ten members of the Geheime Feldpolizei (GFP) – the foot soldiers of the Abwehr – smashed their way into the dining room. All Van Hooff could see was the grimace of bloated German faces. He felt something hard strike his neck. Then the barrel of a gun was pushed into him. Next he was staring straight into the eyes of a thuggish German. The man had the appearance of a wild boar: a huge face, no chin, a snout and two prominent teeth. His arms seemed to end with huge paws. He was Walter Brodmeier, leader of Section 530 of the GFP and an officer with a reputation for brutality.

Van Hooff saw the others being stripped naked to check for weapons. He knew he had one last line of defence. MI6 had given him a cyanide pill which he had secreted behind his ear. One bite and there would be no torture and no revelations from him. But he could not do it. The self-preservation instinct, the hope that there might be some chance of escape or a way out, was too strong. Instead, he tried to make a bolt for a flight of stairs which led out the back, but he fell right into the arms of a German soldier waiting for just such a runner. A whole battalion had been mobilized that evening. The Germans were taking no chances. Van Hooff was met with a volley of kicks and punches. Within a few minutes he and the others were being bundled out of the house and ferried to the city's Saint-Gilles prison. The Germans found forged papers and other information, including sketches of military facilities, letters and the false documents to be used on the escape line. The extravagant feast lay on the table uneaten.

For Michelli, meeting with so many people on the night of 6 May was dangerous. To have such a large group linger for a dinner party increased the risks. But people like Michelli and his friends were not professional agents. They were patriots who had become spies to help save their country. They were not suspicious enough. The idea of having to worry about infiltrators among their own had not yet sunk in. They had not quite got the measure of the Nazi threat. The resistance would have to learn the painful way to fear traitors within.

On the other side of the street, watching the arrests from the café, was the dark-haired woman Madame Roberts had brought with her that afternoon to Michelli's office. She was the mistress of a dangerous man but also a danger in her own right. Her name was Florentine Giralt (also known as Flore Dings), and she was the mistress of Prosper de Zitter, the man tasked by the Abwehr with infiltrating Comet and hunting those helping the escapers. De Zitter himself was street smart but something of a thug. However, his dark-haired, Spanish-born mistress was better educated and better spoken. The 37-year-old Giralt had met de Zitter before the war when she was married to another man. She played the final role in the entrapment of Michelli, Van Hooff and the others. When she had confirmed that they were all in the building, she tipped her hat. That had been the signal for the Germans to move in.

What had gone wrong? Madame Roberts – who lived two blocks from Michelli – may have been too trusting. She was proud of her role in the clandestine world, and had boasted that she had two agents sent from England try to signal from her own house. One of those she told was Florentine Giralt, who had then managed to work her way into Michelli's office that day. Michelli and Roberts must have talked about the dinner that evening, and the opportunity was too good for the Germans to miss. Madame Roberts had been guilty of naivety in her choice of friends. She later defended herself by saying she had been introduced to Giralt by another man she trusted. There were few more important attributes needed to stay alive than being a good judge of character.

But in truth, her slip had only provided the final tip-off to create the most opportune moment for an arrest. The investigation into Michelli had been running for weeks if not months after news had come in that someone was sheltering British airmen. The Germans had Michelli under surveillance well before 6 May. A few days before the raid they told people in a neighbouring apartment to move out and installed their own counter-espionage officers to watch. No doubt Florentine Giralt's report that a party was planned for the evening of the 6th provided them with the perfect opportunity to wrap everything up at once, but the operation and surveillance had been in existence well before that.

The rot went deep. The British intelligence networks put together in Belgium by both MI6 and SOE were starting to collapse like a house of cards. Worse, they had been rotten for some time, yet no one in London had realized how badly compromised they were. One aspect of the problem were the messages contacting Michelli that had been passed through Jacques Van Horen, SOE's agent Terrier, just before the arrests.

Van Horen had been dropped 'blind' – with no reception committee – over Rochefort in Belgium just before midnight on 2 March. He had two pigeons in a container around his neck, but during the drop the cord had become detached and the container dropped to the hard, snow-covered ground. The pigeons were dead on arrival. It was perhaps an omen of what lay ahead. The snow made it hard to hide his parachute and his radio set but he made his way to Brussels. He arrived the next day at the Café de la Paix and looked for a waitress who was the daughter of the owner, and who was supposed to put him in touch with another agent. When the contact arrived in the evening he gave her the password, but she either did not understand or would not accept it. So instead he went to his parents. He retrieved his set and tried to radio back to London to explain what had happened. Word soon reached him about another agent who had been betrayed and he wanted to tell London. His parents acted as his protection team to keep watch as he transmitted late at night in early April. But he stayed on air for an hour. Far too long.

Van Horen's father burst in and said there was movement in the street. Van Horen sent off the last two groups of letters which London had asked him to repeat. While he was transmitting, the doorbell rang. He told his parents to go to bed immediately, turned the light out and listened. Through a window he saw that a house-to-house search was in progress. He took everything that was on the table and shoved it into the suitcase that normally held the radio, put on his coat, drew his weapon and waited. After a while, hearing nothing, he gently opened the back door and looked out. The coast seemed clear. He slipped out, hoping to hide his set. But as soon as he stepped outside the yard was filled with men. He dropped his suitcase next to a staircase in the yard and tried to make a run for it but was caught. His wrists were handcuffed behind his back and his ankles tied. The Germans searched him and found a pistol. They struck him in the face. When they found the radio, they struck him in the face again. His parents were arrested, while he was taken away for interrogation.

They asked how he knew certain named individuals from SOE and Belgian intelligence, and whether he had enjoyed a stay in London hotels. He was told several agents were already working for the Germans. When he did not answer their questions, a rope was slung over the door and he was hung by his handcuffs for between fifteen and twenty minutes, he later said. The Germans then brought in the text of messages sent to him from London. They had been recorded, and now they had his codes they were able to decipher them. Next, he said, he was forced to watch as another man was tortured in front of him. The man had open sores on his feet, on which the Germans painted on some kind of liquid which foamed on contact – probably acid. The man was told to walk. He fell and was then beaten and told to stand. The process was repeated. Van Horen was asked if he understood the lesson.

A few days later, Van Horen was blindfolded and taken to another house. A lift carried him up to the top floor, where there were three or four radio sets. Van Horen's own set was placed on the table and he was told he had to send a message which they handed to him. Van Horen claimed after the war that he had refused, and that a highly proficient German operator started transmitting using his set and imitating his style.

London certainly assumed that the messages were from Van Horen himself, and both SOE and – it seems – MI6 continued contact over the coming months, sending among others the message for Michelli at the end of April. London even dropped containers of material as Van Horen apparently reported successful sabotage attacks on generators and bridges. Van Horen's story after the war was that he had never cooperated with the sending of such messages. But he may have been forced to send and receive messages using his own codes on behalf of the Germans in order to save his parents.

British intelligence is frequently given credit for its work on deception. Among the schemes it employed was Double Cross, which involved playing back German double agents dropped in the UK by turning them and then using them to feed false information by radio. But the Germans could play that game too. The messages London had been sending to Van Horen asking him to contact Michelli and to work on getting Van Hooff and Thonus out had been received by German intelligence. The Abwehr had realized Michelli was a key contact. Using Van Horen's set it had been sending messages back to London asking for more guidance, and had also sent collaborators to Michelli using the agreed codenames.

These were not the only compromises. Another agent – code-named Intersection – dropped in Belgium in January 1942 was arrested on 27 March whilst transmitting as a result of German direction-finding. He had no one watching his back. Intersection agreed to work for the Germans. Within days everyone he had talked to was arrested. London, even though they could see that his signals were not up to his previous standard, continued to use him as a contact for further agents who were to be parachuted in. Those agents literally fell into the hands of the Germans as they arrived. British intelligence did not know it, but its Belgian operations were largely run by the Germans as 1942 progressed.

In a square in central Brussels on 7 May, the British airman Larry Carr waited nervously with his Belgian helper. He was expecting to meet a guide who would take him out of the country on the Comet line and back to Britain. He was due to meet another pilot and, although Carr did not know it, Marcel Thonus was also supposed to accompany them on the journey out. But after an hour no one had turned up.

The only person who arrived was Ron Shoebridge, another member of his flight. It was the first time they had met since the crash. But they soon realized there was no sign of the guide. Word reached them that the men who were due to get them out – led by Michelli – had been arrested.

The Germans' search of Michelli's house had uncovered false papers, including passports that had been made up for the pilots. Now new plans had to be made to help them make their way out through the line; Carr eventually crossed the mountains that bordered France and Spain with Andrée de Jonge, wearing berets and disguised as Basques. Two others from his crew, Shoebridge and Bill Ralston, were captured by the Gestapo.

The Germans had been watching Michelli, but they had no idea who the others were that they had picked up in the raid. It was only after combing through the documents that they realized they had found two agents – Thonus and Van Hooff. They did not know about the link to Raskin. But Bodicker and Plate already had another team on him.

Jean Starck had been one of Thonus's helpers, moving him around Brussels. When he felt the hand of the Germans approaching, he decided he too had to get out. He was told Raskin would help and provide false documents. He had not met the priest and was told to present himself to Raskin with some Chinese money which would act as a token of recognition that he was legitimate (no doubt Raskin had brought it back from China and no one else could get hold of something similar). He was told the priest would help put him on a route to Gibraltar. But then he heard something had gone wrong.

CHAPTER THIRTEEN

Interrogation and Infiltration

On Friday, 1 May Joseph Raskin was at the mission headquarters of Scheut. He celebrated an early mass and had breakfast before going to work in his room in the large brick complex. Around nine in the morning, the doorman knocked on his door to say he had a visitor. In the reception parlour was a local man called Laurent. He asked if Raskin was the father who had been to China. Raskin said yes. The man said he was a stamp collector. He wondered if Raskin would be interested in seeing some of the Chinese stamps from his collection. Raskin said he would be interested and that his visitor should come again. He walked the man out of the door of the reception building. As the visitor stepped out, he gave a signal. Two Germans walked in and grabbed Raskin by the arm.

They ordered the stamp man to tell Raskin in French that he had to take them to his room. By now, it was clear to Raskin that the stamp man was working for the Germans. He was Augustin Leduc, Bodicker and Plate's best agent, sent to track down the priest who was using pigeons. Bodicker himself had been deeply involved in the case. Leduc's orders were to confirm the identity of Raskin as a priest who had been to China. They knew for some reason that this was the key to identifying him as the priest who had been making use of pigeons. Leduc had been given orders to identify if the priest was there, and to give a signal to the Germans waiting outside if he was.

Others in the building realized something was going on. A milk-man had just left after making his delivery to the basement but walked straight back in again to say the Germans were outside and they had guns. In just a few minutes, the building had been cordoned off. A car came into the grounds. Raskin was ushered into the back and before anyone else had the chance to say or do anything, it drove off, Raskin unable to utter a word. Their catch secured, the soldiers melted away and the priests and students began to emerge. Upstairs, the entrance to Raskin's room was sealed. Printed on the seal were the words *Sicherheit Polizei*. The Germans conducted a thorough search after the arrest, taking away two suitcases full of evidence. They discovered a lab for making microfilms and canisters ready for the pigeons. But the statue of the Virgin Mary lay untouched in his rooms. Inside were the microfilms themselves. Everything had been ready except the pigeons.

Raskin was taken to the castle-like fortress of Saint-Gilles prison. It was a grim new home, crammed with prisoners who lived like troglodytes in bare stone caves surrounded by vaulted tunnels. The stench of cabbage and urine hung everywhere. But even here, resist-ance was possible for the determined. Raskin was alone, but other prisoners were given the job of bringing soup or bread or cleaning out his cell. 'Call me Jan,' one young man said as he emptied out a bucket. His next words were careful, since a guard was watching. 'Prepare a message,' he whispered before he left again.

Jan was able to go in and out of the cells to carry out cleaning duties. Next time he came, Raskin was ready and slipped a message to Jan, who placed it in his pocket. The prison was full of political prisoners who had learnt the skills of the clandestine world. A message had to be smuggled out person to person within the confines of the prison before it could reach someone who could take it into the outside world – a tiny replica of the long courier routes used to get messages out of Belgium and to England. One method was to use cigarette papers, onto which a message would be encoded, transcribed and then sent out.

Raskin wrote a series of notes and letters in the coming days which made it out through different routes. One was for the missionaries of Scheut and to Father Verhaeghe, who had known of his clandestine work. 'I am sure about my death sentence,' wrote Raskin. 'Without grace or a miracle, my days are numbered. But God decides those days and I accept it completely.' But, ever the spy as well as the priest, he was not going to give up without doing his best to survive, and to save others. He had a vital message. They must destroy the compromising documents he had hidden, and which the Germans had not found despite their search. The message was met with alarm by the leadership of Scheut, who feared what would happen if their headquarters came to be seen as a den of espionage rather than a place of prayer. So they decided to burn not only those documents but all Raskin's papers. A case was found in the attic full of his notebooks, Chinese papers, drawings and water-colours, a life's mementos of a cultured man. One father with an artistic eye saved some of the pictures and photos, but everything else was consigned to the flames.

Another note outlined the need to protect the broader Leopold Vindictive network. Raskin knew some in his network had not been arrested and he wanted to warn his friends. There was a list of names and addresses. These were people who had to be told as soon as possible of his arrest. He also wanted to assure people that he would not talk. 'I name nobody,' he wrote in this note. 'But the others?' The risk was that others would speak. 'Mr Joye and Voske [Devos] should disappear immediately,' he wrote. 'Mrs Roberts also. It's too dangerous.' The Lichtervelde group should not worry,

Raskin added. He would tell the Germans he had caught the pigeon without the Debaillies' knowledge. Since he frequently stayed in their house and had his own room, he would simply claim he had found the pigeon, locked it in the bedroom and then released it. They were to say that it was normal for him to keep the door of his room closed and that they had known nothing about the bird. It was a barely believable story, but the best he could manage.

Raskin realized he was not the only one in trouble. He reported he had seen some of those he knew in the prison – including Van Hooff – and had heard the name Michelli. These names had to be passed on to others, especially Madame Roberts, he explained. Someone had to go to a shop called 'The Little Doll' in Antwerp and ask a series of women to pass her a message. The messenger must take care not to be followed, but the message was urgent. 'They will all do this voluntarily but it has to be done in one day if possible as the hours are precious and the life of some of them depends on it.'

For some, Raskin's warnings were too late. Madame Roberts had been arrested on 6 May, at the same time as Thonus and Van Hooff. Her ten-year-old son was smart enough to put out a warning signal to others she knew, and also burnt her papers and hid money linked to Raskin.

At a family party in Wallonia, Clément Macq had hurt his knee during a dance. He had been out of town for an operation but came home to his family hoping perhaps that no one had made the connection to him. The Germans rang his doorbell on the morning of 3 August. Leaning on a stick after the operation, even if he had wanted to run he could not have managed to do so.

Fritz Devos fled after the 6 May arrests. He saw a car come to pick up another associate, Julian Praet, who had been a helper moving the parachutists round Brussels. In the car, Devos thought he had seen Marcel Thonus. He believed the agent sent by MI6 was now talking to the Germans. Devos went into hiding, living under a series of false identities.

Hector Joye lay low and went to a friend for a month, but felt uneasy rather than safe. An aunt had tried to persuade him to hide in her convent. But Joye was a family man and he knew this was his vulnerability. If they could not catch him, he knew the Germans would take his wife or children. He felt he had no choice. He went home to Bruges on 10 June. Nine days later one of his sons was walking home when neighbours stopped him, telling him he should not go on as the Germans were there. He went anyway, arriving home to find his parents had been taken away and the house was being searched. His father's office was sealed. His mother was released after a few days. Her small red diary records the transition of her life from worrying about matters to do with the school she ran to visits to Saint-Gilles and from the Gestapo. Appearing many times in the diary over the following weeks is a line saying simply that the Gestapo had come to the house to talk to her. The drawings of the Belgian coast carefully hidden by Joye in the frames of his kitchen door were not found, but the Germans did discover some military maps he had marked.

For the Debaillie family in Lichtervelde, those months as spring turned to summer were bleak. First Raskin, then Joye had been arrested. The pigeon had flown from their house. Arseen had been on the road with Joye. Every day was spent waiting for the knock on the door or the hand on the shoulder. The family feared those around them as well as the Germans. The village remained deeply divided between the blacks and the whites, the pro- and anti-Nazis, and suddenly the family could almost feel the atmosphere become more oppressive, as though they were watched and their activities known about. Rumours began to abound and whispers spread that the family was involved in some kind of resistance work, perhaps to do with the secret army who were said to be stockpiling weapons ready for the Allies to return. Denunciations spread and arrests began. The fear took its toll.

Michel – the fancier who had released the pigeon from the roof a year earlier – had always suffered from a weak heart and on 4 August 1942, the gentlest of the brothers was found dead early in the morning next to his bed. Amidst the anxiety over German arrests, he had suffered a heart attack.

On Saturday 8 August, the family gathered at 11 a.m. at the cemetery near the centre of Lichtervelde to bury him. The plot lies in the middle of the small cemetery, straight down a path from the single entrance by the road. Grief was mixed with fear for Arseen and Gabriel. The two surviving brothers had worried about the risks of being there that day. But to miss their brother's funeral would confirm any suspicions the Germans might have. And they wanted to say goodbye.

Mourners waited in line by the grave to sprinkle holy water onto the coffin. Two men in civilian clothes strode down past the dark headstones that lined the avenue. They were neither friends nor family. They walked up to the black-clad Arseen and pulled him by the sleeve out of the line. They were not Germans but Flemish collaborators. Without saying anything he stepped away with them. Gabriel, standing beside him, was left alone. Young Rosa stood and watched as Arseen was led away to a waiting car, only dimly aware of what the others in the family knew – that they had come to bury one brother that day, and now had lost another.

Soon after, the Germans came to the house to look for Gabriel. Marie and Margaret said they did not know where he was. He had scurried into a hay loft and shifted to hide in the gap under the sloping roof of the house until morning, when he was sure they had left. He then stayed for a while with a friendly farmer. Word went round the village that he was dead – a letter from Gabriel to his family said he was going to drown himself. Instead the family had come up with an ingenious hiding place. In a downstairs room was a table for ironing with a cloth across it. The family dug down beneath the floor and created a hatch which opened up to a space only a metre or so square. Just enough for a man to curl up. Gabriel never left the house for the rest of the war, retreating into this space at the first sign of unexpected visitors or trouble. He never slept in his own bed for fear the Germans would come in the night. Even if he heard them coming and had time to hide, he was afraid they would notice that his bed was warm.

The question on everyone's mind was the one that haunted all resistance networks. Had there been a traitor? Or had people just been sloppy? And had anyone talked under duress after they were captured? A bleak and depressing blame game began.

Some in the network were suspicious that Muylaert had talked after he was picked up in October 1941. Macq seemed to think Muylaert's pride meant he was too boastful and not careful enough about whom he told of his work with them. Being a spy was not about showing off and vanity, Macq complained. He said he had always warned Raskin and Joye to be careful of him.

Certainly the Germans had interrogated Muylaert. We do not know what they did to him. Any fragments they may have obtained – perhaps over time, perhaps with torture – might have been used to complete the jigsaw puzzle of their investigation into who was in touch with the British. But there is no real evidence that he talked, and the time lag from his arrest to that of Raskin was too long – seven months – to account for it.

Some of Raskin's Brussels helpers who worked with Michelli claimed Thonus had denounced the whole group after he was arrested, perhaps being treacherous even earlier. The Belgian Sûreté's investigation shows no proof of that, although it does raise the possibility that Thonus was under surveillance, perhaps owing to his highly visible and reckless behaviour and general sloppiness after he arrived with Van Hooff. Thonus denied betraying anyone. He said that many people with whom he worked were not arrested, meaning he could not have talked. But, according to German police files, Thonus does appear to have given a partial confession, although exactly how it was extracted is unclear. He, like Michelli, may have been badly mistreated by the GFP. This led to further discoveries in what the files say was the basement of an insurance agent, probably Devos. Van Hooff's last residence in Liège was turned over and his radio set found in working order. Slowly the Germans worked their way through the Brussels network and its wider connections across the country. Belgians and British airmen in hiding were found. At least forty people were initially picked up for interrogation. By November 1942, the number had risen to 225, according to German police reports.

Raskin was linked in the view of German investigators to the Dehennin group, which had been rolled up in October 1941. Since Raskin was arrested only in May 1942, and since Thonus and Van Hooff – the two agents sent in to contact him – were taken five days after his arrest, it may appear that all the May arrests were connected. But the same German team under Plate seem to have been following parallel tracks and only later realized there were connections between the priest and the others taken on 6 May.

The networks had been badly compromised. And because they were not compartmentalized, one compromise quickly spread to another. Large networks like Zero and Luc/Marc overlapped with smaller ones like Leopold Vindictive. They were all being rolled up too easily.

Raskin himself knew many people – that was his strength, and his weakness. That and his impatience. And as the hoped-for second pigeon failed to materialize, his desperation had driven him to try more and more routes. He had tried so many channels to get the map of the Belgian coast back to England that all it took was for one to be compromised for the authorities to be able to find him. In the end it looked as if more than one route was discovered.

After the church and his friends, Raskin's smuggled messages also sought to protect the other pillar of his life – the royal family. Raskin warned that the Germans would have found two letters from the Comte de Grunne in his room. These were dangerous as they potentially revealed a connection between the royal court and someone now accused of being an MI6 spy. He told Father Verhaeghe to send a message to de Grunne saying that, if asked, they had only talked about family matters and the King's marriage – and nothing else. In order to reassure them, he told Father Verhaeghe to let others know that he had said 'I will never tell what connects me closely to the King.'

The danger of being linked to the royal family did however offer one hope for clemency. 'The King (who knows me well) should ask the Führer to treat me mercifully,' he asked. De Grunne had been alerted by Raskin's sister to the arrest on 3 May, two days after it took place. On 11 May he wrote to her saying he had been away for a few days and had only just seen her letter. He said he would show it to the Queen Mother, Elizabeth, who knew Raskin. He added that he was sure she would try to intervene as far as she could, while warning that 'in the present circumstances' there could be no assurances as to what the result of such an intervention would be. Raskin still hoped that, despite all the incriminating evidence, his connections might get him out of the worst trouble. One thing he would never lose was hope.

But the royal route was slow. The Queen Mother was out of the country. It was only on 30 May that the royal court made a request to the authorities for the release of Raskin. By then it was already too late. He and his friends had been subject to what was known forebodingly as *Nacht and Nebel* – night and fog. Hitler had signed a decree six months earlier ordering that those found to be involved in resistance in occupied territories were to be secretly transferred and taken beyond the reach of normal criminal proceedings. Their families and friends would know nothing about their fate. On 11 May Raskin had already left Saint-Gilles. His destination was Germany. To his family, he had simply disappeared.

Word reached London on 5 May that something had gone wrong. A three-word telegram arrived at MI6. 'Leopold Vindictive arrested,' it read. It was from Van Hooff. The next day he too would be arrested. What had happened to them all, and why, was a mystery. On 1 July a message came in about the arrest of a radio operator; alongside it was another strange message saying 'Vindictive is safe and has money.' A mistake? Or a German deception message?

All this time MI14(d) and the Columba team had been in the dark. And that had been deliberate. Melland and Sanderson, who had so carefully unfurled those pages of rice paper in July the previous year, had no idea that MI6 had managed to establish contact with their precious source, let alone that they had gone so far as to parachute in agents to establish a connection. The MI6 files are closed, but one letter in the Columba archives points to what happened. The letter is dated 30 May 1942 and is from MI14 in response to a letter sent by MI6 two days previously. There seemed to have been a complaint from MI6 about an MI14 broadcast to Leopold Vindictive made on the BBC. MI14 confirmed that they had sent acknowledgements to Leopold Vindictive in July and on 25 September 1941 via BBC radio but had made no further broadcast until one which seems to have been transmitted just before the letter in May 1942. 'I quite agree that in general it is perhaps inadvisable for messages to be broadcast to organizations on the continent with whom you may possibly be in touch, and I have instructed

Melland to advise APS [Army Pigeon Service] not to arrange for broadcasts in these cases until we have discussed the matter with you.'

Then comes the damning sentence: 'Had we known that you were in touch with Leopold Vindictive we would have spoken to you about him before.' This makes it clear that MI6 had established contact with Leopold Vindictive but had not told MI14 – the organization whose pigeons had been the reason the network came into existence. 'I very much hope that the broadcasts were not the main cause of his capture by the Boche. As he was, I understand, picked up by them early this month i.e. some eight months since the last broadcast using his nom-de-guerre, I feel this is on the whole unlikely,' concludes the letter.

MI14 had been trying to re-establish contact through BBC messages without knowing that agents and radio operators had been sent out to meet Leopold Vindictive. It was only when MI6 heard those broadcasts that it suddenly felt the need to tell MI14 what it had been up to in order to get them to stop broadcasting. But by then it was too late. Word had been received already that Raskin had been arrested and the network rolled up. And poor MI14 was left in the position of having to argue that it was unlikely that its earlier broadcasts were to blame for the recent arrest. It is a damning indictment either of the secrecy of British intelligence or its lack of competence and coordination that two branches of the intelligence service could not keep each other informed about their links with the same resistance network. As SOE also found, such travails were a particular problem when it came to MI6, since it so jealously guarded its sources. That might be for the understandable reason of wanting to protect them against compromise by word getting out too widely, but it might also be simply for the bureau-cratic reason of wanting to claim the credit for a successful source. In this case, the mistake seems particularly hard to forgive: it was

MI14 that had first been in contact with Leopold Vindictive via the pigeons, and so it could hardly be blamed for trying to continue that relationship. And it was MI14 and Columba's pigeons that Leopold Vindictive kept asking for.

For Brian Melland at MI14(d) there seems to have been something deeply personal about the connection with the bearded chaplain, whom he never actually met but whose words he deciphered with a magnifying glass. Melland seemed to remain anxious to solve the mystery of his fate. On 27 August 1942, he received a letter saying two people in England had arrived from a church in Flanders and knew about the evacuation of certain priests. 'I give you this as of probably interest in connection with the famous number 37,' he was told. Not just at the time but for years afterwards, members of Columba and MI14 would fear that their messages, broadcast on the BBC, had been the cause of the discovery of the Belgian priest. MI6 never seems to have told them the truth and put them out of their misery by explaining that the rot went much deeper.

The intelligence networks of both MI6 and SOE in Belgium were falling apart in the spring of 1942. And the problems were compounded because both organizations were so slow to realize it. Parachuted radio operators like Jacques Van Horen had been captured and their radio sets used by the Germans to send false messages, but it took far too long for London to become aware of this. Van Horen was not an isolated case. British operations in Belgium were badly penetrated by German intelligence (although not quite as catastrophically as in the Netherlands, where every single agent dropped was captured). The story of operations makes for a grim account of arrests, betrayal, failure and denial.

There is often a kind of denial within intelligence services when things start to go wrong, an unwillingness to admit that this is due to more than chance but rather because an operation has been compromised. SOE slowly realized something looked wrong with an operation called Manfriday/Intersection in the middle of 1942, but as late as September senior figures thought it was still running smoothly. Only as they examined the record more closely did it began to dawn on SOE that things had gone badly wrong.

MI5 began an investigation. The verdict was dire. Almost every Belgian radio set was being run by the Germans. By autumn 1942, German success in Belgium meant – according to the official SOE history – that the agency's 'organization in the field was no more than a mirage created by the Gestapo'. The year had been 'operationally disastrous', SOE's own files record. By October 1942, Hardy Amies's Belgian section had dispatched forty-five agents to Belgium. Thirty-two were in enemy hands.

Van Horen, who had been in touch with Michelli, was a prime example of the failure to accept what was happening. An MI6 agent had reported on 28 April – before the Leopold Vindictive arrests – that '*Van Horen arreté et parlé*' – he had been arrested and talked. This was passed onto SOE since he was primarily their agent. But London remained in denial that he might have been captured, let alone worked with the Germans. In late July another message came out through the Zero network to Page at MI6 suggesting there had been arrests. But the truth only began to sink in in mid-October when Van Horen managed to have a letter smuggled out through Sweden. It bore three words: '*Suis en prison*' – I am in prison. By November SOE staff realized that Van Horen and another agent, Weasel (who had been reporting successful sabotage operations on generators and bridges), were under enemy control. It still took until December for British intelligence to realize that Van Horen might have been cooperating with the Germans for months before the September message. No one knew for sure since when.

MI5's investigating officer complained about the terrible state of SOE files on Belgium. The organization was often lauded for its daring but it was also sloppy. Agents were of poor quality. The codes they used were weak. In some cases, the identity check an agent was supposed to give at the start of a radio message was wrong, and yet such errors were ignored by SOE because they happened so frequently, making the whole exercise worthless as an indication of whether an agent was under German control. Some SOE agents betrayed everyone – in one case his brother, sister-in-law and niece, even the doctor who had set his ankle, which he broke on his drop.

The damning MI5 investigation also raised concerns over the sending of pigeons for agents. The Van Horen compromise was an example of the danger involved.

Columba itself had been the route for a German deception operation. Containers of money and weapons for the 'secret army' were dropped by SOE for Van Horen at the end of May; further consignments were sent in the following months. Their receipt was confirmed by pigeon messages signed 'Jean of the Reception Committee'. 'A thousand thanks for the money and good food,' Jean wrote on 29 June. Another message congratulating the RAF pilots for their skill ended, 'Long Live the freedom of the United Democracies.' These messages came through Columba and are written on the standard pink sheets used by the team. 'This time we had to wait quite a bit,' reads one message from September, which also asks for confirmation that the last pigeons had arrived in London. 'Please do not forget to send us some more Sten guns for which all the boys are asking.' The last message, in November, sends particular thanks for some letters dropped to pass on to the 'Chief', who is said to be still in France and also asks for two bottles of whisky. All these messages had been sent by Abwehr IIIF. One can only think that the German intelligence officers who had been running the network enjoyed their drink very much.

MI5 noted in its investigation that the pigeons carrying these messages sometimes only returned with the acknowledgement a month after the containers had been dropped. And 'Jean of the Reception Committee' was not a prearranged form of signature. The MI5 investigator assumed that SOE did not have a clue who this person actually was. The use of pigeons in Van Horen's mission and that of another compromised agent was 'thoroughly unreliable' and 'highly undesirable', the MI5 officer thought. 'It appears to me to amount to little more than presenting the Germans with a channel of communication to this country by which they can send any message they like.'

The MI5 investigation also noted that as well as SOE's problems with the Belgian Sûreté (who broke off relations for a while), MI6's secrecy did not help. MI5 knew about their sister service's operations in Belgium. 'SIS have also got some finger in the pie, but exactly how they operate is not known,' the MI5 officer notes, adding that communications from SOE agents, including some letters, were often received through MI6. This was the confusion in the field which had caused such a problem with Michelli's network. Some of the SOE agents who came into contact with agents run by MI6 and the Sûreté in Belgium and asked for help were refused, MI5 noted. This was on MI6 instructions, the order being given on the grounds of security because MI6 feared further compromise. The 'bad blood' between the two services was thereby increased.

MI6's secret – one that it kept from MI5, SOE and others in London – was that it, as much as its rival service, was struggling in Belgium. Thonus and Van Hooff were among a number of trained wireless operators sent into Belgium by MI6 in the spring of 1942, and the supply of intelligence had initially appeared to improve. By June they seemed to be receiving comprehensive railway and troop information. But they too were losing agents. Many were being captured almost immediately on arrival – far more than would be expected assuming the normal level of risk.

In March 1942, following a wave of arrests linked to the Zero, Beaver and Brave networks in Belgium, Claude Dansey had begun to worry. In the same month that Page and MI6 sent Van Hooff and Thonus to contact Leopold Vindictive, he told Page that 'unless some drastic steps are taken with or without the consent of Lepage you will soon be without any agents left in Belgium.' In light of the SOE experience, Dansey wanted to check if any wireless operators in the field were compromised. Then they could 'devise some steps to save what is left'. The knowledge of compromise did not, it seems, stop more agents being sent in, including the men sent to meet Raskin.

Urgent meetings with MI5 would be held in late 1942 and early 1943 to try to establish what was going wrong. MI5 wondered if the problem was due to compromised wireless sets or if something more serious was going on. Could there be a traitor, not in Belgium but in London? Remarkably, some even wondered if Lepage himself – the head of the Belgian Sûreté – could be the traitor. As agents paid the price in the field, the war between SOE and Lepage became even more vicious. Starting in spring 1942, SOE had drawn up a dossier of accusations against the head of the Sûreté. Too many agents were burnt. There were too many 'coincidences' – an agent was arrested a few days after Lepage complained about a Frenchman being used as a saboteur in Belgium. A whole network of people linked to the case appeared to have been arrested in quick succession. Together this had all 'cost the lives of several men'. 'It is a remarkable coincidence that in every case of an independent agent becoming known to the Sûreté he has immediately become under suspicion and has subsequently been arrested,' SOE argued. The charge could not be more serious – that Lepage was selling out SOE operations to the Germans, resulting in the arrest and death of agents. A senior officer at SOE jotted a footnote on a report from Amies saying there was a rumour that the Sûreté sent over to Belgium photos and descriptions of SOE men so that they were always caught.

The extremes to which SOE was willing to go are surprising. There was discussion as to whether they could use a contact who had gone to work in the Sûreté to steal any incriminating documents from a safe. They wondered if someone 'would be able to get something just or unjust' on Lepage and perhaps plant an incriminating letter from the Germans in the diplomatic bag to frame him. SOE's anger had blinded it to its own faults. Lepage was difficult and was playing his own game, but there was never any evidence he had deliberately blown operations. It was all too easy to look for someone else to blame.

MI6 also received warnings of possible treachery in London. A CX report – the name given to an item of raw intelligence – of 13 June 1942 came from a courier. It was passed on to SOE, although with reservations that it had not been confirmed. It said: 'Germans have full knowledge of projected parachute landings in Belgium.' A few months later, another man who arrived in Britain as a refugee passed on a verbal message he had been given: 'Mme Sauvage of Liège wishes to inform the British Intelligence Service that Parachutists destined for or released over Belgium, are betrayed by someone in London, and there are frequent arrests soon after their landing. The capture of such men has taken place after the arrest in London of the paymaster of the Parachutists Corps here. Mme Sauvage insists on the fact that it is quite impossible for the Germans to find out in Belgium the exact place and date of such landings and she is quite sure the leakage must be looked for on this side of the Channel.'

Could a traitor inside British intelligence be responsible? There were fears of treachery everywhere, but the MI5 verdict was that the source of the problem were agents in the UK, who after their training were often loose-lipped about their work, sometimes in London's bars and nightclubs. Such was the worry that a person was planted at the instruction school to keep an eye on whether operations were being compromised there.

But if there had been a compromise – perhaps the man who had approached Van Hooff at his hotel – there is no sign it was discovered. There were some traitors within MI6 in the war, notably one called Hooper who had become an agent of the Germans in the late 1930s and ended up working for MI5 and then MI6 on Dutch operations. But no one has ever been discovered dealing with operations in Belgium at the time. Treachery was too easy an excuse. The truth was that SOE and MI6 were in a mess in Belgium, poorly organized, their teams overlapping and easily penetrated, and so were struggling against an effective enemy.

For some in London, the knowledge that agents were being sent into terrible danger was a source of real pain. Hardy Amies struggled over whether the lives lost were worth it – especially because he felt the gains from SOE's sabotage activity in Belgium were relatively meagre. 'There were many moments – and I still have a guilt complex about it – when I felt once or twice I ought to resign because I thought my heart was not in the thing,' he reflected after the war. 'I thought this is lunacy – we are just sending people to their death.' His only reason for staying was that even if the successes were few they kept up morale, and that if he quit someone would just take his place.

Claude Dansey at MI6 had a different view. When his man in MI9, Jimmy Langley, wanted to do more to help agents working on the evasion line who had been captured and condemned to death, Dansey lashed out. 'One of your failings is that you are too damned weak,' he said. 'Your trouble is, Jimmy, that you love your agents.'

And as the members of the group that represented its greatest triumph lay in a Brussels prison, Columba itself was about to go

The map of coastal defences drawn up by Hector Joye,
Joseph Raskin and others which never made it back to Britain.

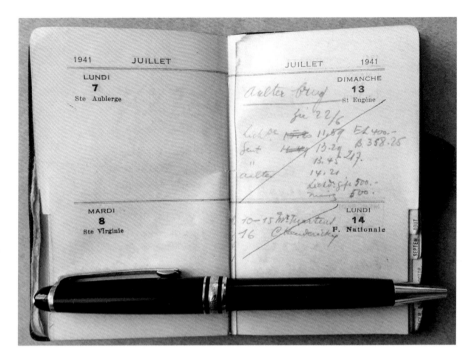

Joseph Raskin's diary, July 1941, with the pages torn out to
remove any evidence of his activities.

The scene at Wijnendale on 27 May 1940. On one side is
Roger Keyes with King Leopold's aide-de-camp. On the
other side, the King is talking to Joseph Raskin, his chaplain.

An earlier version of the coastal defences map.
Detail was progressively added to each version.

Hardy Amies, fashion designer and leading light of SOE's Belgian section for much of the war.

King Leopold III of Belgium.

A hawk – Ursula – swoops to kill a pigeon during wartime. Trained Peregrine Falcons like Ursula were used to hunt German pigeons thought to be carrying messages from secret agents working undercover in Britain.

RAF flights carried pigeons so they could release messages in the event of a crash.

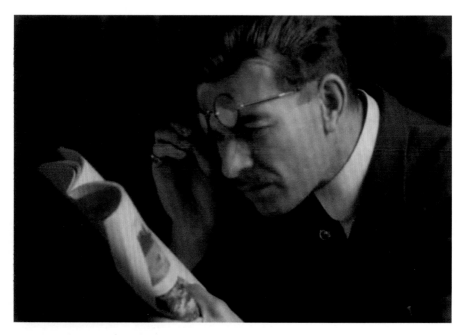

Hector Joye of the Leopold Vindictive network.

William Dex Lea Rayner, the 'pigeon supremo' of the Air
Ministry who frequently clashed with the Columba team.

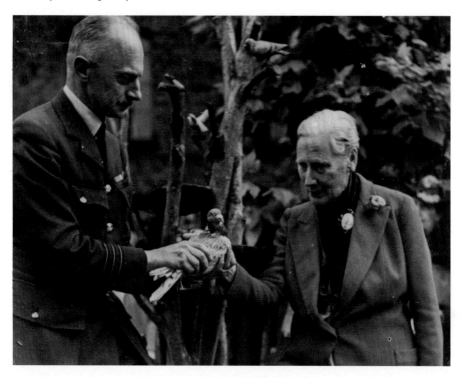

Frederick Jempson – also known as Major Page – the head of MI6's Belgian section during the war.

MI5's Falcon Destruction Unit – the team that went around British cliff-tops to try and destroy hawks in order to protect the pigeons of Columba.

The National Pigeon Service Committee outside the House of Commons
– on the far left is Selby Thomas and on the far right is William Osman.

Group photo of the Special Section (Carrier Pigeon)
in the Army's Royal Corps of Signals.

through its own darkest hour amid accusations of betrayal. The two founders would depart, and pigeon politics, with its bizarre personalities – including an occult-obsessed viscount – would nearly consume Columba's work.

CHAPTER FOURTEEN

The Viscount

At half past ten in the morning of 19 April 1943, a secret court martial was convened at the Duke of York's Headquarters in Chelsea. In the dock was one of the most bizarre characters to grace the story of Columba. Evan Morgan – the last Viscount Tredegar – was an aesthete, occultist and animal lover in charge of the Army's Columba work. He was almost fifty but looked younger, with an aristocratically long face, his receding hair swept back from his forehead. He stood accused of breaching the Official Secrets Act and revealing the innermost workings of MI14(d). But this was no spy story involving subversion and betrayal by Nazi or Communist agents. Instead, the Viscount was accused of revealing these secrets to a group of Ipswich pigeon fanciers, a major in the Army who loved animals and – almost beyond parody – a pair of Girl Guide leaders.

It is tempting to see the world of pigeons through rose-tinted spectacles as a wonderfully British story of eccentrics who all somehow managed to get on and pull together in the war effort. Tempting but not true. The reality is that the pigeon world was filled with the kind of petty bureaucratic and personal rivalries that festered even at a time of national crisis. And Morgan's court martial reveals that the flight path of Columba's pigeons was not always without turbulence and dangers at home, as well as over European skies.

Evan Morgan was – quite literally – a character out of the novels of the thirties. He was the epitome of the pleasure-seeking, bright young things of the era, and was such a flamboyant figure that characters based on him can be found in novels written by his literary friends, including Aldous Huxley who described him as a 'unique fairy prince of modern life'.

He was born in Chelsea in 1893 to a family whose seat was a grand house near Newport in south Wales. A vast estate had been in the family since the fourteenth century and their wealth had been enhanced by the industrial revolution. Military men and politicians populated the family tree. It was however a family in decline. Morgan's father had only limited success in both career paths – becoming a captain in the Navy in return for donating a boat in the First World War and then failing to make his way in Parliament. Evan never looked likely to follow the family line. From his childhood the boy, surrounded by servants, was physically sickly and foppish. He took the classic aristocratic path of Eton and then Christ Church, Oxford and never even came close to getting a degree. His friends would later say they did not even know what subject he was supposed to be studying. He inhabited the world depicted in Evelyn Waugh's *Brideshead Revisited*, his rooms at Oxford hung with Chinese silks and rugs from Persia and Russia. After Oxford, he travelled through North Africa and Spain, writing flowery poetry and confirming a reputation as a gay aesthete before he returned to hang out with the Bloomsbury group. He was rich, and this brought hangers-on whom he would often indulge with booze and cocaine after drinks at the Café Royal or dinner at the Savoy.

Thanks to Morgan's sickliness he did not see much service in the First World War. He had then tried to get a job at 10 Downing Street, but it was decided he was clever but 'degenerate'. In the 1920s he briefly converted to Catholicism and took off to Rome to study for the priesthood. His valet – whom he had brought with him in his Rolls Royce – took all the classes before Morgan himself had to leave after falling for an Italian 'youth'. In 1932, Morgan had been visiting Germany and attended a private dinner just outside Munich. Amongst the other guests were Rudolf Hess, Hitler's deputy, and the then head of the SA, Ernst Rohm.

Morgan had been adopted as a Conservative parliamentary candidate in east London in the twenties but never stood a chance. He did however still make it into Parliament. In 1934, his father – who knew a thing or two himself about living the high life – died at the Ritz, where he had been with his mistress. As a result Morgan became Viscount Tredegar and a member of the House of Lords. The previous year, his first wife – an actress – had petitioned for divorce on grounds of sodomy.

As well as art, drugs, men and booze, Morgan also became obsessed with the occult. Black magic had gripped a sliver of the British elite in an era when Christianity was losing its hold and when dark rituals offered a justification for the more extreme forms of hedonism and individualism. Morgan became friends with the dark master of the times – Aleister Crowley. A man obsessed with excess and devil worship, Crowley took immense pleasure in building a reputation as the 'wickedest man in the world' for his depravity.

Morgan's other primary interest was animals. He travelled round with a menagerie of birds, monkeys and even a rat. Invited to lunch at a house, he brought a crow which would peck the guests' ankles and which once laid an egg on a dressing table. In the grounds of his stately home, he created a private zoo filled with baboons, venomous spiders, vultures and a boxing kangaroo, asking people if they wanted to fight it. 'Chips' Channon wrote in his diary following one visit to Tredegar House: 'glorious house, but the feel and even smell of decay, of aristocracy in extremis, the sinister and the trivial, crucifixes and crocodiles'. Morgan was said never once to have visited the ordinary people who worked at the family estate he inherited, even as he threw dissolute parties and as men like Crowley and H. G. Wells came to stay, some of them witnessing black-magic rites with owls swooping around them in the house. By 1939, as war approached, Morgan had remarried. This time his wife was a Russian princess called Olga who was terrifyingly beautiful and had appeared on the cover of *Tatler*.

What use could be made of such a bizarre character as Morgan during the war? I know, someone from the Army thought, he likes animals. So let's put him in charge of pigeons.

Morgan succeeded Rex Pearson in early November 1942 as the Officer Commanding Special Section of the Army's Carrier Pigeon Service. The precise reasons for Pearson's departure from a service he had helped create are not recorded, but it does not appear to have been by choice; a reference on Christmas Eve 1942 to his 'removal' seems to confirm as much, as do other references to it being 'at short notice'. Perhaps the demon drink that had destroyed his time in Switzerland with MI6 had once again undermined his ability to carry out a job he loved.

Whatever the reason, the man who had first persuaded the doubters that Columba might work was now sidelined. On his final day, Pearson wrote to his contact at the BBC that he was having to 'relinquish command of this unit today and am being relegated to a unit in the country'. He finished his note by explaining that 'One Lord Tredegar will take over but your side will all be done by Captain Kleyn to whom I beg you to extend the same good help you have always given me … he is very keen.'

In the type of bureaucratic tangle that frequently visits itself on the British state, MI14(d) was at the heart of pigeon operations – deciding where to drop the birds and analysing the intelligence that returned. But the Special Section (Carrier Pigeons) of the Army's

Royal Corps of Signals, which Pearson and now Morgan ran, was in charge of supplying the birds for MI14 to use. This meant that Morgan, from his office in Wing House, was nominally in charge of the critical element of Columba – making sure there was a steady supply of pigeons – but without being involved in the secret side of MI14.

Morgan immediately clashed with the man who had just been appointed to the Army Pigeon Service by MI14 to liaise with Columba and was running its day-to-day operational work. Pearson, before he left, had complained that he did not have enough support but the Army had been unwilling to provide more men. In July, MI14 asked its own teams how much value it derived from Columba. Only MI14(a) said they got nothing. Sanderson said that while the value of the operation with respect to invasion plans had obviously declined, if that possibility arose again it would be 'invaluable'. Melland pointed out that it was a valuable source 'over which *we* have a fair measure of control.' MI14(b) said it was of 'considerable value, both in itself and as a check on CX reports' (those produced by MI6). A major challenge was the identification of new German divisions and their locations. One message showed that an SS division was still in northern France and had not moved to Italy as other sources suggested. And the great advantage of Columba was speed. The time lag at the start of 1943 for a courier getting a message to Military Intelligence was at least a month; Columba could get the information in a day. It was described as 'amazingly current'.

The verdict helped justify the arrival of a new intelligence officer at the rank of captain attached to the Army Pigeon Service. John Leonard Kleyn had been born Johannes Leonardes Kleijn in the Netherlands in 1893. He had come to Britain after his family's plans to build a shipping line had been dashed by the outbreak of the First World War. Kleyn worked for Royal Dutch Shell and travelled around Europe, becoming fluent in Dutch, English, French and German. That had been one qualification for the job. Another was a love of animals. In the thirties he had given up the Shell job to breed dalmatians in the south of France, returning to Britain just before the war. His final qualification was his motivation. When war broke out, his father was taken by the Germans from Rotterdam – perhaps because of some suspicion the family were Jewish (they were not). He died on his way to the concentration camp. That left John Kleyn with a lifelong hatred for Germans. As war started, he had first joined the Pioneer Corps, where he was given manual labour tasks. But his fluency in languages was spotted, and he was sent over to the Intelligence Corps and quickly promoted to captain.

Kleyn would occasionally travel abroad on secret missions, writing reports on his return. On one occasion he wrote in Dutch to speed up the process. He discovered that the report had been translated from Dutch by an Englishwoman at MI6. Twenty years his junior, Diana later became his (fourth) wife. Now in his late forties, he was broad-shouldered and had been a good footballer. He liked a challenge and had a direct manner, capable of charm but also unafraid of confrontation. It is fair to say that he and Evan Morgan were never likely to be close.

Kleyn was the link between Melland's MI14(d) and Morgan at the Army. Each month different departments would submit to Melland priority lists of where they wanted pigeons dropped, and Melland would pass them onto Kleyn. Kleyn would collect pigeons that Morgan had organized via the National Pigeon Service and escort them to the RAF teams at Tempsford, discussing with the team there how many birds could be carried and when. Between two and three hundred birds might be dropped in a single night. Kleyn reported to Melland and not to Morgan. All Morgan was supposed to do was ensure there was a supply of pigeons.

Morgan's arrival could not have come at a worse moment. In the autumn of 1942 rumours had started to surface that Columba was to be terminated. Brian Melland of MI14 was the first to hear of it – though not via official channels but in corridor talk. The push came from the lieutenant colonel responsible for the pigeons on the Army side, who claimed the whole service was overvalued. He wanted the Special Service to be folded back into regular Army pigeon operations. On 9 October, Melland wrote a memo over his head to a colonel in Military Intelligence, defending the team. The lieutenant colonel was in no position to judge its effectiveness, he wrote, since he did not see the intelligence, pointing out that his adversary had not even asked other departments if they valued the intelligence they received. If the Army were tired of this service, then MI4 itself should take it over directly. It was at this moment that Morgan took office on the Army side and the alarm bells started to ring in MI14(d). They soon noted that changes were being made which 'may not prove wholly beneficial'.

One of Morgan's first moves was to stop the payment of cash bonuses to loft owners for birds which returned with a message. For poorer pigeon owners the money was a lifeline. In the first week of January 1943, it was warned that this could be calamitous, since it might mean pigeon fanciers would no longer provide their best birds. 'We may send a thousand out and none of them fit to get back with a message,' it was warned. A real commitment was needed to train birds for Columba when only one in ten made it back alive. The point about breeding pigeons was that you invested heavily in trying to develop a 'strain' that would be successful. Ensuring your 'strain' or family of birds that had been carefully built up was not destroyed through the excessive demands made on it was important. And so there was a tension between the racing interest and the national interest. Fanciers did not want to be at a disadvantage compared to fellow racers. From 1942, Columba was organized so that local pigeon supply officers would keep records and make sure the burden was shared equally in each area. Morgan was now dispensing with the services of certain pigeon loft owners who had specialized in training long-distance pigeons and had returned some of the best pigeons. Fanciers, like Bert Woodman, referred to the Channel as the 'moat' – they knew 'it was the graveyard-to-be for hundreds of our best pigeons'.

In November, Kleyn was told some of the equipment used for transporting pigeon baskets to the aerodrome was no longer available since his 'alleged operations' were less important than some others for which it was required. On 30 November Melland complained to the head of MI14 that Army officers were 'belittling the value of the Special Service'. There was also a complaint that – without MI14 being consulted – operations over Christmas were cancelled, leading to the loss of four possible flying days.

Morgan's lifestyle would also have jarred with Melland, Kleyn and others. The Viscount would frequently stroll from Wing House down Piccadilly for tea at the Ritz, and would invite young men out to the best restaurants in London and back afterwards to his Mayfair house. Kleyn and Morgan – who had neighbouring rooms in Wing House – began to clash more and more. Kleyn was no longer getting support from the Army to visit pilots in the aerodrome before they took off. 'It seems the Columba service is suffering as a result of the departure of Major Pearson and the "new order" established by his successor Major Viscount Tredegar,' read a note from Melland in December 1942. MI14 may have started to wonder if Morgan was inept or if he had been ordered to deliberately undermine their work.

Kleyn and Morgan were moving to a war footing. Both knew that in the battle of the bureaucracy only one would survive. In the intelligence world, the best way to get rid of someone is to suggest they may be unreliable or leaky. Quickly, both sides began to whisper. SOE was one place to start. The Viscount and his allies seem to have suggested Kleyn was untrustworthy – particularly because he was Dutch. Since agents would often visit Kleyn at Wing House for training and he would go to the aerodrome, he knew a lot about the timing of drops and details of the agents involved. He should be moved or investigated, it was said.

MI5 and SOE began an investigation, but realized they were caught in cross-fire. On New Year's Eve 1942, Major Frost of MI5 told SOE that Melland had approached him in order to express doubts about the discretion and efficiency of Morgan, Viscount Tredegar. For SOE this was all a bit bewildering. The leadership asked Hardy Amies's Belgian section, the main users of pigeons, what was going on. They were told 'there is a war in progress between Kleyn and Tredegar factions', with MI14 backing the former. An SOE officer went to see Kleyn on 6 January 1943. Kleyn said the newly established hierarchy were endeavouring 'to get rid of him on the grounds that he has not enough work to do'. But this was clearly 'a political move', since there was in fact plenty to do supporting MI14 and SOE. One problem was that the Army hierarchy knew little about Kleyn's work for SOE, since he was instructed to keep secret his visits to the aerodrome on their behalf. Kleyn asked SOE to put in a good word, and this it did, writing to Frost at MI5 the next day saying Kleyn had always been helpful and that security would actually be endangered by his removal: 'It seems a pity that a man who knows our side of the business so intimately should be removed and another put in his place.' A letter to Frost later in the month further emphasized the point: 'Our people say that they have been very satisfied with the discretion and services rendered by Captain Kleyn. With regards to Morgan, I am afraid I cannot help.' The attempt to use MI5 to remove Kleyn had been foiled.

By late January, the situation had reached a crisis and a meeting was called in MI14 to discuss the problems. Morgan's brief tenure was so calamitous that they decided they had to get rid of him. The only question was how.

Three months later, on the morning of 19 April, Morgan listened as three charges against him were read out at his court martial. The first was that at Ipswich on 4 February 1943 he had unlawfully communicated information about pigeon operations to a group of civilians. The second was that on 3 February he had improperly informed a major from the Army Medical Corps about secret aspects of the Columba operation. The third was that he had broken the Official Secrets Act by communicating details of the pigeon operations to two women. To all three charges, he pleaded not guilty.

The prosecution then laid out its case. First – having already stressed that no detail should leave the court – it revealed to those sitting in judgement what Columba was. Next it dealt with the first and most serious charge of breaching the Official Secrets Act, which regarded the Viscount's dealings with the pigeon fanciers who supplied their birds through the National Pigeon Service.

Owners in a town would club together around existing local pigeon racing clubs with an agreed leader. Groups like the 'Folkestone Fanciers' or Dover Group had twenty lofts, each with at least thirty birds. For Bert Woodman's Plymouth Group, the day before a drop, members would get a call – 'goods required tonight', they might be told. A van would trundle around the suburban streets and collect the birds. They would be taken to 18 Cecil Street in Plymouth, a large terraced house in which two back rooms had been converted to store up to seven hundred birds. Then the baskets would be picked up and taken either by van or by rail to Wing House in London, and finally by Kleyn to the airfield. Lofts nearest the target would be picked so the flight path would be as short as possible; Ipswich birds would be sent to the Netherlands, Belgium and Denmark, whilst south coast birds would be used for France (Denmark was the most distant of Columba's targets, with two birds returning in July 1942). Kleyn was the keeper of log books that showed which pigeons were sent out day by day, where they were dropped, which ones returned and what they brought back. This was the sacred record of Columba's work and successes.

At the end of 1942, the court martial heard that Morgan had got hold of the log books and told a sergeant to copy out a summary of operations by pigeons belonging to one group of Ipswich breeders. Then, on 4 January, he had gone to Ipswich to meet the group, which numbered about two dozen and was led by its pigeon supply officer, Herbie Keys. It is not too hard to imagine what a bunch of largely working-class Ipswich pigeon fanciers made of the aesthete viscount. They were worlds apart socially. But at a hotel, Morgan had read out the summary to the breeders. This was information, the court martial was told, that could be useful to the enemy. It revealed at which locations birds were being dropped and from where they had returned. Put those together and the Nazis could potentially work out where agents were oper-ating – like the Belgian team – and then try to find them. 'If any hint reached the enemy of those facts the Gestapo would not lose a moment of time in combing the locality in question for persons who had sent any message,' the prosecution alleged. That was the first charge.

The second charge involved events a month later. A Major Cassidy had come to the Columba offices on a social visit late in the afternoon. He was a statistician who worked on a different floor of Wing House and had no reason to know anything about Columba's work. He knew of the Viscount's job title but not what the Special Section actually did. He had been brought there by a mutual friend, a Major Carruthers. Cassidy was a bird lover and had been told by Carruthers that the Viscount had a rather interesting book about animals from around the world. Inside the office – in which the skeleton of a pigeon was displayed above a bookcase – they looked at an atlas of birds of the world for a while and also talked about whether microgram slides could be enlarged to carry information, since it was something that Cassidy knew about. Then the discussion turned towards pigeons. Cassidy said he had seen plenty of them in Wing House. He said at times he had found it difficult to get in the lift for all the pigeons.

At that point, Cassidy recalled, one of the men – he could not say whether it was the Viscount or Carruthers – said something like 'Let's show him the secret stuff.' At this, the Viscount had a sergeant bring out a live pigeon, a parachute, the instructions and a cylinder and demonstrated how each of these was used. There was also a gesture towards a large map of Europe on the wall behind the Viscount's desk. Here locations were marked by pins which Cassidy surmised were the places that the pigeons were dropped. This amounted, the prosecution said, to conduct to the prejudice of good order and military discipline.

And finally, in the most bizarre of the three alleged transgressions, the prosecution outlined the events of 15 March. The Girl Guides had come to Wing House. This was all part of a publicity push for the Baden-Powell memorial fund – named after the founder of the Scout movement who had died just two years earlier. Arrangements had been made for pigeons to be dropped in Scotland with red containers who would then fly back to Wing House bearing messages. Photographers would be waiting on the roof to grab a picture that might make the papers. They had already tried to do this on 25 February, but the weather had been terrible. The thick London fog meant the pigeons had no chance of finding Wing House. So, on 15 March, they were trying again. It was still foggy, but not as bad, and a few birds had made it. Lady Baden-Powell herself, the widow of the founder, was up on the roof.

The Viscount then invited two of the Girl Guide leaders into his office. The show on the roof had been disappointing and he felt the need to entertain them. Morgan explained how pigeons were brave, dependable birds that could fly through anything – shrapnel, gas, bombs and shells. He once again asked a subaltern to bring in the equipment and then demonstrated – with a live pigeon – how the container and the parachute worked. He explained the different types of cylinder that could be attached, and even the secret of their colours. Green, grey and red with a coloured disc were linked to the Special Pigeon Service; green meant Columba. Plain red was the normal Army Pigeon Service. Blue was RAF (and with a white patch was an RAF SOS message). Black was civil police and yellow was commercial. He also drew their attention to the map on the wall; pointing to a spot on the map north-west of the Zuyder Zee in the Netherlands, he told them this had been the site of an enemy radar station whose details had been brought back by pigeon. This was one of the successes that had so excited R. V. Jones, and the Viscount explained that RAF planes had attacked the site.

Captain Kleyn of MI14 was in his office next door. He knew exactly what was going on even though he was not present. The subaltern had come into the office he shared with Kleyn to pick up one of the containers that were kept there for testing to show the Guides. That may well explain what happened next. On Sunday, 21 March, Lieutenant Colonel Cullinan told Morgan that he had been reported by the two subalterns for events with the Guide leaders on 15 March. He was told he should sign off sick and resign his appointment.

Two weeks later, Morgan was informed there was a formal allegation against him. He was apologetic. But it was too late, and two more charges were added relating to the earlier incidents.

At the court martial, it seemed an open-and-shut case. Plenty of witnesses – not only the sergeants and subalterns but also the Girl

Guide leaders and Major Cassidy – produced evidence, if occasionally a bit hazy, about what Morgan had shown and said in their presence.

But Morgan was a well-connected and rich man. And that meant a good lawyer. In this case it was Sir Walter Monckton – a man who had served as an adviser to King Edward VIII during the abdication crisis and would later himself become a viscount and Conservative cabinet minister. He offered two lines of defence. The first was the more effective. Why had Morgan gone to see the Ipswich fanciers? Was it off his own bat? Why, no. He had been ordered to go to see them by his superior.

The problem was that the Ipswich breeders – led by Keys – had been very unhappy with the scale of the losses. Too many of their birds were going out and never coming back. The burden may have been shared between them, but they felt that groups in other parts of the country may not have been sacrificing as many birds. So great was the Ipswich group's discontent that there had been a danger they might even withdraw cooperation. So Morgan had been given orders to win them over. He had gone there to appeal for their cooperation to continue under him as it had done under Pearson.

Monckton went over the conversation in Ipswich. Morgan had read out the summary of the 250 or so birds that had flown and the number that had come back carrying messages. When he had finished, Keys stood up and said, 'The number is wrong. You have left out two.' Morgan had acknowledged to them that he had missed two birds that had made it back. Then Monckton made his point. If the information was so secret, then how on earth would Keys know that Morgan had missed two birds out? Of course, the answer was that the loft owners all knew exactly how many birds had returned because they had come back to their lofts.

Furthermore, Monckton pointed out that Morgan had not told the sergeant to copy out the most sensitive parts of the log book

– the details of any message or who had sent it. Under cross-examination, the sergeant revealed that the summary had been prepared not only under the orders of Morgan but also those of the officer above him, Lieutenant Colonel Cullinan, who was responsible for all pigeon operations and not only those supporting Columba. He had given orders for the summary to be written out to support Morgan's mission to win the Ipswich team over. How had he got hold of Kleyn's log books? Kleyn had handed them over. Why had he handed them over? Because he knew instructions had come from Cullinan. In other words, the Viscount was simply following orders. And it had worked. Ipswich had continued to supply pigeons.

And when it came to the demonstrations of the pigeon, the parachute and the container to Cassidy and the Girl Guides, was this really a secret? Monckton pointed out that the whole point of the contraptions was that they were dropped over occupied countries. The Germans were surely in possession of hundreds of them already. What further secrets could be exposed? They might not know how precisely they were used, or that the green cylinders carried secret Columba messages. But still.

Furthermore, after Morgan's appointment in early November 1942, Monckton asked, was it not the case that Lieutenant Colonel Cullinan had himself frequently brought army officers into Morgan's room and ordered him to carry out a demonstration to them? Morgan in a statement said that his predecessor, Major Pearson, had frequently shown documents such as questionnaires to visitors.

Yes, there was a map of eastern England and the continent on the wall, and it was marked with coloured pins. But those on the continent had been affixed by a Dutchman – a Mr Ray – who had escaped from the Netherlands and placed pins at locations where he thought Allied sympathizers might be prepared to revolt against the enemy in the event of a landing. Plenty of people came through the office but no one had objected to the map before.

Morgan himself did not give evidence in his defence. But a statement he had given previously was read out in which he recalled that the facts of the Zuyder Zee site had been given to him by Lieutenant Colonel Cullinan, 'who also told me that he had been congratulated by Guide Leaders'. It was public knowledge that pigeons were dropped on the continent, since the Girl Guides had to admit they were already aware of it. The vague gesture to the site in the Netherlands was imprecise, Monckton suggested, especially since all the others in the room could not agree whether he had pointed with his finger or a stick, or what precise words he had said.

Brian Melland tried to fight back when he appeared as a witness. He emphasized that the places where pigeons were dropped were secret. He confirmed that the location of the site and the events at the Zuyder Zee were secret. Yes, the enemy was in possession of parachutes, but they would not know the method of release. He even tried to maintain that the difference between red and green canisters was highly significant. He did his best to pile on the pressure, but under the most intensive cross-examination of the entire proceedings, he had to admit that the Germans had probably captured a lot of containers, parachutes and pigeons themselves. It was becoming clear that the conversations that the Viscount had had were either authorized or not that unusual.

Then Monckton made his final plea. Yes, the Viscount had made an 'error of judgement', but it was important to take into account his personal and medical history. The Viscount's childhood, his lawyer explained, had been desperately unhappy. His mother suffered from what was called a 'divided personality'. By one account she had built herself a large bird's nest in her sitting room and then sat in it wearing a beak. The young Evan Morgan had been a spoilt child, allowed to run riot and live an irregular life. His sister, like his mother, had suffered mental health issues and the Viscount was physically sick, never having passed a medical board. From May to November 1942 he had been on continuous sick leave, and frequently after November as well. Monckton brought in Morgan's doctor, who had known him since he was twelve. He had repeatedly warned the Viscount of the risk of mental or physical breakdown. Morgan was a man who would have been more at home in fifteenth-century Italy than the War Office of the 1940s, the proceedings were told. The doctor said he was very surprised when he heard Morgan had been accepted for service in the Army at all, let alone for secret work. Truth be told, Monckton explained, he was 'ill-equipped for his station'. And at this moment his domestic life was also crashing round him. Princess Olga was seeking a divorce. With all this in mind, Monckton pleaded that the penalty should not be too harsh.

Colonel Prescott, presiding over the court martial, returned with his verdict: not guilty when it came to the charge regarding Major Cassidy but guilty when it came to Ipswich and the Guides. But the sentence was light. No imprisonment, simply a severe reprimand. Monckton could not have hoped for more. He had done his job. But Morgan was no longer to be part of Columba. In that sense at least, Melland and others had got what they wanted.

That summer Morgan's divorce from Olga came through. The black magic practitioner Aleister Crowley was staying at Tredegar House in Wales once more. Morgan showed him his magic room and they engaged in some occult readings. There were rumours that Morgan had asked Crowley to cast a spell on his former commanding officer to make him sick. But Morgan himself was the one who was sick. In 1949, he died aged just fifty-five, the last of his line. Four years later Tredegar House was turned into a school.

The Viscount's desire to cast a spell on his superior reveals that he well understood what lay behind the court martial – personal animosity. It is clear from the evidence that not just Kleyn but Melland, Cullinan, the subalterns and sergeants had all taken a deep dislike to their aristocratic colleague almost immediately after his arrival and were determined to get rid of him. They were willing to suggest that he was engaged on trips like Ipswich off his own bat, when in fact he was following orders, or that he was taking a risky step by demonstrating pigeons when others had done the same. That may be brutal but it was also understandable. Melland, Kleyn and others took their jobs seriously. They were engaged in a secret intelligence operation and there were people whose lives were on the line in France, Belgium and the Netherlands. Careless talk could cost lives. And to have their work compromised by a bizarre, occult-loving viscount would only have made matters worse.

The Viscount's brief tenure was only one example of the 'pigeon politics' that surrounded Columba. A sad letter arrived at the Air Ministry in early May 1943, just after the court martial. It was from Rex Pearson. He was now out of a job, writing from his cottage in Hampshire. 'The time seems to be ripe for consideration of a separate pigeon Intelligence Service as distinct from Wing House – not to replace it but to augment it,' he wrote to the head of Air Intelligence. This new version of Columba could carry a questionnaire focusing purely on issues that mattered to the Air Ministry, he explained. 'I would very much like to organize this service for you,' he pleaded, asking for an interview. He was essentially proposing to create another Columba, but this time out of the hands of the Army.

The letter was dismissed by the Director of Intelligence Operations. A note in the file remarks that 'there is something gravely phoney about the letter', saying that other officers would not touch the proposal either. Poor old Pearson was casting around for some kind of role. After a few months, the one place that would take him was the BBC, where he found work in the European

Intelligence Department. Even here he tried to keep involved in Columba, trying to pull a 'fast one' in Kleyn's view by getting questionnaires revised without proper permission.

Pearson's letter was tapping into a deep antipathy between the Air Ministry and the Columba team. The long-running battle between the Army Pigeon Service, which ran Columba, and the Air Ministry, which technically was responsible for all pigeon operations, was intensifying.

William Dex Lea Rayner at the Air Ministry – supposedly Britain's military pigeon supremo – absolutely hated the fact that the Army ran their own service. What drove him particularly crazy, sitting in Adastral House in Kingsway, was that the War Office down the road would not even tell him what Columba was up to, perhaps out of a genuine desire to keep intelligence operations secret but perhaps also out of sheer bloody-mindedness. The bad blood spilled over into relations with the National Pigeon Service.

At first NPS and Rayner's Air Ministry had been allies against the Army and the War Office. In January 1941, an Army colonel launched a scathing attack on Rayner and the NPS for excluding him from meetings. That October, the NPS complained of the same colonel assuming a 'dictatorial attitude to the committee'.

But as Columba grew, the Army began to work directly with the NPS, and it became clear to the fanciers that the Army and its Special Section was where the action was. It was they who were using birds and supplying food in return. Feathers flew. What really galled Rayner was that the NPS Committee (whose work he paid for) knew more than he did about this secret work and kept it from him. The result was 'undignified, unnecessary, and even insulting', Rayner complained as he demanded details of the number of birds used, the losses and returns and the value of the information. Rayner became furious when the War Office refused to give answers on grounds of 'security'; he subsequently tried to undermine Columba, telling people that his colleagues in the RAF did not consider it useful. 'If the whole scheme is a War Office "racket" then it is not an Air Ministry function to facilitate it,' he complained.

The most vicious 'pigeon politics' was within the pigeon fancy itself. There were accusations of favouritism and bullying. Some pigeon fanciers complained to MPs about the 'autocratic' approach of the NPS committee, who would turn up and demand pigeons were supplied even from depleted lofts. Owners said they would be threatened with removal from the register and the termination of free food coupons if they did not comply.

But the NPS's most acerbic critic was the man who had helped found it, William Osman. Like Pearson with the Army, this founder of pigeon work did not last the course.

Osman had been invited to join the committee in May 1939, but that November he wrote a spectacularly bad-tempered letter to the NPS chair, G. Barrett, saying that the situation was 'quite intolerable' and if NPS failed then Barrett 'can go on being a sub-postmaster and grocer'. Osman began by complaining about the NPS secretary, Selby Thomas. 'He has never kept any pigeons – merely budgerigars – and unlike myself has had no experience whatsoever of pigeons in war.' He was angry at not being consulted and claimed the NPS was being turned into a 'one-man show', failing to learn the lessons of the last war. 'There is no one on the committee – or for that matter in the country – knowing as much about pigeons for war,' he said in a three-page rant. In a fantastically over-the-top comparison he went even further. 'I am not prepared to acquiesce in the doings of a Führer.' Osman's rivals rebutted his claims, telling the Air Ministry that he had failed to turn up to meetings and do any work. Osman was soon kicked out of the NPS.

He then pushed for a position as a paid consultant to the Air Ministry. In a veiled threat, he suggested that if a suitable role was not found, it might be better 'from the point of view of the nation' that he retained his independence so he could 'point out mistakes that are made, and perhaps right some injustices'. 'The number of questions likely to arise upon which I should feel in need of Major Osman's advice are very few,' Rayner wrote to his superior, pointing to the problem of his conflicts of interest with his role as editor and proprietor of the *Racing Pigeon* and in the sale of pigeons. This was all despite Rayner originally having been one of Osman's allies. One official claimed that Osman and his relatives and friends had supplied or controlled the supply of pigeons in the First World War, 'and judging by the instances I have of prices charged it would appear that he must have made a very good thing of it'. His activities were 'not in accordance with his professed patriotic motives', an official noted icily.

Osman used his editorship to snipe at his former colleagues. The journal printed extracts from supposedly 'restricted' documents which related to Columba. MI14 was called in. Melland despaired. 'The main point about this storm-in-a-teacup is that it is purely a quarrel in the pigeon fanciers world,' he wrote. MI14 cared only for the intelligence product – it was up to the Air Ministry and Signals to sort out the 'private feelings of pigeoneers'. Nevertheless, Melland wrote to MI5 and asked them to take a look. 'It all sounds a bit hysterical to me, but we certainly don't want any trouble in our particular feathered world.' A long list was drawn up of all the disparaging articles in the *Racing Pigeon* which criticized the Army Pigeon Service and the National Pigeon Service.

The fear was that the attacks might undermine the willingness of some fanciers to offer their birds, or might lead an angry pigeoneer to defend the operation publicly – and do so by revealing Columba's secrets. A scathing report on Osman was written later by the War Office. 'Major Osman conducts his paper in an aggressive fashion, encouraging controversy,' the report noted, adding that he seemed 'slovenly' and to drink heavily. But, at the end of the day, Richard

Walker from MI5 suggested that no action should be taken, partly for fear of publicity.

By the summer of 1943, the court martial was over and the threats to close down Columba had been seen off by MI14(d). Instead plans were put in place to increase its staffing because it had been proved to be so successful, and to increase the scope of Columba's activities. The pigeon fancy remained committed despite some wobbles. Columba would still have one more important role to play. At its inception, its mission had been to spot German plans to invade Britain. Now it would be needed to prepare the way as Britain and its Allies planned to invade Europe; it would play a role in deceiving the enemy and hunting its most dangerous weapons.

CHAPTER FIFTEEN

Trials and Tribulations

Joseph Raskin arrived in Germany in May 1942, as the country was slowly realizing that the war would not be over as soon as Hitler had promised. In the East, the invasion of the Soviet Union had stalled and was turning into a brutal war of attrition. Allied bombers were beginning to pierce German defences, thanks to the work of R. V. Jones and others. But the German hold on Western Europe remained firm and the Nazi secret police were determined to maintain their grip, by means that included enforcing their version of justice on enemy spies. Raskin and his friends were first taken to Brauweiler prison in Cologne, which had begun life as a Benedictine abbey in the Middle Ages but now belonged to the Gestapo, a place where social and political 'undesirables' were kept. It was one of the strange ironies of the priest's journey through Nazi Germany that so many of the places he visited had been built for Christian worship, a grim reminder of the subversion of faith in that country.

Hector Joye was able to get a letter home from Brauweiler that July – the only one his wife Louise received after his arrest. There was no high drama in it, just hope and domesticity. 'I am well. I hope to see you all in a few months. Would you send a good shirt and a new warm jacket,' he wrote, adding, as an afterthought, a request for a large piece of soap. In August, Arseen Debaillie was taken to Brauweiler and reunited with his friends. He sent a letter back to the family saying they should pay money to try to get him released, something the Germans sometimes suggested would work. 'I'm doing well, thank God. Life is very monotonous, but there is also nothing to be done,' he added. When the Gestapo delivered the letter to Lichtervelde, they demanded 20,000 francs.

Spying had been expensive for the family. They had already tried paying out once for Arseen and had given money to help Devos escape. The family pulled together the money and handed it over. Nothing happened. Then came a demand for more money. Again a sum was handed over, and again nothing came of it.

There were no letters from Raskin. He had a red note attached to his identity card, unlike the other men, which may have been why. All of them were allowed sometimes to walk on a small patch of grass but never to talk to those they knew.

Brauweiler was where the interrogations began. The Germans wanted confessions. For all the arbitrary exercise of power and violence inherent in the Nazi system, they still wanted to put espionage cases through a formal legal process. Otherwise, the risk was that spies would be seen as martyrs. And if it was going to go to court, then the most effective way of securing a conviction was through confession. The Germans began the kind of patient work that their best interrogators excelled in. They were trying to draw out as much as they could by playing the men off against each other. They would reveal details of what they learnt from one man to the others in order to make it sound as if they knew more than they did, bluffing that others had already told all.

Leopold Vindictive's interrogation was revealing about what the Germans did and did not know. Bodicker from Abwehr IIIF in Brussels sent on details of what his team had been able to gather. Everything revolved around the first pigeon and the contact with the group around Joseph Dehennin, whom Raskin had first tried to use to ask Britain for more birds. Clément Macq's account provides the only insight into how the Gestapo tried to break the men. Macq was transferred to Brauweiler on 5 August and interrogated for the first time on 17 August. He was read a declaration which contained details regarding his own role and what he and others had discussed with Joye and Raskin. The Germans also seemed to know the times and places of meetings with René Dufrasne, the man to whom Macq had passed Raskin's message to Britain. Macq denied everything and said it was all untrue. After a few hours he was back in his cell. He was never tortured apart from receiving one blow with a stick.

Joye was brought into the room with Macq next time and a declaration supposedly from him was read out. The interrogators spoke about a specific document Joye had given Macq. Joye made a tiny signal with his finger to indicate he had admitted only to giving Macq one document. Joye was asked if he maintained his previous statements and he said he did. Macq at this point continued to deny everything.

Next Raskin was brought into the room. The Germans asked Macq if he knew who Raskin was. Macq said they had been in contact regarding a cinema projector for the priest's lectures. This was true and provided an alibi. Fortunately, Raskin had said the same. Both men then said they had never discussed espionage.

Now they brought in Dufrasne. He was unrecognizable to Macq. He had lost weight and his eyes were dead. There were no direct signs of torture but he could see this was a man who had been broken. The interrogators read to Macq a statement by Dufrasne which seemed to contain precise details of their relationship and meetings with regard to Leopold Vindictive. They asked Dufrasne to confirm this verbally. He did so. Then emotion seemed to overwhelm him. He said something about how Macq had to think of his children and the consequences. Macq later insisted that he had continued to deny everything. Before being taken away, Dufrasne asked the interrogators to tell Macq that it was not he who had denounced Macq. The interrogators confirmed this.

The interrogators now spoke to Macq alone. They said it was no use denying everything any longer. He had now heard the confessions of Joye and Dufrasne. Macq knew he was in a corner and played for time to try to think up a story which would correlate with their statements without incriminating him too much. It was lunchtime and he asked for something to eat. His interrogators consented. But when they came back they insisted on a confession. He said he needed a few moments to digest his food. He was taken back to his cell and offered a pencil and paper, but refused them saying that what he had to say could be summed up in a few words and that it was not necessary to write them down. The Germans must have realized he was stalling and he was left alone again.

A few weeks later, on 15 September, Macq was brought back to see the Gestapo. By now he had had time to think up a story. He said that Joye had told him about an organization called Leopold Vindictive which Joye and Raskin were involved in. Its aim, he had been told, was to help ordinary people under occupation – a kind of underground charity. Joye had asked if he knew about getting some kind of contact with England for the work – perhaps requesting food and supplies from the United States – and this is what he had passed on to Dufrasne.

In his declaration, Dufrasne had talked about a pigeon. Macq denied ever hearing anything about pigeons and said Dufrasne must have been mistaken and perhaps heard about it from Raskin, if anyone. The interrogator insisted that he only needed enlightenment about the pigeon in order to liberate Macq.

A translation of his 'confession' was then given to Macq. There was a sentence that Macq thought was ambiguous and so he refused to sign. The interrogator became indignant and said something about German justice being more correct than Belgian justice and they did not want him to sign anything false. But the declaration was duly altered and Macq agreed to sign.

The Germans had hard evidence. When they had arrested the Dehennin group back in October 1941, at least two hundred documents were found during the search of Dehennin's father's house. His interrogator put them in front of him and asked him to clarify the source of every one. There were other details that only someone close to Dehennin and whom he met almost every day could have known. Dehennin could not hide his astonishment at all the details and feared that a friend or a member of his family had betrayed him. He still did not know that it had been his brother-in-law, Pieren.

There was little he could do to deny he had been the leader of a network. Amongst the documents they had also unearthed copies of the telegrams and messages that Leopold Vindictive had given Muylaert to try to get to London.

Faced with the growing stack of evidence accumulated by the Germans, some of the men must have felt they had to confess to certain details. Joye's defence when he was faced with documentary evidence would be that he was only passing details of factories and installations where ordinary Belgian people worked to England so the RAF could avoid bombing them. Raskin had to confess to some activity, but deliberately hid the role of some of his contacts in Brussels who had passed on information and claimed much of the material that had been collected had been destroyed in April 1942. The advice among the resistance was always to confess only to what you absolutely could not deny, while trying to find some reason for it that did not implicate others. But the Germans were still able to use those details with other prisoners. Slowly, painstakingly, the Gestapo built their case. It feels easy now to ask who talked and who did not. Perhaps Dufrasne did. Perhaps others made partial confessions. But under what duress and what manipulation? And perhaps they sometimes confessed when confronted with incontrovertible evidence, but tried to hide other facts or the role of other people. The recollections of some of the men are full of confusion and fear over who might have talked, often based on a fragmentary picture since they were unaware of the full extent of German penetration and knowledge. Without knowing who the real traitors were or how evidence had been collected, the men went through their own grim, painful internal interrogation and mental torture, wondering which of their friends might have either betrayed them before the arrest or talked afterwards. Macq came to believe that Raskin had offered himself up as a sacrifice, taking all the blame on his shoulders and saying he was the sole person to have been behind Leopold Vindictive.

At the end of October 1942 the initial interrogation was over and the men were moved by car to Bochum. As in Brauweiler, the prisoners in Bochum wore their own clothes. It was winter now and Arseen had to cut a deal with a French cellmate to borrow a green pullover, a khaki shirt, a maroon wool scarf, several blue handkerchiefs and a pair of shoes which did not quite fit.

Next they were transferred to Wuppertal. The days began at a quarter past five in the morning, when they were woken in their cell – this was a good fifteen minutes of lie-in for Raskin compared to his days as a missionary. But now he was on his knees scrubbing floors rather than praying. Breakfast was either a slice of bread and half a litre of watery porridge or two slices with jam. Days would be spent sewing leather clothes for the German soldiers who occupied their country. Lunch was cabbage soup, dinner three slices of bread, perhaps with cottage cheese. Raskin wrote some notes but never managed to get them out. One letter survives:

Arseen, Hector and I are now in the prison of Wuppertal. We are all very healthy: please do not be concerned. Our crime is not dangerous. Only after the war will they allow us to go back home. We are monitored very strictly and receive no letters or parcels. We cannot go to Mass, nor receive Holy Communion, or see a priest. There is not the slightest difference between our guards and real pagans … We rarely see each other and there is no way to talk to each other … The Lord is among us and the Blessed Mother blesses us, how could we be afraid? The Belgians are about 300 in number … we will undoubtedly return to our country so our families can rest assured.

Hope was still there.

The prisoners may not have been allowed to go to mass, but on Sundays Raskin held his own service from within his cell. He would break the dark prison bread, bless it and pray. As this happened, a knock would go from cell to cell allowing those who so wanted to kneel in their cells as if they were back in church at home and not in a German jail. Some would hear the prayers, while those who could not would at least know they were being said. For a few moments in their cells they were not alone. Macq and Dufrasne had cells next to each other and could talk through the walls. Raskin communicated with Macq and others by hiding messages in a hollow stick which he would drop to the ground during walks, signalling to the person the message was meant for. He tried to send notes to Joye, worried over the man's health and the careworn expression he could see on him when they passed.

A week later, on his fifty-first birthday, Raskin scribbled a prayer card with the addresses of four families back in Belgium whose relatives were in jail with him. He wanted them to be informed that there was no danger and they would return after the war. 'There is absolutely no risk,' he assured them. He even asked his family to make sure that moths were kept out of his clothes. It was another indication that he was sure he would be home eventually. Raskin felt optimistic that the war would be over soon. 'The Germans have long lost all hope,' he said. He could see that shortages were beginning to take their toll, even on food. The German war machine was starting to judder under the strain. 'The victory is near: Long live our homeland.' The message never made it out.

On 24 June 1943, the Allies bombed the city of Wuppertal. Two weeks later, the planes were back again and this time the prison caught fire. One hundred and sixty-nine men, including the members of Leopold Vindictive, were taken from Wuppertal to Esterwegen on 7 July. Now it was prison clothes – black trousers and jacket, hardly brightened by the yellow lines that marked out a political prisoner. Their heads were shaved, although Raskin presented a strange sight since he was still allowed to keep his full beard on top of the bald scalp. Those who knew him there say he also retained his optimism. He was held in a barracks occupied by fellow Belgians and, exempted from certain tasks because he was a priest, continued to hold to some extent to the life of religious ritual that had governed his years before captivity.

In barracks number six, Macq worked some of his old engineering magic and somehow managed to construct a radio, from which prisoners could occasionally grab a muffled BBC broadcast which spoke of progress against the Nazis in the war. They might hear the coded *messages personnels* and wonder what men and women had now taken their place. Raskin was held in a different block but during a walk, the priest told Macq he had written to the German Ministry of Justice about their case, and had mentioned that in the campaign of May 1940 he had saved the lives of two German officers who lay wounded in a burning building. He hoped that might help them. He was already planning for his return.

The priest also found time to go back to his old First World War pastime and sketched out scenes from camp life. In small print he recorded in a notebook a few lines of a diary during his days there. Three days after his arrival he noted that there was nearly one death every night, usually from dysentery. Arseen Debaillie was among those who were ill but just about made it through. Muylaert and Joye were also hospitalized for long periods with fever. A month after arriving, he recorded a bitter warning of the other way death haunted the cells. 'Saturday 7th August. This night suddenly twelve of the sixteen sentenced to death taken away.'

By May 1943, the Germans had written up their indictment and the men were told they would stand trial. On Wednesday, 25 August Raskin noted in his diary that the trial had now been scheduled for 31 August at 9 a.m.

In Belgium, no one knew what was happening. The friends had simply disappeared. Hector Joye's wife Louise heard nothing of her husband: 'What can I answer my sons when they ask for their father again and again?' she wrote to the Red Cross. Rumours swirled around. One was that Raskin had been condemned to death but was pardoned after the intervention of the Queen Mother of Belgium.

When the morning of the trial came, the men's prison clothes were taken away and replaced with their well-ironed civilian clothes. Raskin unfurled his priestly garments. But the Germans objected, saying the robes were akin to a uniform, which was banned. Instead he was given a blue suit. His friends' sense of humour had not been dimmed by their confinement as they joked that it made him look like a car mechanic. Those left in the barracks also promised they would pray. Then came a thirty-kilometre drive through a beautiful sunny landscape.

Normally the court – grandly named a 'Tribunal of the People' – would sit in Berlin, but it was temporarily sitting in the Ursuline convent of Papenburg. The People's Court had special jurisdiction over political crimes – it was a component of the system of terror within Germany and occupied lands. The President of the Court was to sit in judgement on Leopold Vindictive. He was dressed in a blood-red robe, giving him, in the eyes of the accused, a satanic appearance. The eyes themselves above an angular nose were also demonic, the Belgians thought. He had the look of a man who seemed to relish his work.

That impression was accurate. Roland Freisler was not a lawyer who had reluctantly collaborated with the Nazi system, he was an intrinsic part of its evil who had been instrumental in taking National Socialist ideology and expressing it in the form of law and decrees. He had authored a legal decree against 'national parasites' and had attended the Wannsee conference in 1942 to provide legal advice on the plans for the 'Final Solution' which would eliminate the Jews. His trials always began with a Nazi salute and he brooked no diso-bedience in his courtroom. Theatrics were important to him – he had learnt as much from attending Soviet show trials as an observer before the war. The outward façade was of a normal legal process – a judge, lawyers, dossiers of evidence – translated to the dining room of a convent for girls with a large cross hanging on the wall.

After the salute, the accusations against the group were read out. The accused sat on two benches, a line of bald heads except for one woman – the nurse, Hélène Dufour, who had passed messages in sealed envelopes for Dehennin. Two linked groups were on trial. One, around Dehennin, included the others who had worked with him; the other, around Raskin, included Joye, Macq, Dufrasne and Arseen Debaillie. All were accused of secretly collecting informa-tion about the German army and passing it on to the enemy or others. Additionally, some were charged with smuggling people out of the country, listening to non-German radio transmissions and being in possession of anti-German material.

It was explained to the court that they were two independent circles of espionage: one, under Dehennin, under the influence of the French Deuxième Bureau and occasionally the English intelligence service; the other, under Raskin, working only with the English. Muylaert was the only common point which brought them together.

The evidence the Germans had accumulated and now presented to the court was weighty. The meetings between Dehennin and his French contact were described in detail, as was the specific intelligence that had been handed over. There were names, codenames, dates, and details of the money that had passed between him and the French, as well as their work helping people escape the country. There were the lines of contact between Muylaert and MI6 and the attempt to pass telegrams, including those from Raskin.

Next they came to Leopold Vindictive. It had begun, the Germans said correctly, when the 'racing' pigeon descended by parachute with its questionnaire – although they had the timing wrong, saying it had been in May 1941. The German allegations described the way the three accused friends – Raskin, Joye and Arseen Debaillie – had met in Lichtervelde and then divided up the intelligence gathering between them to collect material to send back to Britain attached to the pigeon. They knew Raskin had been the one to write the final report. There were precise details of what the pigeon had carried back and of what each man had contributed – for instance that Arseen had reported about copper wires on the Bruges–Ghent railway line whilst Joye had reported on what he had seen around Bruges. The pigeon had not been intercepted, so had someone talked under duress – or had the notes and drafts the men used for their first dispatch been found somewhere? It was noted that Raskin had taken a photograph of the pigeon and that Arseen had developed the picture. The codename Leopold Vindictive 200 and its origins were explained, including the meeting with Keys.

Here was their story, of which they were so proud, now turned into an accusation.

No one else was alleged to have collected any of the material – so at least the names of some of the others who provided details to Raskin in Brussels had been protected. Raskin himself was singled out as the central figure, having given orders to spy on military buildings in Ostend after the first pigeon was sent home. Their desperate desire for a further pigeon was noted. The friends' travels in August and September after the sending of the first pigeon were also listed, including Michel and Arseen's drive along the coast with Joye to make observations which could be transferred to drawings. Painful as it must have been, the group realized that some of them had talked. The Germans also produced the text of telegrams that had been passed to Muylaert to try to get to England, found during the October raids, as well as details of further intelligence that Muylaert had given Raskin.

The telegrams bore the general name Leopold Vindictive, not the names of the men, so they would not have provided enough information to catch the individuals involved straight away. The mystery of the gap between the October 1941 arrests and those of May 1942 remained. A few details were revealed about the meeting with Thonus in April 1942, and the telegram he had been given asking for a further pigeon was produced – the Germans had found that. But there was far less about the second Brussels group, with which Raskin had actually become far more entangled; they did not, for instance, know the real name of Devos. None of those arrested in May 1942 at Michelli's house – including Thonus and Van Hooff – were put on trial with Leopold Vindictive. There were limits to the Germans' knowledge. The telegrams – the ones given to both groups to send to London – were the most damning written evidence. They were the bitter legacy of the group's failure to establish a reliable channel to London.

The Germans had also managed to intercept a message Raskin had tried to send Joye soon after their arrest. 'The very strong anti-German feeling by the accused Raskin is very prominent in a secret message to Joye. He tried to influence Joye to give false information to the officers of the German departments who were interrogating them,' the German indictment reads.

The defence lawyer for Raskin and Arseen Debaillie was a 64-year-old who received the indictment only a few days before the trial and was able to speak to his clients for just half an hour before it began, but Raskin still felt he was doing his best. After the accusation had been read out, the defendants had to leave and then return one by one. The judge asked them how they pleaded. If they did not plead guilty, he said he would give them a minute more to speak the truth.

Macq denied everything. Dufrasne said he had acted as a Belgian officer and done what such an officer had to do – his duty. Arseen said his brother, now deceased, had been the one responsible. At this the judge laughed. Joye suggested that some material had been passed to Raskin but it had all been destroyed and not sent anywhere. At 4 p.m. on the first day, the court broke up. Raskin's mood was dark. Only now, it seems, was the promise of release disappearing from view. The next day, the defence lawyers made their case – some saying the evidence was hearsay or lacking, or that the men were former soldiers who were doing their duty. Only two offered up neither denials nor excuses, apologies or mitigating circumstances for their actions. They were Hélène Dufour and Raskin.

Dufour spoke in French of her pride in her country and her actions. Raskin spoke in German, the language of those who sought to judge him. His tone was confident and dignified. No official record remains of what he said; a German began noting it down but when he heard what was being said he stopped taking notes. Raskin was then silenced. 'I will never forget his attitude in front of his judges,' Macq later recalled. 'He said he had done what he had to do as a Belgian. He took all responsibility for the group as its leader.' Raskin said he felt no regret in the service he had given his country: 'In conscience and before my God, I have done my duty.' The judge responded harshly, describing him as an enemy of Germany.

There was plenty of evidence, but no full confession from the central players. The chances that they would all be found innocent were slim. But they hoped one or two might be. And the penalty for those found guilty still lay in the balance. A prison sentence would only hold them until the day that was surely coming soon, when the Allies would fight their way to Germany. Under the cross in a convent dining room, they awaited their fate.

CHAPTER SIXTEEN

Deception

In May 1943, a pigeon on Special Section duty returned to its loft in Oxfordshire. Home was not the suburban terrace of most working-class pigeon fanciers but a creeper-covered Victorian house on the village green in Tackley. The pigeon had originally been bred by a Barnsley fancier, but its home was now with Mary Manningham-Buller. Tending to a secret loft was not solely the province of men, nor even of the working class, although the sport had traditionally been a male-dominated environment. 'I suspect that many a man found peace and quiet with his pigeons away from the woman's world of kitchen and scullery,' wrote a member of the Osman family. But, during the war, women often ended up looking after lofts and collecting messages if the men were away. In Manningham-Buller's case, her husband Reginald was elected to Parliament (he would become attorney general, while his daughter, Eliza, would later become the head of MI5). During the war Mary was largely alone in the picturesque village with her pigeons.

As well as the presence of the pigeons and a strange corporal, the neighbours may have wondered about the motorbikes roaring up to the house to collect messages. The same pigeon that arrived in May 1943 would make a number of journeys from behind enemy lines, a performance which would win it the Dickin Medal. Manningham-Buller's pigeons – which returned from France twenty times – were particularly valued since some brought back news relevant to an urgent priority for British intelligence, the hunt for Germany's most advanced weapons.

It was one sign of Columba's shift of gears in the mid-war period and its move towards a more focused role rather than the random appeals for information it had begun with. The first attempt to target intelligence gathering had come in August 1942 when a batch of Columba pigeons was specially dispatched to establish reactions to the Dieppe Raid. Allied troops, mainly Canadian, had been trying to probe German coastal defences (the kind of attack on the Belgian coast for which Leopold Vindictive's maps would have provided invaluable assistance had they reached London). The losses proved terrible. News of the raid was brought back by a pigeon called Beach Comber, but MI14 and Columba had been tasked with gauging German reactions. A special questionnaire was drawn up to ask about the nature and extent of any damage, the effect on enemy morale and the effectiveness of a warning for locals broadcast on the BBC. 'There was an extraordinary wave of hope on the day of Dieppe,' one Columba return said.

The wake of the Dieppe Raid saw a particularly lengthy message arrive from someone who signed themselves with the intriguing codename 'The Father Christmas of Normandy'. 'Your disembark-ation at Dieppe made the French people very happy,' they wrote on 27 August. Drivers of motor lorries were told at gunpoint to drive over reinforcements, they explained, but he and friends had managed to stop some troops being captured. There was plenty of useful information about German positions and listening posts, but also some interesting personal appeals. These included a request for a message to be sent over the BBC that a particular gendarme in the area would do well to lie awake and think of his future after the war ended. The author promised that there was a 'strong nucleus' of men ready for action who just needed support in terms of weapons and radios (as well as ideally some coffee, chocolate, tinned food and cigarettes). If the material could be dropped, then a message should be sent out on the BBC saying 'Father Christmas of Normandy will see his children tonight.'

Dieppe was the first of four occasions on which aircraft were specifically sent to carry out Columba pigeon drops. The other three specific missions were carried out in support of 'Crossbow' – the hunt for intelligence on V1 and V2 rockets.

By December 1942, messages tallying with earlier rumours started to reach R. V. Jones from human sources about the possibility that Germany was developing rockets to hit Britain. Finding out about these rockets became a top priority for Jones and his colleagues, who were desperate for information while the weapons were at the research stage and before they were put to deadly use. At first there was little more to go on, but from March 1943 transcripts were made of the conversations of captured German officers held in Britain. In a highly productive intelligence operation, the interrogation centre in which they were held was bugged. This provided real gems, including a conversation between two generals about progress on the 'rocket business'. 'They've got those huge things which they've brought up here,' one said to the other. 'They've always said they would go fifteen kilometres into the stratosphere and then … You only aim at an area.' Turf wars complicated the hunt as Jones had to play second fiddle to a team led by the Conservative politician Duncan-Sandys (who was married to Churchill's daughter).

The pigeons that returned to the loft in Mary Manningham-Buller's Oxfordshire garden in the summer of 1943 brought more details, supplied by an agent. Work was taking place at Peenemünde on the Baltic coast, where previous reports had already suggested the rockets were being designed. The weapons had not yet struck but Jones and others knew they were being prepared. Finding any launch sites already constructed in Western Europe was a priority. On Christmas Day 1943, MI14(d) received a specific request from MI14(h) for 'Crossbow: Pigeon Intelligence'. They were told to organize drops at precise spots in northern France. Cherbourg and Pas-de-Calais had been identified by Jones as possible locations. The race was on to find what were called 'ski sites' because the launch pads had been identified as looking like ski-boards. The search involved both aerial reconnaissance and pigeons; indeed these were the largest ever drops for Columba. Brian Melland sent over to Kleyn three specific drop points on the French coast to be passed on to the teams at Tempsford. The aspiration was to drop eight hundred birds in all. Two hundred pigeons were dropped from each Halifax bomber, which meant it took the dispatchers twenty minutes to release them all from the hatch. This, everyone knew, was risky for the crews.

R. V. Jones may have come to appreciate the role of pigeons, but his colleagues at MI6 were only just realizing they could carry back useful intelligence. MI6 gradually began to appreciate the value of pigeons carrying microfilms on which maps and drawings could be sent. Some of the most advanced work on this was carried out by the Middle East pigeon section in Palestine. But it was the Dutch section of MI6 that eventually made most use of the technique: 'On one occasion a most valuable packet of microfilms of enemy operations was brought back at a critical moment by this means,' MI6 noted. It was carried by Scotch Lass, trained at RAF Felixstowe, which was dropped with an agent in the Netherlands in 1944. Even though the bird was injured, hitting telegraph wires in the semi-darkness when it was released at early dawn, it managed to carry back on the same day, over a distance of 200 miles, thirty-eight microphotographs 'of the utmost value'.

MI6 had finally cottoned on to the value of pigeons. But it was late to the game – too late for Joseph Raskin and Leopold Vindictive. Raskin had his microfilms of the German coastal defences ready for a pigeon three years before Scotch Lass made her flight.

As Raskin and his friends languished in prison, Columba was entering its final, critical phase preparing for the liberation of Europe. Leopold Vindictive were waiting – hoping – that this might come in time to save them from whatever fate Nazi Germany had in store. At the very moment they awaited their trial, hundreds of extra Columba pigeons were being dropped in specific locations in northern France, suggesting invasion was imminent. The purpose, though, was not liberation but deception.

At 3.15 p.m. on 9 July 1943, a major 'Pigeon Conference' was held in Room 254 of the War Office. Around the table sat representatives from the senior military commands, as well as Brian Melland from MI14. Brigadier Kirkman, Deputy Director of Military Intelligence, gave an overview of Columba. It was still proving its worth. 'It is desired to state how highly this source is appreciated,' GHQ Home Forces had written the previous month. 'It will become increasingly valuable as the time for operations approaches. It is very much to be hoped that Columba's range and resources will be continually increased.' German divisional movements and locations had been supplied, as had the sites of more of the radar stations that R. V. Jones was after. The RAF Special Duties Squadron had honed their dropping skills into a 'fine art', and operations took place every month in an arc from Denmark in the north to Bordeaux in southern France. A 'go slow' policy had recently been pursued in order to build up a sufficient stock of birds – which now numbered 15,000 – and also to avoid making the enemy too 'pigeon conscious' before the final push. Kleyn had written a detailed paper outlining the ways in which the Germans watched

Columba. But was there now a way to take advantage of the enemy's pigeon-mindedness?

The Columba team had been aware from the start that their pigeons could be used to trap locals as their opponent became 'pigeon-minded'. They had also heard that the Germans sometimes put their own pigeons in Columba baskets so that a pigeon would fly to a German loft with its message. One woman observed a fat German placing a basket in her garden. She subsequently took the pigeon out and attached to its leg a rude message to the Gestapo. 'She was arrested,' MI5 reported.

Sometimes the fear of planted German birds was enough to put locals off. At one point the returns from Columba in the Netherlands dropped to zero. The reason, the team learnt, was that word had gone round the resistance that the pigeons falling from the sky were German rather than British. 'How do they know that these pigeons actually fly to England? *We know better. They are German pigeons. Gestapo pigeons,*' a clandestine Dutch newspaper reported on 2 November 1942. Reports claimed that pigeons which arrived asking for shelter for a British pilot, or connections with resistance organizations, or help for Jews were all from the Gestapo. This caused consternation at Columba HQ. They had been enjoying a fair degree of success in the Netherlands. But in the six months following the newspaper article, there were no returns whatsoever. A report passed on from the French Secret Service in London likewise raised the concern that Gestapo pigeons were posing as British birds. A source said the pigeons were being dropped with a packet of English cigarettes to prove their authenticity and asked for the name of local patriots who could help in the event of the imminent invasion by the Allies. The French resistance had developed a slogan to raise the alarm – '*fumez les cigarettes – mangez les pigeons*': 'smoke the cigarettes – eat the pigeons'. The MI14 team debated whether to advertise the differences between the real pigeons and the German impostors. But the fear was that a warning could confuse people. 'It might result in the less intelligent leaving both kinds alone,' Melland wrote, pointing out that asking people to avoid mentioning their locality would make nine out of ten messages useless.

MI14 had also understood that the Germans might be using pigeons to feed back false information to London as part of a deception operation – the type of operation they had run using radios and pigeons with the SOE agent Van Horen. An MI6 report from Chimay in Belgium on 18 October 1942 claimed that some Columba pigeons had been delivered to Germans, who sent them off with false information. From the very start, Melland had been sceptical about some of their returns. The fourteenth message received by the team came from a pigeon that had been dropped on 13 May 1941 but took twenty-five days to come back looking 'fat and in good condition'. The writer, near Cherbourg, asked to be put in touch with local agents and made a request to drop messages at a particular crossroads. MI14 deemed that suspicious.

By the following May, the Columba team thought they had seen half a dozen messages planted by Germans. One 1942 message actually came back written in German by two 'old soldiers' and was described as having 'contained only abjurations written in the purest Goebbelese'.

Because a high number of birds were known to fall into enemy hands, MI14(d) decided to treat all messages as possible plants. They carried out basic counter-intelligence checks, looking for corroboration. The Germans typically added extraneous military detail that a civilian would not know. 'They are apt to give too much false information instead of inserting one important but false item between a lot of correct stuff which they do not mind our knowing or which they think we know already,' it was noted. Typically, a German message would claim the sender was about to get some new, vital piece of information and needed to be put in touch with a local resistance agent. 'Such requests are naturally suspect.' But if the Germans had used Columba for deception, could London do the same?

At MI5, the tartan trouser-wearing T. A. Robertson (known as TAR) had been mulling over the possibilities of pigeon deception. Since many of the Columba pigeons were captured by the Germans, the service could be used for a feint. 'It occurs to me that this is a possible means of putting deception over to the enemy by the careful framing of the questionnaires, as presumably the Germans must, if they capture some of these birds, take notice of the type of question which is being asked,' he wrote to Major Petavel at the War Office on 24 June.

Columba was being drawn into a new operation, known as Cockade. The decision had been made that an invasion of Europe could not take place until early in the summer of 1944. But, just as the Germans had tried to keep Britain on edge in 1941–2 over its plans, so now the favour would be returned. The idea of Cockade was to draw German forces away from Italy and the eastern front by feigning to attack in France and Norway in late 1943. This was to be accomplished using tools like commando raids and agents. Columba's role was in having extra pigeons dropped in very specific places. The original questionnaire had already been changed to ask not about preparations for an invasion of England but German preparations to defend Europe against Allied invasion. But with these new drops it would be tweaked again to focus on very specific areas like coastal defences and locations which might be used to land airborne troops. The idea was that the Germans would notice the different questions and the extra pigeons in certain locations, and that this would make them think the Allies were preparing to land at those places in the near future.

In August 1943, the total number of pigeons to be dropped was increased from 750 to 1,000, the extra 250 being dropped in the area of Pas-de-Calais. The RAF teams at Tempsford were given unusually specific instructions to release the birds at a rate of thirty per village, down a particular road. Others from the existing allocation were dropped in Brest, which formed another part of the feint (as did Norway, where the possibility of employing Columba had been investigated, although it had been deemed too risky for the RAF to fly so far for it). This all had to be done carefully, Melland explained, to prevent it being too obvious.

But one intelligence officer raised a concern overlooked by others. What would the dropping of extra Columba pigeons mean for the villagers on the ground? Or for the patriots who picked up those birds? It would create additional anticipation of an invasion. That was unfortunate but not too serious. The much greater risk was that the Germans, if they saw more pigeons coming down and bought the idea that this was to generate more intelligence for an invasion, would increase their vigilance and hunt for members of the resistance in those places. That might lead to disaster for anyone brave enough to respond to the pigeons they found. Deception in this instance was not simply a clever wheeze but something which risked civilian lives. Ordinary people would potentially gather intelligence and risk their lives by sending it back when it was all simply part of a trick. So, did the benefit of deception outweigh the risk to those finding pigeons in the areas where nothing was actually going to happen?

These were the moral choices of intelligence work. Only a few in London seemed to worry about such consequences, and there is no evidence that their concerns had any effect on the decision to go ahead. But nor does it appear that Cockade itself had a significant effect on German thinking. There were some signs of German agitation and increased intelligence activity, but Cockade as a whole and the pigeon drops may simply have been too subtle for a German war machine which was now under strain.

At MI5, Richard Walker came up with an even more complex deception operation as winter took hold. This one he called the 'contamination plan'. It was based on the knowledge that a stray or lost pigeon would find its way to a nearby loft rather than stay in the wild. His idea was that if some 'second rate' British pigeons could be disguised by putting German rings on them and then released by plane over Europe, they would eventually find their way to German-controlled lofts. The pigeon might then be given to a German agent sent to Britain; the bird – back in its home country – would fly to a British loft instead of delivering the intelligence. But the more likely outcome was that the Germans would eventually spot that something was amiss, perhaps by seeing two pigeons with identical ring numbers. They would then realize that their pigeon stock had been contaminated by imposter British birds and wonder how many more of their birds were phoney. The only thing they could do would be to recall all their birds, undermining their trust in their own pigeons. And by the time they had checked them and identified any fakes, Walker would have delivered more. It was a cunning plan, Guy Liddell agreed – the avian version of the Double Cross system.

The contamination plan might throw the Germans 'off balance' at just the right time. But it needed plenty of assistance. Replacing the rings was the hard part, since they were put on when a pigeon was less than a week old and the claw was still flexible. Walker tracked down a Professor Briscoe, as well as two captains (Swann and Hope), to help. Briscoe discovered that the British Aluminium Company had developed a new type of solder which had not yet been patented, but which they offered to MI5 so long as they agreed to keep it secret. It allowed them to make an invisible joint in the rings. Walker took the German pigeons that had been found on the east coast and used their Wehrmacht rings as the basis to make copies. The last challenge was to drop them. They must not materialize in a British container or parachute, so instead British parachute experts at Henlow came up with a special weighted hessian sack which could carry six or seven birds at a time before it was pushed through the floor of an aircraft. A weight forced it down, and an elastic band fixed to the aircraft pulled the bag open and turned it upside down, depositing the poor pigeons into the air from where they could fly off. In all, 350 phoney pigeons were released over Belgium and the Netherlands.

A Wehrmacht soldier who looked after pigeons was captured and interrogated later in the war. It was reported back to Guy Liddell at MI5 that one of Walker's 'Double Cross' pigeons had been picked up dead in Belgium or the Netherlands. The German said it was impossible to put a new ring on the bird without the soldering being spotted. This was excellent news for Walker and Liddell. 'He is wrong of course because this is precisely what we have done.' It meant the Germans were unaware of the possibility of deception. But in the end, 'contamination', like Cockade, was a dud. When the German military officer in charge of the pigeon service was interrogated after the war, he said his lofts could never have been infiltrated since it was impossible to attach a new ring to a pigeon. No one had noticed the phoney birds.

Amidst all the deception, decoys and feints, plans for the real invasion were now gathering pace, including the role of Columba. And that meant some new arrivals in the pigeon world.

CHAPTER SEVENTEEN

The Americans are Coming

W hen the 2nd Platoon 280th Signal Company disembarked from SS *Audacious* on 12 September 1942 in Glasgow, audacious is probably not the word they would have chosen to reflect how they felt. Their pigeons, which had been brought from America, were in a sorry state from the long journey. About a fifth were sick with colds, 'rattles' and lameness. And it did not help that some of the company's specialist equipment had been mistakenly shipped to Iceland. The officer who greeted the platoon informed them they would have to wait a month in a Glasgow transit camp while their birds were quarantined before finally heading south.

Eventually the men and their bedraggled birds made it to Tidworth. The company was headed by two leading pigeon officers, Lieutenant Thomas H. Spencer, previously a partner in a lumber business from North Carolina, and Lieutenant Irwin F. Salz, a New Yorker and a long-time member of the Sandy Hook pigeon racing company. In Tidworth they settled down to work with the British Army Pigeon Service, sharing birds and advice on an experimental basis. The young American birds struggled at first with the British climate even though they, like the troops, looked stronger thanks to a better diet. 'The dampness of the English climate seemed to cause an undue amount of respiratory troubles in the American pigeons,' it was noted. But the American pigeons – like some of their soldiers – soon began cross-breeding with the local population, often quite successfully. The goal was to take the birds into Europe.

America had pedigree when it came to pigeons. When the US military arrived in Europe during the First World War, it had quickly seen their value and had established its own service in 1917. This began with two officers and twelve men, but by the end of that war more than 330 men were involved. British owners gave 600 young pigeons to the US Army in addition to 10,000 purchased from American fanciers. In the interwar period, homing pigeons found a use with bootleggers during prohibition as the carriers of messages between ships and land. By 1938, the US Army had built twenty new lofts for a breeding and training centre at Fort Monmouth, New Jersey, and in June 1941 the 280th Signal Pigeon Company – out of which other units would be hived off – was stood up. A month after Pearl Harbor in December 1941, things really moved up a gear when the War Department made a call to the American fancy for help. It asked for champion racing pigeons which had flown 200 miles to be loaned, gifted or bought at the price of $5. Support flooded in from American owners, who donated thousands of birds and volunteered to work in the Signal Corps. Around 40,000 birds from domestic fanciers were shipped out to tactical units in the field. US Army pigeons were incorporated into twelve special Signal Pigeon Companies, each of which had three combat platoons using 1,500 pigeons apiece. At its peak the US pigeon corps had 3,000 men, 150 officers and 54,000 pigeons. 'Cheer up, Men, Birds May Also Be Drafted', read one newspaper report. There were even the same fears of German pigeon spies as those that haunted Britain's MI5. In January 1941, America's top code-breakers were asked for help dealing with an exhausted carrier pigeon found on Long Island carrying a message with some kind of coded coordinates and emblazoned with a Nazi swastika.

America's pigeons soon saw action. A 'North African Pigeon Platoon' arrived in Casablanca in November 1942 and moved to the front, where pigeons were trained to home to a Tunisian loft. Their value was apparent when radio silence was required or to convey requests for ammunition and supply, as well as to carry important or secret messages. On 17 March 1943, a pigeon named Yank brought in the first news of the American advance on Gafsa, Tunisia. In early April, during the battle of El Guettar, four messages were carried by a single bird. Two of those were from General Patton, marked secret and urgent.

The North Africa-based pigeon company moved on to Italy after the invasion of that country began in September 1943. Pigeons were given to partisans around Bologna and as far north as Modena. They would sew birds into their coat pockets or use a special jacket devised by the Americans. The birds could then carry back messages and maps regarding gun positions and troop movements. They were also used when troops were physically so close to the enemy that using a radio would have risked them being overheard or spotted.

Units isolated in mountainous terrain in Italy found pigeons invaluable. One patrol deep in enemy territory, under heavy fire and running out of food, blankets and medical supplies for its wounded, sent back an urgent request for help by pigeon which led to a parachute drop of supplies within a few hours. American pigeons even saved British lives in Italy. The US 56th Infantry Division was trying to break the German defence's lines at a heavily fortified village called Colvi Vecchia on the morning of 18 October 1943. It called in bombers to help. What it did not know was that earlier that morning the Germans had retreated and the British 169th Infantry Brigade had moved into the village. Attempts to cancel the bombings by sending radio messages failed. The only hope was six-month-old GI Joe, who had been hatched in Algeria. He flew twenty miles from the 10th Corps HQ in twenty minutes and arrived as the planes were preparing to take off to bomb the village. If he had arrived five minutes later, a hundred British soldiers might have been killed, as well as civilians. GI Joe would be the first non-British bird to be awarded the Dickin Medal for gallantry by animals and enjoyed the honour until 1961 when he died at the ripe old pigeon age of 18.

The Office of Strategic Services (OSS) – the forerunner of the Central Intelligence Agency, the CIA – also found pigeons 'very beneficial', dropping them with teams behind enemy lines in Europe and with agents in Asia. The US developed a strange-looking contraption called the 'pigeon bra', which made it easier for agents to carry the birds on their person. In the fight for Papua New Guinea, US marines sent a patrol to the village of Drabito. The patrol's radio was damaged during a firefight and so they released two pigeons to warn HQ of the Japanese counter-attack. These pigeons were shot down by the Japanese. One pigeon was left, trained by the 7th Australian pigeon section but attached to the US 6th Army. It was released during a short lull in the fighting and came under heavy fire straight away, but covered the thirty miles back in forty-six minutes. The Japanese positions were then bombed and the patrol saved.

Some of the most impressive OSS results came in Burma. A four-month-old pigeon called Jungle Joe was parachuted behind enemy lines to Allied scouts gathering intelligence on nearby Japanese troop and gun positions. He was their only means of communication, and flew back 225 miles through bad weather and over steep mountains with his information, which was said to have helped capture what was described as a large chunk of Burma. Another team from the OSS and Office of Naval Intelligence took thirty birds on an epic journey by rail, ship and air from Florida to China so they could train Chinese guerrillas in the event of a possible invasion of the Chinese coast.

The war was global and so was the deployment of pigeons. Britain's pigeon service extended across the Mediterranean, the Middle East and West Africa from Alexandria to Bahrain, the Seychelles to Dar es Salaam. The Middle East Pigeon Service, with its HQ at Cairo, carried out operations from Turkey through Syria to Lebanon and down to Jerusalem. The Indian Pigeon Service had operated in the North West Frontier Province in the 1930s. British pigeons sent there as reinforcements must have been bewildered by the change of climate but worked successfully behind enemy lines in Burma.

In Europe, the Americans were integrated into pigeon services from late 1943. The US had already been in on the secret of the Columba operation. In August 1942, they had actually looked at developing their own version of Columba. After discussion with Rex Pearson, the Office of War Information created a mock-up of an American questionnaire. What is noticeable about the American version is that it featured pictures – small cartoons of marching soldiers, ships and gun emplacements – to illustrate the kinds of information people should send back. There was also a focus on which American radio broadcasts could be heard in Europe. But now they had arrived, the Americans were to be part of Columba itself. Once they had settled after their long journey, Lieutenants Spencer and Salz and the other pigeoneers from 280th Company were assigned Columba lofts for their use. Their mission was to prepare for D-Day. Spencer worked on plans for pigeons to be used for gathering intelligence from behind enemy lines and as a means of contact for advancing Allied forces when the use of radios was not possible.

Early in December 1943, Bert Woodman in Plymouth received orders to report to Wing House one Saturday morning. His pigeons had been shifted from RAF rescue duty to Special Section work on Columba and there was a show and lunch that day for fanciers who were contributing pigeons to the war effort. Woodman was met by Lieutenant Colonel Montgomery, who ran Army pigeon operations including Special Section. He explained that Woodman was going to be introduced to an American officer. 'You will say nothing to anyone,' Montgomery told Woodman, specifically saying this meant Rayner at the Air Ministry.

Having agreed, Woodman headed off in the colonel's small van that wintry morning to a Holborn restaurant. In the Venetian room, the fanciers ate a rather tasty Viennese steak. The Special Section officers explained to them that more pigeons would be needed in the coming months. In the Drill Hall at Buckingham Gate, the fanciers then toured an exhibition of a thousand pigeons. As Woodman was walking around, he was introduced to a young American army officer. 'Bert, meet Lieutenant Irwin Salz of the United States Army 280th Pigeon Company,' he was told. 'Take the lieutenant outside, find a pub and buy him a drink, he has something to ask you.'

Neither of them was a local, but eventually they found a pub and went into the snug. Salz explained that he had been sent to ask Bert if he would help supply the Americans with a pigeon service for the return to Europe. Bert quietly answered yes, and the New York and the Plymouth fancier shook hands. A special relationship had been born in the pub.

Just after Christmas, a US staff sergeant arrived by jeep at Woodman's Plymouth Pigeon Supply Group headquarters at 18 Cecil Street, to collect pigeons for 'Exercise Duck', designed to test how quickly messages could be distributed after their arrival at a local loft. Woodman and his colleagues showed the American round the locality and its lofts as they sketched out their locations on a big sheet of greaseproof paper spread out on his floor. By February 1944, Lieutenants Spencer and Salz were amongst the few indoctrinated into the plans for the invasion in Normandy, so that they could work on pigeon communications. They began training birds from Plymouth lofts by tossing them first from the coast and then from US Navy ships in the Channel as far as twenty miles offshore. Some days they were taken out on landing craft, and guns would be fired to simulate the conditions they might expect to meet.

There had been the inevitable battle between the Army and the RAF once Rayner at the Air Ministry eventually learnt of the plans. Rayner even proposed a test to prove his RAF birds would perform better over longer distances. But in the end, the US First Army was largely supplied by Columba's civilian lofts in Portsmouth and Plymouth, which were well used to cross-Channel work. In all, British pigeon fanciers supplied 46,532 birds to the Americans during the war.

As the Allied armies gathered for the decisive moment, Columba continued to collect intelligence to prepare the way. Nearly four and a half thousand birds were dropped in the first six months of 1944 from the thousand lofts supplying birds. A total of 202 messages made it back despite some terrible weather. The priority lists stating where Columba pigeons should be dropped were now provided by SHAEF, the Supreme Headquarters Allied Expeditionary Force (which also now coordinated SOE). The importance of up-to-date intelligence had never been greater. 'It is considered essential to approach the question of Columba targets entirely afresh at this critical stage. Now if ever is the time for the old lady to show her paces,' the team wrote on 26 May. A set of priority targets was drawn up, consisting of inland areas of France and Belgium which were to be covered by a far greater concentration of birds.

The intelligence the pigeons brought back was richer than at Columba's inception three years earlier, and it was filled with the useful minutiae that only a local could provide. A small tunnel in one place was full of mines. A train filled with ammunition passed through a specific station at the same time every day. Mines had been placed in a particular harbour. Information on the German order of battle was especially prized, pointing as it did to the movement of armour belonging to 1st Panzer Korps from Belgium to the Beauvais area.

Comment was often made on the fragility of German morale. One writer noted that many Germans possessed civilian clothes which they intended to put on as soon as the Allies arrived. There were now more details of collaborators, and a renewed push to go after them; the information was sent to Rear Echelon SHAEF 'at their special request'. At Sequedin, near Lille, a named grocer was said to be an informer of the Gestapo who entertained them at his home. Meanwhile at La Basse, on the Rue de Lille, a certain woman was said to be a tenant of a small restaurant reserved for the Germans who denounced patriots to the Gestapo. 'It would be a good thing to warn the inhabitants of these localities over the radio,' the message writers said.

The intelligence had become more detailed in part because more people were now willing and able to help. Resistance had evolved since the summer of 1941 from the small, amateurish groups of friends like Leopold Vindictive. Birds were now falling into the hands of organized and semi-organized resistance groups which were growing in number, strength and confidence. In France, the Maquis operated in the countryside – young, armed men in hiding who carried out sabotage and prepared for war. The messages were now much longer and more precise in terms of intelligence. They show a far greater understanding of the value of tactical military intelligence than the early crop.

At MI5, the priority was to keep Allied plans for D-Day secret from any German spies in Britain. As a result, catching enemy pigeons mattered more than ever. The needs of espionage and counter-espionage collided around the cliffs of Britain. The

Falconry Unit – with its hawks trained to go after German pigeons carrying secrets – could only cover a few miles of coast, but the desire was to expand operations to stop enemy birds. The original plan was to put the unit into action around Colchester, but the hawks' abysmal failure to tell the difference between friend and foe led to concerns that friendly pigeons – including those from SOE, MI6 and Columba, as well as those the Army was planning to use for D–Day – would be more likely than Nazi spy pigeons to fall victim to their talons. The plan was blocked. So Richard Walker at MI5 cooked up another idea.

Homing pigeons are dedicated but sociable creatures. If they spot a flock of friendly pigeons, they will often decide to hang out with them in the hope of food or rest. Not long before D-Day, all the fanciers living within ten miles of the coast, from Cornwall to Norfolk, were approached through the NPS and asked to come to a local meeting. At each meeting, Walker turned up and asked them to assist in a scheme to lure into their lofts any single enemy birds that might be flying out of Britain. They were asked to arrange the times at which they let their birds out for their daily flight so that there were always pigeons in the air to attract exhausted enemy birds. This 'screen' of friendly birds was the pigeon equivalent of the chaff of R. V. Jones's 'Window', so effective at confusing German radar. However, no enemy birds were caught, as there were no active German agents sending back information. 'Had they done so it is fairly certain that the loft screen would have bagged a fair proportion of them,' explained Walker, ever the optimist about his plans.

The Germans also began to prepare on the pigeon front for an Allied invasion. On 1 March, the Military Commander for Belgium and northern France decreed that it would be forbidden to keep pigeons in a number of districts. The rings of all pigeons killed had to be surrendered as confirmation. Forty-five thousand pigeons were moved from coastal towns to Brussels to prevent their use by the enemy. There had been some hopes in Britain that the Germans might leave existing pigeon lofts intact, but it was now clear that a stock of young English birds would have to be brought over.

As D-Day approached, the weather was bad. Cold winds, heavy rain and poor visibility made it hard for the RAF Special Duties team to drop Columba birds. Seven aircraft were lost on the nine operational nights that month (all but two before D-Day itself). On the night of 5 June, the BBC crackled with *messages personnels* instructing agents to carry out special sabotage operations against railways and other targets. Bert Woodman took a walk on the promenade in Plymouth with his wife that evening. Out on Plymouth Sound, he could see row after row of invasion craft, arrayed in straight lines like a company of soldiers, with a cloud of barrage balloons hovering above them.

On 6 June, Allied troops landed on the heavily fortified Normandy beaches under unimaginably ferocious and brutal bombardment. Amid the gunfire and the chaos and the blood, pigeons flew free above the men's heads back over the Channel to bear news of the unfolding events. The pigeons had been issued from Portsmouth and Plymouth to formations in marshalling areas just before they embarked for France.

In Britain, the fanciers waited by their lofts. The wind was picking up to a gale and no one was sure a single bird would get through. Gustav was the first pigeon to arrive back, in five and a quarter hours. He carried a message from a Reuters correspondent dispatched from the beach as the first landing took place (Gustav later died when someone cleaning his loft accidentally stepped on him). Paddy, bred in Northern Ireland, was the fastest pigeon – flying 230 miles in four hours and fifty minutes. In Plymouth, alarm bells began to ring as pigeons returned to their lofts and American jeeps raced to collect the cylinders.

Not all the arrivals bore messages. Some of the saddest pigeons that returned to Plymouth were covered in human blood. The men had been carrying pigeon drum containers as they landed. They had been struck by gunfire which had ripped through the drums, freeing the birds to fly home but leaving the men who had carried the pigeons to die on the beaches.

The US First Army used hundreds of birds on D-Day, about half making it back. These carried ammunition status reports and emergency messages. In the end, radios worked reasonably well on the day of the invasion and so the need for pigeons was not quite so great as anticipated. As well as messages from troops, a select group of elite birds had been trained to wear a harness which could carry a container of 35mm film. But these never returned with their historic cargo. The combination of the weight of the container, the hostile conditions and rough handling meant they flew inland to perch and rest rather than heading home, and so went straight into the German lines, where they were shot down or captured.

Many of the pigeons that made it back from D-Day were more exhausted than they should have been. The Army Pigeon Service surmised that this was because they did not take the straightest route. Due to the smoke and noise of battle, rather than fly in a straight line of 125 miles they took a more circuitous route up the French coast to Dunkirk and then across the Channel before homing, tripling the distance. Afterwards, the APS and Rayner of the RAF inevitably battled as to whose birds had been more effective and disputed details in each other's reports.

The Special Air Service [SAS], established as a commando unit earlier in the war, proved avid pigeon users, taking 330 birds from Army lofts around D-Day. Around one in twelve of the birds they were given had already flown Columba missions. One bird sent with SAS troops on 7 June 1944 returned from near the Swiss border on 29 June after spending twenty days in a small container. Long confinement was one reason why many birds did not make it home. Another problem for the SAS was that their need for security meant they could not tell loft owners where they were going, and so could not pick the most suitable birds for the mission.

The American pigeoneers slowly accompanied their troops into Europe through shattered French villages, past the wreckage of planes and vehicles and dead horses. The friendly offer of cider and Calvados eased their path. In combat, their pigeons had to fly through heavy fire, still having to evade hawks, sometimes dazed and suffering shell-shock. The bond between men and birds remained strong – American soldiers' reports tell of the sadness when disease meant hundreds of pigeons had to be destroyed, or of their pride when a bird was awarded his own 'purple heart' for returning back wounded to one of their mobile lofts (which were usually tugged around by a jeep).

The news from the front was not always good. The first word of landings by 1st British Airborne at Arnhem in September came from pigeons. They reported that the British paratroops held the north end of Arnhem Bridge and were waiting for the 2nd Army to arrive to support them. But the reinforcements were delayed and German resistance was much heavier than they expected. On 19 September at 10.30 a.m., a pigeon named William of Orange was released to fly from Arnhem to London. Travelling 260 miles, 135 of them over sea, in a speedy four hours and twenty-five minutes, it carried a message that the situation in Arnhem was desperate. The troops urgently needed resupply. Thanks to the pigeon's message, an effort was made to do just that. The aircraft had to take off from the Midlands as the south was covered in a blanket of fog. By the time it arrived, the drop site to which it sent the supplies was in the hands of the Germans. By the next day things were even worse; the British troops were nearly out of food and ammunition and under heavy fire. Eventually they would have to withdraw from what had indeed been a bridge too far.

As the Allies began to push through France, messages flooded in to Columba as if a dam had burst. Extra drops were organized behind enemy lines to gather intelligence, and people were now willing to take more risks. 'We await you impatiently and hope to see you soon to get rid of the dirty Boches who have poisoned our country for four years now,' wrote a pair of 22-year-old Frenchmen who signed themselves Lulu and Riri and riskily identified the small locality thirty miles from Chartres where they lived. 'Come and liberate us soon and bring cigarettes, tea, sweets, etc. Kick the Boches out of here,' read another message. Some, excited by D-Day, started to fight too soon and would die as the German grip took longer to loosen than they had anticipated. Columba carried messages that described members of the resistance being killed and one girl being tied to a wheelbarrow and beaten for having a radio transmission set.

The French resistance shifted from sabotage to more organized warfare. They provided updates through Columba on supplies sent by parachute, with references to which containers were the most useful – they said they now needed less explosives and more equipment that would be useful for guerrilla warfare, rather than the sabotage of the past. They also pleaded for battery-powered radio sets to be used in the field and even for bicycle tyres for messengers, since this was the only means of getting around. One group said a German motor car had been fired on by the resistance, killing a colonel and wounding a general. In reprisal, the Germans hanged eleven young people whose bodies were left exposed for days in the streets of Carhaix. A pigeon with a message from 'Julien and Jacques' dated 4 July 1944 provided detailed intelligence. 'Do not worry, dear Allies. We have been standing firm for 4 years now and we know all the defeatists, collaborators and especially the turncoats.

We shake you by the hand. Together we shall win.' It warned that one group of Maquis had been discovered by the enemy; thirteen were killed, despite an 'energetic defence'. They also warned that 'Your supplies by parachute on the night of 29th–30th June fell in the hands of the enemy.'

One of the more startling messages came on 13 July from an organized resistance group in Brittany who wrongly thought they were being deceived. 'As we suspect that this is a German pigeon, we are sending you some news which you will find interesting,' the group wrote, explaining that they were now well supplied by the Allies and were making preparations to 'teach you the lesson which you deserve'. They claimed that there were deserters from a German army which consisted mainly of teenagers. 'In the end you will pay your debts to the prisoners, the families you have shot and those you have tortured.' It offered a warning as well to the Germans. 'For us, as from today, 10 Boches for one Frenchman, Suffering for suffering, an eye for an eye, a tooth for a tooth. Remember that we FFI [the French Forces of the Interior, as de Gaulle christened the resistance] will go and occupy Germany and make you pay. Already we have done in many Boches and know that we have the arms we need you will learn very shortly.' It was signed 'Marag' – a chief of section of a group of Bretons – and ended with the phrase 'Mort aux Boches'. This message was noted to be sent to MI6, no doubt interested in who this highly motivated group of partisans might be.

Out of the blue, the Columba team at MI14 received a letter from their old colleague Rex Pearson soon after D-Day. He had not given up. On 16 June, Pearson wrote a personal letter to Brian Melland from the BBC, where he was still working. 'Forgive me for being so importunate – I think that's the right word,' he began. 'This is a chance of a lifetime and more and if you can get me sent over I'll guarantee good results within eight weeks.' His suggestion was to avoid the Channel crossing by having pigeons return with messages to a base in Normandy. They could be delivered by plane or even, he suggested, by balloon as he had done in the First World War, as this would provide independence from the RAF. The rates of return of Columba would be improved enormously, he was sure. 'Will you have lunch with me on Monday or Tuesday,' he ended pleadingly. Melland replied on 19 June with thanks and explained that the idea of using Normandy as a base was already being discussed. 'I'm afraid I'm booked for lunch tomorrow Tuesday, but may I give you a ring when the position is firmer?' he wrote.

Pearson was no longer in the loop and so could not know that the idea of basing Columba in France had indeed already been looked at. The aspiration had been to open a base in France in August so flights could start in October. But that proved difficult because of the initially uneven speed of the Allied advance, followed by a rapid German retreat once the Allies broke out of Normandy. Instead, Columba continued to run from Britain, with Kleyn sending lists of priority areas to match the locations where the Allies were preparing to fight their way through.

A week after D-Day, residents of Britain heard a new, terrifying sound. The buzz of an engine overhead which suddenly spluttered out. Next came silence. Then an explosion. In response to the arrival of the Allies on the Normandy beaches, the Germans first unleashed their V1 – one of the earliest just missing MI6 HQ at Broadway. A few months later came the V2 rockets. In London, Churchill grew deeply concerned about the possible impact. Did London need to be evacuated?

Columba offered help in minimizing the deadly toll of the rockets. The challenge was to find their launch pads. In July, eighty-nine Columba messages which returned gave information which helped identify ten flying bomb emplacements. One message lists two 'flying torpedo' emplacements in their area, another lists four. As with night-fighter radar, the strangeness of the new technology made the launch sites distinctive enough to be spotted by locals.

The Columba returns helped provide targets for the RAF and Allies to strike as they desperately sought to stem the tide of rockets. At the start of August, a message from Totes in Normandy from a local Frenchman who signed himself Le Favue provided some of the richest information. He detailed targets for railway lines used by the Germans, but also specified emplacements for what the author called 'robots' with their runways in the sports grounds of a college.

Totes was one of the sites targeted by Allied planes as the location of German V1 positions, and as the French writer then explained there was an addendum in English from 'your captain' and some of his colleagues who 'reached us from the sky'. The crashed airmen – from the Royal Australian and Canadian Air Forces as well as the US Air Force – went on to use the pigeon message to pass on their own detailed wealth of intelligence about German anti-aircraft positions and infantry movements as well as V1 sites, knowing enough to explain what type of catapult was being used for take-off. They explained how Germans had originally said London would be 'kaput' in ninety-six hours after the launches began but after a week recognized that many were failing. They also explained that the V1 flying bombs were proving only partially successful. Of the first four fired from one position, two fell within 200 yards and another not much further off. Only one successful shot per installation per day seemed to be the average.

The airmen even critiqued their own side's bombing tactics:

The use of heavy bombers at high levels on 'No Ball' [V1 launch sites] and other pin-point targets is to be deplored as they very, very seldom hit any military targets, but do a great deal of damage to French property and make many enemies. As instance on the afternoon of 14th July, many Lancs. [Lancaster bombers] came over and bombed above cloud. The markers went down *near* the little factory but the heavies let go up to five miles off and bombs fell uselessly in the fields and villages and caused much damage. I saw at least ten sticks fall that did no military good whatever … On the roads, the fighters are hitting a lot of French civilian traffic, but are doing good work keeping the Hun quiet.

The team went on to ask for more pigeons to be dropped in specific nearby fields where locals would be helpful. 'We are told to wait here for "Monty",' the message concluded, a reference to General Montgomery, then pushing through France.

The bleakest messages are those that detail civilian casualties from Allied bombing raids. 'I would ask you, my friends,' wrote a French farmer who found the pigeon in his beetroot field in Mayenne, 'to warn the population a few minutes before the bombing because you kill many civilians who are your friends. Very few Germans get killed. It is nearly always the civilians who suffer from your aircraft. If you circle before dropping your bombs, the population would have time to withdraw from the town, thus avoiding many French victims. You must spare your friends and kill the Germans.' The farmer ended with a plea for liberation as soon as possible since all his friends had been taken by the Gestapo. 'Please send us arms, rifles, revolvers and ammunition by parachute,' he wrote, signing himself Jean du Coin Larue. Numerous messages contained pleas to respect the white flags that civilians sometimes flew (despite the risk of a fine) since they were being hit.

Others too warned of the dangers of Allied aircraft hitting civilian targets. In some messages, anger comes through. 'Aviators should be very, very, very careful,' one author who called himself the 'refugee boar' from Parthenay, Deux-Sèvres, wrote in a long message in July 1944, explaining how four fighter bombers targeting a viaduct failed to hit it or kill a single German but did kill a mother of four children. The author provided extensive details of which bombing raids over the previous two months had missed and instead killed civilians. A dairy truck had been hit, and soon afterwards a father of seven was killed by fire from an aircraft. 'The military results obtained have not warranted the losses and destruction suffered by the French population. Amongst those who are wildly anti-Boches many complain bitterly of poorly aimed Allied attacks.' The writer provided detailed suggestions on how to be more effective – for instance, that trains should be attacked between stations and from the side so the driver and his fireman (who were always French) were not hit. One message from the Netherlands said, 'I implore you not to shoot on trains and vehicles with innocent people. Last week about 250 people were killed or wounded in Holland. You cannot call this fair play and the war cannot be won that way. It is not an act of heroism to shoot on trains with civilians by low flying aircraft.'

In Belgium, Joseph Raskin's family witnessed the power of Allied bombs. On the morning of 9 May, the air raid siren sounded in the town of Aarschot where they lived. Heavy bombers flew over the town but no bombs fell. But two and a half hours later, more US Air Force planes came, and this time they targeted the town's important railway station and depot, close to the Raskin family house. Buildings were reduced to rubble and fires raged. The bridges over the river were destroyed.

As troops moved through Europe, the worry for Allied pigeon experts was increasingly about the presence of enemy pigeons, and about the Germans developing their own version of Columba. An observant military policeman at the harbour of Le Havre spotted birds flying suspiciously away from a hillside not long after it had been captured. A search party was sent and found a camouflaged tunnel entrance. Inside was a team of Germans who had been spying on Allied shipping in the harbour below and releasing the details via pigeon to maintain radio silence. The Germans also enlisted other locals and pigeons to spy in stay-behind networks.

André, a 33-year-old Belgian hotel proprietor from near Ostend, had returned in March from sick leave after being forced to work on the Russian front. In a café, he fell into conversation with a man who said there might be a way for him to avoid going back to the front. All André had to do was work for the man by sending messages via pigeon. A few days later he was given pigeons and forms and told to practise, using the cover name Sabot. His job was to provide details of Allied troop movements if they arrived in the town. André had been recruited into the German 'stay-behind' pigeon network.

Intelligence had reached Allied Command in late 1944 giving precise details of how the Germans had established these networks to provide intelligence or help organize resistance in Belgium, France, the Netherlands and Germany itself as the Wehrmacht were pushed back. Captured enemy agents said there were twice as many agents using pigeons as there were those using radio sets. In a mirror image of Columba, they had been given instructions to supply details of Allied troop movements by means of pigeons which would fly back to German-controlled lofts. In Belgium the agents were located mainly near the coast. Some, Richard Walker of MI5 explained in a note, operated clandestinely out of houses with birds hidden in attics, others used birds from larger military-run lofts such as one in Brussels. 'Personally, I consider this constitutes a very real danger,' T. A. Robertson at MI5 wrote as he forwarded the paper to Dick White, the intelligence liaison for SHAEF (and a future head of MI5 and MI6). Troops were ordered to report any lofts they found and to wait for the Army Pigeon Signal Company to come and literally clip the birds' wings so they could not carry messages. Riflemen were sometimes ordered to shoot down any birds

suspected of carrying messages. Detailed interrogation questionnaires were drawn up for any captured Germans who might have
knowledge of pigeon activities.

Captain G. F. Swann was in charge of pigeon counter-espionage
for the 21st Army Group and found evidence to support Robertson's
fears as the troops advanced. This included a coded message from
an agent who had since been captured, and which his interrogators
could now put to him to try and gain useful intelligence on the
cipher system German intelligence was using to encode their
messages. Details were sent back to MI5, and Walker tried to crack
the codes of the various messages received.

André the hotel owner was arrested the day Canadian troops
entered his town – local patriots had suspected him all along. He
tried to bluff his way out by claiming he was working for the Allied
underground movement, but a message from an agent working
with him was found on the roof of a building in Ostend. Similarly,
Bertrand, an agent in Yquelon in France, was given 4,000 francs a
month to release pigeons, but at the first sign of an American tank
he got on his bicycle and made off. He was later arrested in Paris.
Pigeons were used extensively by the German Army before D-Day,
but in practice they found it harder to keep using them afterwards,
so rapidly were they forced to retreat.

As the Allies prepared to make the final push into Germany,
intelligence mounted relating to extensive pigeon preparations by
the enemy in their homeland. Orders were given to Allied units that
one of their first missions on entering German towns was to identify pigeon fanciers and their lofts and then interrogate them.
SHAEF even made plans to bomb a particular German loft thought
to be supplying Nazi networks.

Allied forces had entered Belgium at the start of September 1944.
For the second time, the towns of Belgium felt the full force of war,
but now the Germans were retreating rather than advancing. Hitler

counter-attacked in the Ardennes in December and it would not be until February that the whole of the country was liberated, but the pace of the Allied advance in the early days surprised even those who were part of it. 'Every time we halted, we had fruit and wine showered on us. We looked like flying greengrocer's shops,' one British soldier remembered. Joseph Raskin's brothers and sisters and their children watched the Allies pass out chocolate as they made their way through. Crowds lined the streets to welcome the troops with cheers and 'V for Victory' signs. Flags and banners were retrieved from cellars to be flown from houses.

The Germans fell back from Brussels quickly, and by 3 September the Allied convoys were struggling to get through the crowds that thronged the street to welcome them. The cafés blazed with light that night. Champagne stored by the Germans in the cellars of the Palace of Justice was brought out. Brussels 'fairly swam in wine', soldiers recalled.

There was a bitter harvest in the following days. Wives and mothers in Brussels had to be restrained from taking out their fury on captured Germans. Some Belgian men grabbed weapons and went hunting for Nazis or for collaborators.

That included the men who had betrayed Leopold Vindictive. Pieren, the brother-in-law of Dehennin, is thought to have been shot in Brussels on the day of liberation. Leduc, the man who had arrived at the mission house of Scheut to aid Raskin's arrest, was reported to have been killed by the resistance near Lille, although there were later reports that this was a case of mistaken identity and that he might still be at large.

Major Page from MI6 and Lepage from the Belgian Sûreté landed in Arromanches in Normandy on 11 September and arrived in Brussels two days later. In the Hotel Metropole, Page continued his work gathering intelligence, his primary targets being the identification of V2 weapon sites and an effort to run agents into

Germany. Hardy Amies headed to liberated Brussels to work with the Sûreté running agents into Germany and got himself into typically Amies-style trouble. As an old friend of the editor of *Vogue* magazine, while in Brussels he helped one of the magazine's star writers with a story on female members of the Belgian resistance. Amies took the writer, Lee Miller, a muse to Man Ray in Paris – and herself the subject of investigation by MI5 – to meet the 'baby-faced' Countess Thérèse.

The Countess had carried millions of francs in her handbag for arms, bribery and sabotage, the journalist's resulting copy read breathlessly. Miller recounted in the story how Amies offered to take her to 'a reception'. Fearing it would be a boring 'hand-shaking' event, the *Vogue* writer was delighted to find that it actually involved acting as the reception committee in a field for a parachute drop containing weapons. By the time the military got on to the matter, most of Miller's article – including pictures of Amies, described as a 'famous couturier', had already gone to the printers. As an investigating officer noted, it seemed extraordinary 'that a serving officer should lend his secret service background in the interests of his private affairs' through a 'gaudy publicity stunt' which 'will cause a flutter in many feminine hearts when they realise that their handsome couturier is after all, the "Scarlet Pimpernel" of this war'. The editor reluctantly agreed to delete a 'spicy tit-bit' about Amies's work for SOE.

Pigeons were among the spoils of war that soldiers were given explicit instructions to seize. As they pushed into Belgium, the Americans were ordered to commandeer German lofts. The 282nd Signal Pigeon Company established its headquarters in Verviers on 12 September and captured from the Germans over a thousand birds which it then trained for its own use. Just as crack teams were sent to capture Nazi scientists, so there was a concerted effort to capture the best German pigeons to harness their skills. The 285th

Signal Pigeon Company managed to commandeer one of the most famous German racing pigeons, a bird called Meister, who was then made a 'naturalized American' so he could be used for breeding.

When one German headquarters building in Belgium was seized, Allied soldiers made a surprising find. In the adjoining loft buildings and storage rooms were a huge number of containers from Columba. And in the lofts were birds with British rings dating from 1940 and 1941. These seem to have been local birds who had British rings re-soldered on to them in an attempt to trap locals who thought they were using Columba since the birds would fly to German lofts. This was final proof of just how pigeon-minded the Germans had become. They had taken the threat of Columba seriously enough to try to organize their own large-scale deception operations.

In April 1945, Britain's own deception expert, Richard Walker from MI5, went to Brussels and Paris to work with the security services of liberated countries on pigeon spies. This included sharing details of 'double cross pigeon agents' and of how to enlist civilian fanciers to spot enemy birds, as well as the technique of using a screen of friendly birds to draw enemy pigeons away from their destination. He even offered the use of the MI5 falcon team to the French, who were worried about pro-Vichy groups who had gone into hiding in remote areas and might be communicating by means of pigeons. In Brussels, he found that pigeon fanciers were desperate to resume their sport, and their 350,000 members formed an impressive political lobby which pressed for the ban to be lifted. The war was nearly over and they wanted to get back to normal.

By then, Columba had done its work. The operation had been scaled back in late 1944 and was halted when Allied armies reached Germany. It was formally closed on 14 February 1945.

★ ★ ★

But what of the authors of Columba's most famous missive? Lichtervelde was liberated on 8 September 1944. Gabriel Debaillie finally came out of hiding in the house – although he would struggle for many years to be comfortable in other people's company, never talking much. There was no sign of his brother Arseen. And for the families of Leopold Vindictive in Belgium, even the ending of the war brought them no answers as to the fate of their loved ones who had disappeared. For that, they would have to wait still longer.

CHAPTER EIGHTEEN

Fates

Fear and trembling have beset me;
horror has overwhelmed me.
I said, 'Oh, that I had the wings of a dove!
I would fly away and be at rest.'
Psalm 55: 5–6

The war in Europe came to its end in May 1945. But for the family of Joseph Raskin – like so many others – the waiting did not. They had no inkling at the time that he was involved in espionage and knew nothing about why he had been taken, or where.

Day after day passed without word from the priest and his friends. Some prisoners who had been detained in Nazi camps began to trickle back, but there was no sign of the three men from Lichtervelde. That allowed just a glimmer of hope.

One or two former prisoners who had known them wrote letters to Raskin's family saying that they had seen him in Esterwegen and other prisons along the way and passed on what they knew. Letters full of rumours went back and forth amongst members of the family – one rumour was that he was alive and might be swapped for some Dutch prisoners. Slowly as the weeks passed a picture emerged of his path through Germany.

On 26 May, one of Raskin's sisters received a letter from Jean Starck, who had worked within Leopold Vindictive's Brussels network and helped shelter Marcel Thonus. He had just returned from Germany. He did not know for sure what had happened to their relative but the message was bleak. 'Regarding Father Raskin, you have to prepare yourself for bad news,' he wrote. 'All the signs are that he was executed in Germany in 1943.' Another letter received on the last day of May was from a Benedictine monk who had heard Raskin's confession at Esterwegen and knew he had been taken from there. 'My personal impression – my belief – is that your brother is no longer of this world … That's all I know about a man who was a hero and who – if he is dead – had the satisfaction that he can say he had caused grave damage to the Germans.'

As May turned to June, the last vestiges of hope were fading but still the full story of the men's fates was unclear. For two months the families asked, searched, questioned. By August the family learnt the truth. The answers finally came in the form of letters and court documents that revealed the story of Leopold Vindictive's final days.

On the second day of the trial in August 1943, at the stroke of midday, Raskin, Joye, Debaillie and most of the others had been sentenced to death. Only Dufour, Dufrasne and Macq had been given prison sentences, since they were judged simply to have passed on information rather than collecting it themselves. Despite all his hopes of freedom being dashed, Raskin accepted the sentence against him calmly as he was taken back to the prison camp. Each night as he waited for his fate he would say the rosary and give sermons.

His demeanour was sterner than before, Clément Macq wrote to the family, but there had still been joy. In the following few weeks he had participated in what Macq called musical soirées at bedtime. On one particularly memorable night he performed a mix of folk songs, Chinese tunes and religious hymns. But the hour was getting late. One day the Germans came and announced that all those condemned to death were to be taken away the next morning. That night Raskin blessed the other prisoners one last time. Macq never saw him again.

The next morning, 15 September, the condemned were loaded into a truck. They included Raskin, Joye and Debaillie along with Muylaert, Dehennin and one of Dehennin's fellow spies, Marcel van Caester. They were handcuffed in pairs, Raskin with van Caester. Their destination was Dortmund.

At least three hundred people met their end in Dortmund, one of the killing grounds for Nazi Germany. More than a third were political opponents of the Reich and resistance fighters. Almost two-thirds were German, often criminals. But foreign resistance workers and agents were also held there – even one young Australian who had been living in Paris as war broke out and was caught working for an escape line. The largest group of foreigners were Belgians, the youngest of whom was 18 years old, the oldest 55.

Even after arrival, punishment was not swiftly delivered. There would be more waiting. Paperwork still had to be filled in.

The most detailed account of Joseph Raskin's final days came from a man who was among the last to see him alive. The man's role seems disconcerting and may have been perplexing to Raskin himself. His name was Steinhoff and he, like Raskin, was a Catholic priest. But his job was to serve as chaplain for those facing death in Dortmund. It was Steinhoff who passed details of Raskin's last moments to his sister after the war.

'Your brother [after his arrival at Dortmund] … was under strict guard, and I was not allowed to speak to him,' Steinhoff wrote. The cells for condemned men were full, so Raskin had been held on another floor. It was only in the last three hours that Steinhoff had been allowed to speak to Raskin properly. The Belgian had received that strange offer of a final meal – consisting in this case, perhaps, only of better-quality soup or cheese. Most prisoners found the extra ration of cigarettes the greater comfort. Raskin had been calm and dignified as he gave his confession and took communion. Afterwards, Steinhoff returned to bring him a cigarette, which Raskin declined because he said he wanted to spend the next moments praying. Steinhoff told Raskin's family that he had written some hymns and also – on his last days – drawn a sketch of a chapel he wanted to have built.

The type of bureaucracy that suffused Nazi Germany remained in evidence. In the afternoon, each of those facing death had to appear before a prosecutor, a registrar and the director. The judgement and sentence was read out. The refusal of clemency was noted. A man was asked if he had any final statements. There would have been no contact with families before and final letters could now be handed over. These were never sent on.

The execution took place in a purpose-built annexe. Steinhoff saw Raskin again as he and two guards accompanied the priest down the corridor. As Raskin walked he recited the Magnificat, so loudly that everyone within earshot could clearly hear him. Steinhoff spoke the words he said to all the Belgian and French prisoners he saw on that same walk: 'This evening, you will be in paradise.' Raskin responded by saying, 'I hope so, Father.'

Most men were calm as they faced their fate. Steinhoff found it difficult when those facing death were over-emotional. One condemned man tried to embrace him and asked him to pass the accompanying kiss on to his family. Steinhoff recoiled. Signs of sympathy carried risk for him, since the guards were watching and might report him to the Gestapo. He told the resistance prisoners that one day there would be a plaque in their honour back in their home countries to remember their patriotic sacrifice. Steinhoff kept a list of those killed. He had to keep it secret from the Gestapo, who would have seen the act as disloyal.

It is hard to know what to think of Steinhoff. Was he a man offering final support for fellow believers at their darkest moment, or was he somehow complicit in the murderous Nazi machine? Steinhoff perhaps understood the ambiguities of his position. He would encourage the condemned men to pray for him when they reached the other side. Where Raskin's faith had called him to challenge what he saw as the abuse of power in the world around him, Steinhoff's focused on the afterlife. The German priest wrote to the Raskin family soon after the war ended. 'Sister, perhaps my message helps to strengthen you in the belief of the sacred death of your brother,' he said. 'I am firmly convinced that his death is an atoning sacrifice before God for the sins of men. I am convinced that by his death more grace will be upon us all than through any work he could have carried out here on this earth.'

Steinhoff waited outside as they arrived at the room. He was only allowed through the final door when it was a German prisoner.

The room was divided by a thick curtain of dark brown wool. One half, which Raskin entered, served as an office. He was asked by an official to confirm his name. Once this was done, the curtain was swiftly pulled back. The executioner and two assistants stood waiting. Two men seized Raskin. His shirt and jacket were removed so that his torso was bare. His hands were tied behind his back. His shaved head – he still wore the beard that his brothers and sister had found so amusing when it first appeared – was placed by the two guards in a frame. His neck was secured in place with a bolt. Then, with one swift move, the blade of a guillotine did its work. Joseph Raskin was beheaded. His head fell into a container, blood flowed onto the floor.

The whole process from walking down the corridor to affirming his name to death took forty-five seconds. This was a murder machine. Not on the scale of the concentration camps, but still efficient and mechanical in its own way. Two jets of water cleaned the blood away ready for the next prisoner. That day would be one of the busiest Dortmund would see. Seventeen were killed in all.

On Monday, 18 October 1943, the blade had struck Raskin at 18.43. The three friends who had met that day in July 1941 in Lichtervelde died within minutes of each other: Raskin one minute after Arseen, Joye two minutes after the priest. Three friends who had lived, spied and finally died together.

After they were beheaded, Raskin, Joye and Debaillie's bodies were taken to Dortmund's main cemetery and cremated. Their ashes were placed in an urn. Everything had been done in secret. The Nazis wanted no martyrs' graves. When the war was over, the Red Cross confirmed the death and Raskin's brother, Justin, asked for help from a British military officer he knew. On 4 September 1945, Major Shepherd, attached to the Allied occupation in Dortmund, went to the cemetery to collect the ashes. He brought the urn – a simple, closed earthen pot – and a few personal belongings back to Belgium and to the family. Raskin's final letters had gone missing.

The ashes were taken round the family wrapped in a ribbon in the colours of the Belgian flag. Among the flowers and wreaths around it was a photo of Raskin in Lichtervelde, a smile on his face. No one wanted to talk about the way in which he and the others had actually been killed. Discussing the method of their murder seemed just too brutal. Raskin's remains were then laid to rest in the family grave in Stevoort. The ashes of Hector Joye and Arseen Debaillie also came back from Dortmund.

Arseen's family had found out what little they could of his time in prison from a strange source – the Frenchman who had lent him clothes in Bochum. After the war, not knowing that Arseen had died, the Frenchman wrote asking if the clothes could be returned. Marie and Margaret wrote back to inform him that their brother had died but that they would of course pay him back for his kind-ness. He gave them an account of Arseen's last days. The two of them had made plans for life after the war, he explained. He assured them that Arseen would have faced death with all the courage that he witnessed during their brief time together. 'He was a true Belgian,' he said.

The fate of the others involved in their story was mixed. Joseph Dehennin, Maurice Muylaert and Marcel van Caester were killed in Dortmund the same day as Raskin. Madame Roberts spent fourteen months in prison in Belgium before being released. René Dufrasne died in prison from illness. Clément Macq made it out alive. Henri Michelli was sent to Germany in August 1943 along with Andrée de Jonge of the Comet line, but their death sentence was never carried out. When Dachau was liberated on 29 April 1945 by the US Army, they were freed. Marcel Thonus had been held in Belgium for fifteen months before being taken to Dachau, like Jef Van Hooff. Both parachutists survived to be liberated. (The Belgian authorities still had a file open on Thonus for desertion, but the case was dropped.)

The Belgian Sûreté opened a file on Leopold Vindictive at the end of the war in an effort to understand who had been a part of it, in order to acknowledge their service. The result was a messy picture. The investigator struggled to understand who had done what; the three central participants were all now deceased and could no longer tell their story and the few more marginal figures who did survive exaggerated their own role.

Fate dealt its hand to the judge who had presided over the death sentences handed to Raskin and the other men. On the morning of 3 February 1945, Roland Freisler had been holding a session of the People's Tribunal when Allied bombers struck Berlin. The tribunal took a direct hit and Freisler was crushed to death by a column in his own courtroom.

★ ★ ★

As war ended, men who had fought their way through Europe began to return to their pigeon lofts in gardens across the country. In many cases, wives or mothers had been cleaning, feeding and caring for the birds in their absence. About half the 70,000 lofts from pre-war days were still running. 'It was good while it lasted. One by one we are handing over to the men,' wrote one of those women, a Mrs Lawson. She had been uninterested in the hobby before the war, but that had changed as she played her part, forced to learn the difference between a squab and a squeaker. 'Try not to judge us too harshly if you feel our work lacked the perfection of your master touch,' she added wryly. Many women welcomed the return of their men – of course – but also experienced a faint sense of regret at being relegated to the traditional role of making cups of tea whilst the men tended to the birds. But for other women, their men would never come back and the lofts were theirs now, perhaps to tend in the memory of a husband or son or brother, perhaps instead simply to be boarded up. 'There are empty chairs as well as empty perches in the loft,' Mrs Lawson wrote.

What recognition should there be for the birds and their owners who played their part? Should they receive medals? This became the subject of a surreal debate within the Air Ministry after it was pointed out that guard dogs were being rewarded. 'I don't want to be unduly hard on the pigeon,' one officer began, before going on to say it was unfair on guard dogs to compare the two since dogs had been taught to use their brains while pigeons were just following a homing instinct and so could not be considered brave. 'Do pigeons have brains? … please comment,' he wrote. Rayner responded with a long missive. Two pigeons might have had the same training but one would push itself harder to make it home – in other words it was not blind instinct but 'voluntary determination'. The pigeon had to overcome its fear of drowning and take huge risks despite being more naturally timid and nervous than a dog. Pigeons would get their recognition. Those deemed the bravest would be among the animals to receive the Dickin Medal. Broadcasts were also made on the BBC to those in Europe who had passed messages through Columba to write in so they could be acknowledged.

As Columba's work was coming to an end, the Army's Director of Signals had offered some acknowledgement to pigeon owners, partly to encourage those who felt the losses were high and little knew the value of what they had been involved in. A competition was held with more than a thousand birds, one from each loft that had supplied Columba, including one from the King. 'In the past, the work of the Special Section has for obvious reasons been kept surrounded in mystery,' the general told the fanciers, 'but today I am in a position, partially at any rate, to lift the veil and help you appreciate more fully the valuable contribution you have made to the service.' He recognized that many present must have wondered what was inside those cylinders that they had not been allowed to open. He revealed that the information had included details of flying bomb sites and of troop movements. In one case, he said, a message had given such detailed information with regard to a particular headquarters, including the time when officers were present, that a subsequent bombing raid had what he called 'excellent results'. In one case a writer had told a German who was keen to get out of the war to go to a road where he knew the resistance were waiting. Another message, he explained, had included a short note from a grounded airman telling his wife he was safe and well. 'This pigeon, it is felt, certainly delivered the goods.' At the Air Ministry, Rayner was incandescent with rage when he learnt that the director had used statistics about Columba and its success rate – roughly 1,000 messages from 17,000 birds sent – which Rayner himself had never been told. The dreary farce of pigeon politics continued. The next battle was to work out what kind of pigeon force would be needed in the post-war period.

What role might pigeons play in a future war? And what kind of capability – military, intelligence or civilian – should be maintained in peacetime in preparation? The surreally titled 'Sub-Committee on Pigeons, Joint Intelligence Committee' was created to probe those questions. Captain James Caiger, the man running the Army Pigeon Service including Columba at the end of the war, was appointed civilian representative. He also worked as an unofficial adviser to MI5. The committee decided it was 'most undesirable' that it should become known he was acting on behalf of the intelligence services. That meant Caiger was asked to operate undercover on behalf of MI5 in the civilian pigeon world – one of the more unusual assignments for operatives from the security service.

Caiger and Rayner clashed over the future. The RAF had discontinued the use of pigeons for search and rescue in 1944 and Rayner's best hope of becoming a post-war pigeon coordinator was to set out an ambitious agenda. He wrote a paper outlining the way in which a government establishment under the Air Ministry could drive innovation. It might be possible to develop pigeons that could home to a particular object – they might be taught to home to a searchlight carrying an explosive charge, or even deliver bacteria for biological warfare to a specific target. This might even be possible at long range – who needed bomber planes? 'A thousand pigeons each with a two ounce explosive capsule, landing at intervals on a specific target might be a seriously inconvenient surprise,' wrote Rayner. Could pigeons dropped by rocket or balloons drift silently into heavily defended areas? Could they be equipped with metallic foil to interfere with radar? Could agents develop a self-destroying microgram message ('this pigeon will self-destruct …')? If the right release mechanism could be found, might they be sent back with messages from submarines on intelligence-gathering work and unable to radio home (would the birds be launched out of a torpedo tube, one wonders)? There was no end to the possibilities.

Others were sceptical. Rayner was described by one MI5 officer as 'the nearest thing to a pigeon that anybody had seen and that he was clearly trying to make a job for himself'.

MI6's belated view was that the risks of being pigeon-blind were real – 'the past error of dropping all official interest in pigeons as soon as the war is over should not again be repeated,' was their view. The accuracy achieved in dropping by night had enormously increased the value of pigeons for communication from enemy territories. To take advantage of this required practising the use of pigeons in air travel, air release and parachuting. 'Otherwise, when war comes again, there will be (as it was in this war) the best part of two years before satisfactory results can be obtained.' MI6 wanted high-level research and training and a government loft but did not want to pay for it.

Captured documents and interrogations were revealing that the Germans had been ahead of the Allies. During the war, the British and Americans had worked on two-way pigeon flights in which a bird could be trained to go back and forth from a moving location rather than just back home to a static home loft – a technique called 'Boomerang'. Now they were learning that the Germany Army Pigeon Manual of 1925 already included Boomerang as standard practice.

R. V. Jones too wanted to maintain pigeon research. The man of science who had fought the high-tech 'Battle of the Beams' would visit the Air Ministry as the war ended to try to fathom the mystery of how pigeons navigated. (At the same time, he was also trying to work out how male moths homed on female moths from miles away, in order to find out if the ability to sniff chemical compounds could be used to detect a submarine's diesel exhaust or even sniff for traces of nuclear material from a distance.) For a while it seemed as if pigeons would still have a role.

The verdict of MI14 and the War Office was that they might want a renewed Operation Columba behind the Iron Curtain in the next war. But the Army said they could see no further role for it. Walker at MI5 explained that their interest was defensive. Even in the absence of all-out war, Britain might be involved in keeping the peace in 'wilder countries' where pigeons might be used by 'underground forces and local partisans' – such as in southern Europe, the Balkans and the Far East. It would be good for officers out there to have someone they could refer to for advice, but all that was needed was a pigeon expert with their own loft rather than a permanent establishment. Money was the final determinant for cash-strapped Britain as the deadlocked sub-committee defaulted to the civilian option, at a tenth of the price of a new research establishment. Caiger would use his 100 pigeons and keep the committee in touch with the latest developments amongst the fancy at home and abroad.

The pigeon sub-committee approached the Americans. They said there was no formal US intelligence research team, although the Army continued work at Fort Monmouth. Caiger visited America with a list of questions, drawn from British spies, regarding research on areas like dropping pigeons from faster planes, night flying, two-way services, the effect of radio transmissions and new techniques in concealing secret messages. There was also interest as to whether radioactivity affected the flight of homing pigeons. In a post-apocalyptic future, would pigeons still be able to fly over the wastelands left by an atomic bomb? Might a tiny gadget tied to a pigeon's leg indicate if it had passed near an atomic plant? Britain carried out tests, flying pigeons past an atomic source on a boat which emitted a radioactive plume (Caiger himself coming rather too close).

In the House of Commons in February 1948, Reginald Manningham-Buller MP raised the subject of pigeons, no doubt thanks to his wife's experience. He questioned the Secretary of State for Air about an Air Ministry letter suggesting there would be no future role for pigeons in war. The Secretary of State promised to look into the issue. But interest was waning. MI5's worries shrank to fears that Communist British pigeon fanciers might use their birds in the event of war. MI6 went cold. As clashes with Rayner intensified, Caiger threatened to resign. T. A. Robertson at MI5 responded that 'Rayner has always been a menace in pigeon affairs' and lobbied for his removal. Rayner was offered the chance to write a handbook on wartime pigeon use. Caiger himself wrote a short pigeon book, *The Secrets of the Eye*, which was distributed to committee members ('I would pay 10 shillings NOT to have to read this,' one air commodore wrote to Robertson at MI5). The pigeon sub-committee was wound up in March 1950. Pigeon breeding returned to being a matter of competitive pleasure rather than secret intelligence and national service.

But was it really the end for the spy pigeon? A note of the Joint Intelligence Committee in 1948 asked MI5 to inform the London representative of the CIA that 'an attempt was being made to probe behind the Iron Curtain.' No details of what British spies were trying to do have been released. But it sounds as if a spy somewhere had released a bird, or that pigeons had been dropped to test the population's reaction. And the CIA did go on to use pigeons for intelligence gathering in the Cold War. In the 1970s, the agency's Directorate of Science and Technology developed a camera small and light enough to be carried by a pigeon. On release it would fly over the target on its way home and take photos at set intervals. A battery-powered motor wound the film, advanced the spool and cocked the shutter. 'Details of missions by pigeons are still classified,' is all the CIA says about where its spy pigeons flew.

Even today spy pigeons have not entirely disappeared – or, at least, the fear of them stealing secrets is still apparent. In 2008, Iran seized what it said were spy pigeons near its nuclear plant in Natanz, and a few years later, Indian police paraded what they claimed was a Pakistani bird employed in espionage. If anything, the demand for pigeons may return in our technological age. In 2011, Chinese state media announced that a special unit of the People's Liberation Army was training pigeons to conduct 'special military missions'. 'In modern warfare, the pigeon is indispensable,' an officer said, especially if an advanced cyber or electromagnetic attack knocked out electronic communications. Perhaps somewhere the successors to Rex Pearson and Brian Melland are also thinking about how to train pigeons for such a post-apocalyptic future.

At the end of the Second World War, Brian Melland, by then recognized as the leading expert on captured enemy military material, travelled to occupied Germany. He visited the bunker where Hitler had given orders to his once mighty army, whose movements Melland had previously tried to piece together using all the sources of intelligence at his disposal. Melland left the Army soon after the end of the war. He considered returning to the theatre and to acting but decided he was too old. Instead, he went to work in the Cabinet Office helping to organize its war archives.

In the early 1960s, nearly twenty years after the war had ended and just a few years before he died, Melland was working through the files of Columba, an operation which had once been his own. The file was still classified but he was making sure the historical record that would eventually emerge was accurate. The file was bound in one of the standard manila folders used by the government. But on the cover was a cartoon of a pigeon, with Hitler splayed underneath. It was a sign of the humour the team at MI14(d) had always enjoyed despite the life-and-death nature of the struggle in which they were engaged. Checking some of the facts about Columba, Melland exchanged letters with his old colleague 'Sandy' Sanderson. The two men remained close and their letters, still with the odd German phrase thrown in, included references to a plan to meet up for breakfast one day. Melland was trying to ensure that eventually – when the file was declassified – people would have a real understanding of this most unusual of intelligence operations. Columba certainly justified high praise for the birds' owners and those in enemy territory who ran such grave risks, he and Sanderson agreed. The two men's thoughts were also drawn to message 37, which they had opened up together in July 1941 with such surprise. Both agreed that this one message had been different from all the others. It had been the 'outstanding achievement', Melland wrote as he left a note in the file for others, one day, to find. The fate of Leopold Vindictive – whose members were still not named inside the folder as Melland closed it one last time – preyed on his mind, though, as he considered the sacrifice they had made for the small sheets of rice paper tucked into a canister.

What did Columba achieve? Pigeons did not win the war. People did. And that included the hungry, half-starved people who chose not to dine on the pigeons they found in French, Belgian and Dutch fields, or, out of fear, to hand them over to their occupiers, but who instead chose to risk their lives dispatching a bird to Britain with the hope that they might thereby have played some small part in aiding their deliverance. Soldiers and sailors and airmen also won the war. They relied on intelligence to guide them, and Columba's messages played their part – whether in understanding the disposition of Nazi forces, the location of defences which were shooting down RAF planes, or of rockets striking Britain. It is rare for one single item of intelligence to be transformative. The picture is a mosaic made up of many pieces and fragments, and whilst other sources no doubt played a much larger role than Columba, those pink slips often provided a missing piece, or confirmation, that was crucial for the likes of MI14 and R. V. Jones.

Columba was a unique intelligence operation that provided something that no other source could – intelligence from ordinary people in enemy territory, almost in real time. It offered a direct, emotional bond as well as an intelligence link between those in occupied Europe and the pigeon owners, spies and most senior figures in Britain. That was why Churchill himself was shown message 37 from Leopold Vindictive. It was not simply the intelligence – it was what that message signified. It offered hope in both Britain and occupied Europe that the two parties, connected only by a pigeon, could reach out to each other and despite the potential risks, would not give up in the face of appalling odds.

The costs were heavy. Certainly for the birds – of the more than16,000 pigeons sent, only one in ten made it back alive. But for people too. How are we to judge the terrible cost for those three friends from Lichtervelde who paid such a price for their decision to make use of an Ipswich bird found in a farmer's field on a July morning? The team at MI14(d) may have been stunned by the intelligence haul that Joseph Raskin, Hector Joye and Arseen Debaillie provided them, but was it truly worth their lives? One answer is that these were three men who heard a call, bound in patriotic love for their country and underpinned by their own faith. And their decision to heed that call provides an inspiration for others who may one day face their own choice. A choice, when confronted with tyranny, not to submit but instead to resist.

Acknowledgements

The story of Columba and of those who used the Secret Pigeon Service has been pieced together over many years and with the help of many people. I would like to thank the following archives, institutions and their staff for access to material: Britain's National Archives at Kew; the Belgian Security Service archives at the Centre for Historical Research and Documentation on War and Society (CEGESOMA) in Brussels; the US National Archives at College Park, Maryland; the British Library; the trustees of the Liddell Hart Centre for Military Archives at King's College London; the Imperial War Museum archive; the Churchill Archives at Churchill College, Cambridge; the BBC Written Archives at Caversham; the Royal Signals Museum; the British Archives of Falconry; and the British Falconers' Club.

Vital pieces of the puzzle were found in British and Belgian archives, but it would not have been possible to understand the whole picture – and especially the story of Leopold Vindictive – without the assistance of a number of individuals who guided me through the various archives, or who provided advice and, in some cases, their own material. They include Colin Hill (who welcomed me into his loft when I first began looking at the subject), John Clinch, Martin Skipworth, Mark Seaman, Robin Libert, Eliza

Manningham-Buller, Philippe Connart, Andrew Riley, Mark Upton, Tony James, David Horobin, Louise North, Jo Peeters, Martyn Cox, Geoffrey Pidgeon, Emmanuel Debruyne, Nicolas Livingstone, Anna and David Melland, Peter Kleyn and Michael Shepherd. I'd also like to thank Gisela Corera for her help with translations and Steve Gove for his comments and help with the text. My agent Georgina Capel has provided the kind of encouragement and support every writer needs (even when I told her my plan was to write about pigeons). And my editor Arabella Pike at HarperCollins has adeptly guided me in bringing the story together with her astute suggestions. My wife and sons have also shown great patience as I wrestled with my pigeons, and they will always have my thanks for their support and encouragement.

I owe a particular debt to the families of the Leopold Vindictive network. The Debaillie and Joye families provided me with memories and papers that were vital in telling this story. This book would not have been possible without the help of Brigitte Raskin, the niece of Joseph Raskin. Her own research into her uncle's life proved an invaluable guide. And her advice, hospitality and friendship has, I hope, resulted in a British–Belgian cooperation which is in some tiny way a reflection of what her uncle sought to achieve during the war.

References

A note on sources:

References are to the National Archives at Kew unless otherwise specified. The full set of Columba messages has not been preserved in a single place. The first ninety-one messages are in WO 208/3560, with more in WO 208/3561 and WO 208/3555. A photostat copy of message 37 is in CAB 208/3564, the central Columba file. A further set of messages which were of use to the Admiralty are preserved in ADM 199/2475.

The R. V. Jones papers are held at Churchill College, Cambridge.

The Belgian Security Service files are at the CEGESOMA archive in Brussels.

Admiral Keyes's papers are at the British Library.

L. H. F. Sanderson's papers are at the Liddell Hart Archive, King's College London.

US National Archives are at College Park, Maryland.

BBC documents are held in the BBC Written Archives Centre, Caversham.

Documents on Joseph Raskin and Scheut are in the KADOC archive in Louvain, Belgium.

Introduction

8   sent to distant towns: The general historical background is drawn from Andrew D. Belchman, *Pigeons* (New York: Grove Press, 2006); Wendell Levi, *The Pigeon* (1969); Courtney Humphries, *Superdove* (New York: HarperCollins, 2008); Jean Hansell, *The Pigeon in the Wider World* (Bath: Millstream Books 2010).

9   'one in nine families had a pigeon': Belchman, *Pigeons*, p. 199.

11   'the humble pigeon's flight': Steven Johnston, 'Animals in War: Commemoration, Patriotism, Death', *Political Research Quarterly*, Vol. 65, No. 2 (June 2012), pp. 359–71.

Chapter One: Birth

13   handed over by its owner: The most likely bird is listed as coming from Margetts/Routh on Lattice Avenue, judging by the Meritorious Performance List in William Osman's *Pigeons in World War II* (1950). According to a 1935 telephone directory, William Henry James Routh lived at number 60 and at number 58 was Albert James Margetts, so this may have been a loft shared by the two families.

13   behind enemy lines: Details of flights are drawn from a combination of sources including Freddie Clark, *Agents by Moonlight* (Stroud: Tempus, 1999); the website http://beforetempsford.org.uk; Ron Hockey's papers and flight logs, which are held at the Imperial War Museum; Gibb McCall, *Flight Most Secret* (William Kimber, 1981); Hugh Verity, *We Landed by Moonlight* (Manchester: Crecy, 1998); and files at the National Archives.

14   parachuting two agents into Belgium: Ron Hockey's papers, Imperial War Museum; http://www.cegesoma.be/docs/Invent/AA_1098_AA_1100.pdf; http://beforetempsford.org.uk/7-july-1941. There is some confusion between different logs and files as to which operations were flown on this and surrounding nights. One was Operation Marble – parachuting an agent called Paul Jacquemin into Belgium to work with MI6's sole network, codenamed Clarence. Another was Moonshine/Opinion. Nicolas Livingstone, who produced the Before Tempsford site, believes the most likely flight on which our pigeon was dropped was the Moonshine/Opinion mission.

14   'We tried ... good drop': See Frank Cromwell Griffiths' testimony at the Imperial War Museum, Reel 2, http://www.iwm.org.uk/collections/item/object/80012005

14   the next night: http://beforetempsford.org.uk/2016/07/

15 publication the *Racing Pigeon* in 1898: Lt Col. A. H. Osman, *Pigeons in the Great War* (1929); Garry McCafferty, *They Had No Choice* (Stroud: Tempus, 2002), ch. 20.

16 expanded among all the services: Osman, *Pigeons in the Great War*.

16 'When the battle rages ... for succour': Quoted in Levi, *The Pigeon*, p. 7.

16 trapped behind enemy lines: Osman, *Pigeons in the Great War*.

16 not long after the war: A small loft was kept in Egypt with the plan to use it for internal security. But by 1928, that loft was closed, leaving only a small facility in Singapore.

17 the newspaper he edited: AIR 2/2211.

17 concentrated in working-class areas: WO 32/10681; Osman's estimate. There were two unions, the larger being the National Homing Union, and two journals – the bigger being the *Racing Pigeon*, owned and edited by Osman in London, the second *British Homing World*, edited by F. W. Marriott and published in Birmingham.

17 'There was a terrible slaughter': H. C. Woodman, 'War of Little Wings', *Racing Pigeon Pictorial*, 1975–6. All references to Woodman are taken from these articles.

18 hard-up dance band manager: Osman, *Pigeons in the Great War*; WO 208/3565.

19 Z's man in Zurich: Anthony Read and David Fisher, *Colonel Z* (London: Hodder and Stoughton, 1984), p. 231.

20 an adverse impact on his work: Keith Jeffery, *MI6* (London: Bloomsbury, 2010), p. 379 refers to the drink problem without naming Pearson, but the identity is clear when cross-referenced with the account in Read and Fisher, *Colonel Z*, p. 231.

21 taken across the front lines: Read and Fisher, *Colonel Z*, p. 139.

21 Animals were another option: One intelligence officer persuaded a farmer's wife to bribe a German to deliver a hen to her sister on the other side of the wire. The hen would then have a message tied to its leg and be released at night to waddle home. Sigismund Payne-Best, Imperial War Museum Sound Archive interview 4520.

21 carrying important military information: WO 208/3561.

22 by the end of the First World War: WO 208/3564.

22 refused to cooperate: HS 8/854.

22 a source of abiding tension: The first demand for pigeons for intelligence work was made in October 1940, when a mission was successfully carried out by two birds selected from a civilian loft by the Air Ministry.

24 'they may be picked up … pigeon pie': AIR 2/4969.

24 'In our jaundiced opinion … dining table': McCall, *Flight Most Secret*, pp. 46–7.

Chapter Two: The Special Pigeon Service

26 more talented younger men: Noel Annan, *Changing Enemies* (London: HarperCollins, 1995), p. 3.

26 passing on their secrets … Anthony Blunt: Guy Liddell, diary entry, 11 May 1945.

27 just landed in Britain: Biographical details of Brian Melland are from his son, David Melland.

27 New Year's Day 1941: Annan, *Changing Enemies*, p. 2.

28 an invasion was considered imminent: Leo McKinstry, *Operation Sealion* (London: John Murray, 2014), p. 87.

29 if nothing had been heard: Sanderson papers, Liddell Hart Archives.

30 The German navy … close to a year: German Plans for the Invasion of England, US National Archives NR 910.

30 coastal defences between Dover and Brighton: German Plans for the Invasion of England, US National Archives NR 910.

32 many were likely to be rubbish: Annan, *Changing Enemies*, p. 26.

32 'can only be classed … body of sources': WO 190/893. Keith Jeffery in *MI6* makes clear that it was only by the end of 1941 that the Cleveland (then Clarence) network under Walthere Dewe was establishing contacts. Dewe had been involved in the Dame Blanche network in the First World War and had continued working between the wars. His team had been given one-way radio transmitters so his sub-agents could send back reports, but it was proving hard to train people to use the sets and get the networks up and running in the early days of occupation.

33 it had failed to deliver: WO 198/893.

33 nearly a third of a year: Jeffery, *MI6*, p. 520.

34 floodlight the whole of southern England: R. V. Jones, *Most Secret War* (London: Coronet, 1978), p. 65.

36 When the ears … find out more: Jones, *Most Secret War*, p. 426.

36 the intensive manufacture of gas: WO 198/893.

37 Columba message number one … 10.30 a.m.: http://beforetempsford.org.uk

39 'From now onwards … anyone who betrays': Columba message 51.

40 eat them before they were ripe: Columba message 62.

40 taken off with his aeroplane and fled: Columba message 62, August 1941.

41 replace all his own pigeons ... also been killed: Columba message 75.

Chapter Three: Leopold Vindictive

45 what being a patriot really meant: Many biographical details of the Raskin, Joye and Debaillie families have been provided by the families themselves; others are from Brigitte Raskin, *De eeuw van de ekster. Een Belgisch levensverhaal* (Amsterdam: Meulenhoff, 1994).

48 Belgium's war quickly became Britain's: John Horne and Alan Kramer, *German Atrocities 1914* (New Haven and London: Yale University Press, 2001), pp. 26–30.

55 Columba birds were dropped: WO 208/3562.

55 'Rear a couple ... kill all mine': Columba message 506, 28 August 1943.

56 details of what they observed: The Belgian Security Service Archive file on Leopold Vindictive contains details of some of those who provided information, although the precise dates and contacts remain confusing.

Chapter Four: Arrival

62 'I well remember the fascination ... which they contained': CAB 146/431.

62 distribute the information round other departments: Later in the war, these functions would be taken over by Captain Kleyn's team at Wing House.

65 its attempts to send in a radio operator ... had failed: HS 6/217.

66 a day he would never forget: The account of Keyes's visit to Belgium is drawn from the official record, PREM 4/24/4, his own papers, which are held at the British Library, and the account of his son, Roger Keyes, *Outrageous Fortune* (London: Martin Secker and Warburg, 1984).

68 a long-barrelled Luger pistol: Keyes papers; Philip Johns, *Within Two Cloaks* (London: William Kimber, 1979).

72 'Confirmation of the value ... the sender's bona fides': WO 208/3556.

73 shown to Churchill himself: The sending of the message personally to Churchill is recorded in the Columba file, CAB 208/3564, in a draft of Kenneth Strong's memoir.

Chapter Five: Listening

75 'Don't you see … English radio': BBC E2/192/1 File 1a, April–July 1941, p. 24 has detailed reports of Belgian responses to the BBC.

76 permitting her pupils to listen to the BBC: BBC E2/186/4, November 1940–January 1941.

76 'My wife would like … so patriotic': Columba message 85.

76 speaking from London … wanted him to know: Columba message 46.

77 'You have announced … said nothing': Columba message 240. See also Lynne Olson, *Last Hope Island* (London: Scribe, 2017), p. 118.

77 The messages … had arrived in London: The specific codenames are mentioned in a memo of 30 April 1942, BBC E2/90.

78 crossed the Channel with their treasure: The archives are confusing about this message. BBC E2/90 shows that a message may have been broadcast on 14 July after a request on 13 July to Leopold Vindictive 300 in response to requests from the intelligence services. On 15 July the archives show an acknowledgement being broadcast to Leopold Vindictive 200. There is no sign from the Belgian side that the 300 message was heard.

82 as stated in the original message: Notes from the papers of Brigitte Raskin.

82 supplied intelligence to the priest: They included the two sisters Yvonne and Louisa Deloge, and also Elise Ausseloos.

83 lodging, food, clothes and money: Letter of Mme Roberts, Belgian Security Service Archives.

83 'Père Raskin and his group': Joseph Raskin file, Belgian Security Service Archives.

84 The message was relayed … again: WO 208/3556 includes the message and the timing of broadcasts.

84 At 3.35 a.m. the following day … Operation Periwig: Also http://beforetempsford.org.uk/1941/08/page/2/

Chapter Six: Battle of the Skies

87 'The Germans are fully pigeon-minded … make them more so': WO 206/3556 Annex, note by Captain Kleyn.

87 'Our defence against the carrier pigeons was vast': Quoted in *War of the Birds*, 2005 TV documentary.

87 issue a warning: The Channel Islands poster can be seen in the Bletchley Park museum.

87 'In future, the Courts-Martial … all cases of this nature': Philips Adhemar, Ardoye, Columba message 30.

87 'An Italian … The coward!': Columba message 545, 1 September 1943.

87 booby trap underneath: Columba message 376, May 1943.

88 'I do not sign … have been arrested': Columba message 634, 7 November 1943.

88 RAF flight passing overhead: Columba message 547, Loudun (Vienne), 16 August 1943.

88 'marksmen on the coast … from time to time': Columba message 376, May 1943.

89 work of training one: 'How Trained Hawks Were Used in the War', *The Falconer*, Vol. II No. 1 (July 1948).

90 not worth an exhaustive investigation: WO 32/10681.

91 'We find it difficult … fit de-icing apparatus to pigeons': WO 32/10681.

92 killed during their work: There are official accounts in the MI5 files of the Falcon Destruction Unit, but the best details can be found in Woodman, 'War of Little Wings'.

92 assumed he had liberated it: Basil Thomson in Hugh and Grahame Greene, *The Spy's Bedside Book* (London: Hutchinson, 2008), p. 185.

93 released from London: KV 4/10.

94 destroy all non-NPS birds now: WO32/10331; Liddell diary, 17 August 1942, KV 4/190.

95 600 to 800 men looking after them: The whole enterprise was controlled by SS Waffen General Ernst Sachs, who was in charge of long-range communications, and beneath him a fancier called Heinrich Voss. Soldiers would strap on large backpacks which acted as two-storey pigeon carriers and which could carry as many as twelve birds. *Organization of Military Pigeons in Germany*, report in US National Archives, NR 6111; KV 4/10.

95 on the eastern front: Pigeons were used where radio conditions were difficult (for instance in mountainous regions), and where there was a lack of radio sets and trained operators. In wilder areas like the Balkans, outlying agents could send pigeons with messages to central radio stations.

95 taking twelve or thirteen hours: *War of the Birds*, 2005 TV documentary.

96 Germans in the First World War: A pigeon has fifty-two main feathers in the wing and tail, and a prearranged system of spots on feathers could make an almost unbreakable code (KV 4/10).

96 such a bird: Study by Flt Lt Walker of MI5, in WO 208/3556.

96 heighten pigeon-spy fears: KV 4/193. It was feared by MI5 that Germans might land baskets of pigeons by boat or submarine at caves on the British coast where agents might pick them up. Or they might be smuggled in via neutral boats or trawlers (especially through Ireland) or dropped by parachute to remote farms. Perhaps, once taken to Ireland, they might be placed in an overcoat pocket and then put on a trading vessel heading for South Wales, MI5 fretted.

96 given an English loft as home: KV 4/10.

98 'The ones in the Scilly Isles … found to be our own': KV 4/191.

Chapter Seven: Reaching Out

100 still in their containers: RAF operations record book of 138 Squadron indicates a flight on 3 September 1941 which took off from Newmarket at 20.15 on a mission codenamed Conugal. At Courtrai the weather was clear and fine and the agent was dropped, but then it is recorded that bad weather prevailed and the pigeons were brought back.

101 drop pigeons near Lichtervelde: See https://beforetempsford.org.uk/1941/10/page/2/

101 'he will organize … kill individual Germans': HS 6/104.

101 to the west of their target: http://beforetempsford.org.uk/2016/10/page/2/

104 target for enemy action: M. R. D. Foot, *SOE in the Low Countries* (London: St Ermin's Press, 2009), p. 229.

106 newly created 'Commandos': McKinstry, *Operation Sealion*, p. 151.

107 their intended audience in London: A doctor named Husquin who also worked with the resistance provided plans of German emplacements and a map of Ostend on which he had worked during a recent visit.

108 resistance work in 1940: Testimony and interviews of Clément Macq, Belgian Security Service Archives.

109 originally from Hamburg: Belgian Security Service Archives on Abwehr IIIF.

109 spoke English and French: HS 6/750.

110 MI5 in London reckoned: MI5 manual on the Abwehr, July 1944; https://www.cia.gov/library/readingroom/docs/GERMAN%20INTELLIGENCE%20SERVICE%20(WWII),%20%20VOL.%201_0003.pdf

110 use his contacts to work against them: In Brussels, Dehennin began working with Marcel van Caester, a member of the gendarmerie who had access to sensitive information. Hélène Dufour, a nurse, would carry sealed envelopes for them.

110 through the Iberian peninsula: One telegram was handed over to a contact of the Cleveland network, who had a transmitter.

110 a message would get through: Dehennin was primarily linked to French rather than British intelligence. Raskin himself was not keen to work with the French. He wanted to deal directly with the British rather than go through middlemen whom he did not always entirely trust. But he was desperate enough to use the Dehennin contact to try to reconnect with Britain.

110 courier for the messages: Fernand Strubbe, *Geheime Oorlog* (Tielt: Lannoo, 1992), p. 118.

111 did not know his name: Notes from the papers of Brigitte Raskin; Bodicker: report number 35. Also German Secret Police Report of 4 June 1942.

Chapter Eight: Resistance

113 just another regular Columba drop: Devos testimony, Belgian Security Service Archives.

114 The message was given ... between two lectures: Papers of Brigitte Raskin.

115 'One hears ... "before they come"': Columba message 81.

115 'We Frenchmen ... out of this misery': Columba message 91.

115 Columba would halt its operations: Pearson also seems to have been involved in a difficult but unspecified argument with military intelligence in December 1941, according to a note in a file dated 20 December 1941 (BBC E2/78).

115 'You are up there ... spotted by the night-fighters': Leonard Ratcliff in Sean Rayment, *Tales from the Special Forces Club* (London: William Collins, 2013), p. 172.

116 80 per cent ... due to night fighters: AIR 40/3054.

116 discerned from aerial reconnaissance: Columba message 79.

117 'Help our Jews': Columba message 236, ADM 199/2475.

117 'As with every other kind ... answer them': R. V. Jones papers B85, 'Pigeons'.

118 boring, old-fashioned and upright: Details drawn from Strubbe, *Geheime Oorlog*.

119 boss inside the organization: J. M. Langley, *Fight Another Day* (London: Collins, 1974), p. 133.

119 Belgian aviator … called Jean Vandael: Vandael was linked to MI6. His network was codenamed Alex.

120 make their way to England: Although Vandael was convinced that his messages were reaching England, this was not always the case; perhaps the French were unable or unwilling to get them through. Vandael was now trying to use the 'The Three Musketeers' network, which also had links with Zero.

120 taught to see his partner agency: Jones, *Within Two Cloaks*, p. 11.

122 had been a double agent: Verity, *We Landed by Moonlight*, pp. 12–13, 43–4; Foot, *SOE in the Low Countries*, p. 267.

122 pick people up or drop them off: Hugh Verity, Imperial War Museum Sound Archive 32162.

122 reconstruct its contents: It is not clear how London knew a message had gone missing. Possibly Vandael himself told them he had delivered a message, and this was what led London to investigate its disappearence. There is only one note in the Belgian Security Service Archives and the MI6 files remain closed.

123 attempt to reach out failed: Letter of February 1942, Leopold Vindictive file, Belgian Security Service Archives.

123 act as a radio operator: Letter from Commander Vandermies, 23 January 1942, Leopold Vindictive file, Belgian Security Service Archives.

Chapter Nine: Secret Agents

125 taking to Europe: The account of Jef Van Hooff's time as an agent is, unless otherwise indicated, drawn from his memoir, *Je Suis Espion* (Mechelen: Imprimerie H. Dessain, undated). Additional details of the dropping of agents from AIR 27/956.

125 Among those groups … would be Leopold Vindictive: Note from Page of 27 February 1942 in the Leopold Vindictive file, Belgian Security Service Archives.

129 'he made … his interrogation': HS 9/1506/4; Strubbe, *Geheime Oorlog*, pp. 297–8; Van Hooff memoir.

129 could be ruthless: HS 9/29/2.

129 shot or beaten to death: HS 6/272.

129 'None of the officers … described as bitter': HS 7/100.

130 shot as a result: Christopher Murphy, *Security and Special Operations* (London: Palgrave Macmillan, 2006), p. 8.

130 'We were very much the poor child … then it is delayed': Hardy Amies interview, Imperial War Museum Sound Archives 8687.

132 run both organizations: Gill Bennett, *Churchill's Man of Mystery* (Abingdon: Routledge, 2007), p. 267.

132 the agent was actually from MI6: Jones, *Most Secret War*, p. 336.

132 sent out on the BBC: Foot, *SOE in the Low Countries*, p. 37.

132 to MI6 and not to him: Amies of SOE and Arontstein and Nicodeme of the Belgian security service, the Sûreté, had a thunderous argument on 16 March 1942.

133 against their competition: Initially the Sûreté was based at 27 Eaton Place and then round the corner at 38 Belgrave Square, a stone's throw from the Deuxième Bureau at 34 and then 40 Eaton Place (Emmanuel Debruyne, 'Un Service secret en exil, L'administration de la Sûreté de L'Etat a Londres', 2005, http://www.cegesoma.be/docs/media/chtp_beg/chtp_15/chtp15_025_Debruyne.pdf

133 Belgians and other foreign services: Foot, *SOE in the Low Countries*, p. 225; see also Olson, *Last Hope Island*, p. 152.

134 the basis of close cooperation: Read and Fisher, *Colonel Z*, p. 278.

134 'crypto-fascist regime around the monarch': Jeffery, *MI6*, pp. 387–9.

134 nothing to do with the Sûreté: Foot, *SOE in the Low Countries*, p. 231.

134 'bloody liar': HS 6/300.

135 details about his own background: HS 6/232.

135 England rather than Belgium: Lepage grumbled to MI5 about MI6 not letting him communicate directly with agents in Belgium (KV 4/188). On 28 July 1941 he had lunch with Guy Liddell of MI5. 'I gather that he does not much like SIS presumably because they will not allow him to communicate direct with his agents in Belgium. SIS quite rightly feel that they must maintain control of these matters,' Liddell notes in his diary.

138 any investigation by MI5: HS 6/300, 6 February 1942.

138 'so that he could redeem himself': Nicodeme's 1945 letter at the end of the war is in Thonus's file in the Belgian Security Service Archives.

139 undertaken by the Belgian government: Leopold Vindictive file, Belgian Security Service Archives.

139 parachute to the ground: Osman, *Pigeons in the Great War*, p. 48.

140 a fancier vetted by MI5: RAF birds offered more security, it was thought, but were less well trained than civilian birds at long distances. But by 1942 RAF lofts did most of the agent work.

141 find they were in Scotland: AIR 2/5036 and AIR 2/4129, which
correlates closely as to timing with the story in *We Landed by
Moonlight*, pp. 34–6 and that of Freddie Dyke, http://www.bbc.co.
uk/history/ww2peopleswar/stories/57/a2083457.shtml. The same
owner, R. W. Beard, had been supplying pigeons via Rayner for a
month for previous attempted secret missions.

141 those of the Air Ministry: HS 8/854.

141 look after their pigeons: WO 208/3561.

142 HQ at Baker Street: HS 8/854. In 1942, SOE was parachuting an
agent into Belgium to work with pigeon loft owners to create a
news service sending in propaganda films and sending out Belgian
newspapers. The idea was that twenty-five pigeons would arrive
each month with food to a base near Waterloo, although the results
proved mixed (HS 6/92).

143 'For days … saucers of water!': Jones, *Most Secret War*, pp. 404–5.

143 'spasmodic … agents in the Field': In September 1942, a special
exemption certificate was issued for S. J. Bryant, MI6's pigeon expert,
whose birds had been working for Columba, to hold pigeons at
Broadway where he would work with Wing Commander Sofiano,
the man in charge of the logistics of dropping agents (AIR 2/4129;
other files list him as Briant). Bryant trained birds which made three
flights from France for Special Section, and homed on 11 July, 9
September and 29 November 1941.

Chapter Ten: Undercover

151 why he was there: Burr (alias Thonus) testimony, Belgian Security
Service Archives.

151 'constantly drunk': Thonus file, Belgian Security Service Archives.
See particularly note from Marius of 10 December 1942.

151 parachutist had brought for him: Devos's post-war testimony is not
altogether accurate and reliable.

152 'He did not establish … what happened to him': Letter from Page,
26 January 1945, in the Leopold Vindictive file, Belgian Security
Service Archives.

152 buying and selling paintings: Notes on Bodicker, Belgian Security
Service Archives.

154 'King Albert … done that': BBC E2/78, 11 May 1942.

155 after arriving in Belgium: http://beforetempsford.org.uk/2016/05/
page/2/

155 sent to London: Jean Starck, quoted in a post-war letter from Justin Raskin, brother of Joseph. Leopold Vindictive file, Belgian Security Service Archives.

156 'I felt burnt': Thonus's brief testimony, Leopold Vindictive file, Belgian Security Service Archives.

157 most important traitor in Europe: Herman Bodson, *Downed Allied Airmen and Evasion of Capture* (Jefferson, NC: McFarland, 2005), ch. 8.

157 women who were captured: Bodson, *Downed Allied Airmen and Evasion of Capture*, ch. 8; Jacques Doneux, *They Arrived by Moonlight* (London: St Ermin's Press, 2000).

158 come to see Michelli: Albert Mardagar – also known as BAVEY – was dropped on 1 May 1942 to make contact via Michelli with Maurice Vandael, the uncle of Jean Vandael.

Chapter Eleven: Battle of the Skies II

160 using a collar-stud compass: Larry Carr's escape report for MI9. Copy provided by John Clinch.

161 shot down four bombers: Columba message 988, 6 August 1944.

162 German night fighter: HS 9/932/8; http://www.conscript-heroes. com/Art48-Lockhart-960.html; http://aircrewremembered.com/ william-lockhart.html; Columba message 214.

163 consider discontinuing the service: 'When we have considered washing them out in the past,' one officer wrote in January 1942, 'the reaction has been well – we've got them, and they may be some moral encouragement to one or two chaps, and you never know, they may save a crew some day, so we may as well hang on to them.' (AIR 15/716).

166 ground-based interception system: AIR 40/3054.

166 plane back to England: Jones, *Most Secret War*, p. 341.

167 'Pigeons drew … control stations': R. V. Jones papers B85.

168 'Cheerio!!!!! Twee Geuzen': ADM 199/2475.

168 found by pigeon that year: Jones, *Most Secret War*, p. 357.

169 Leopold Vindictive's message 37: WO 208/3564.

170 'I have never seen … profuse message': Jones, *Most Secret War*, p. 390.

171 'This information … so wide a distribution': R. V. Jones papers B85; F. H. Hinsley, *British Intelligence in the Second World War*, Vol. 3 part 1 (Cambridge: CUP, 1988), p. 309.

Chapter Twelve: Capture

174 used on the escape line: Jean-Leon Charles and Phillipe Dasnoy, *Les Dossiers secrets de la police allemande en Belgique*, pp. 377–8.

175 also known as Flore Dings: Florentine was separated from her husband, Paul Dings.

178 in order to save his parents: HS 6/205, Etienne van Hoyer information; Foot, *SOE in the Low Countries*.

178 using the agreed codenames: The Abwehr had sent a Belgian collaborator to Michelli using the correct recognition phrase: 'I am coming from Marcel to know if you are interested in Malaga'. The collaborator asked Michelli to help get messages to France. Michelli had provided the name of a priest who could hide documents under his vestments. The Germans had used Van Horen's codes and radio set to send out another message to London on 4 May, making it look as if everything was progressing fine.

179 no one watching his back: Foot, *SOE in the Low Countries*, p. 272.

179 hands of the Germans as they arrived: HS 6/111. The Beaver network to which Michelli was linked had been penetrated and one of its agents turned. Van Damme – Beaver – had been arrested on 15 January.

179 captured by the Gestapo: Carr's escape report, provided by John Clinch.

Chapter Thirteen: Interrogation and Infiltration

182 hung everywhere: http://home.clara.net/clinchy/neeb2a3.htm

184 'They will all … depends on it': Letter in Brigitte Raskin's papers.

185 a series of false identities: Devos testimony in Leopold Vindictive file, Belgian Security Service Archives.

187 careful of him: Letter from Clément Macq, 11 November 1945, papers of Brigitte Raskin.

187 being treacherous even earlier: Julian Praet was among those who accused Thonus of possible treachery. Another member of the Brussels group, Jean Starck, in a two-page letter to Justin Raskin written after the war on 21 March 1946 (Brigitte Raskin papers), also pointed the finger at Thonus, with whom he had worked for two months. See also Joseph Raskin file, Belgian Security Service Archives.

188 Thonus denied betraying anyone: Thonus testimony in Leopold Vindictive file, Belgian Security Service Archives. Thonus countered accusations by saying he was suspicious of Marcel Allard, a Brussels

contact of Devos with whom he stayed and whom he heard had
been arrested on the morning of 6 May.

188 probably Devos: Charles and Dasnoy, *Les Dossiers secrets de la police allemande en Belgique*.

189 passed on to Leopold Vindictive: http://www.cegesoma.be/docs/ Invent/AA_1098_AA_1100.pdf

190 'Vindictive is safe and has money': Leopold Vindictive file, Belgian Security Service Archives.

191 'I very much hope ... on the whole unlikely': A draft of the letter from DO of MI14/G1H is in WO 208/3561.

192 betrayal, failure and denial: Foot, *SOE in the Low Countries*.

193 'organization in the field ... created by the Gestapo': Quoted in Jeffery, *MI6*, p. 520.

193 under enemy control: Foot, *SOE in the Low Countries*, p. 277.

194 it was also sloppy: KV 6/10.

194 under German control: HS 7/100.

194 broke on his drop: Foot, *SOE in the Low Countries*.

195 enjoyed their drink very much: HS 6/205.

196 'unless some drastic steps ... left in Belgium': Jeffery, *MI6*, pp. 520–1.

196 arrested in quick succession: HS 6/300.

197 they were always caught: Foot, *SOE in the Low Countries*, p. 287.

197 to frame him: HS 6/300/1.

197 'Germans have full knowledge ... in Belgium': HS 6/231. The MI6 note to SOE alongside it commented: 'We have no information as to precisely where this report came from or whether it is supposed to apply to individual landings or some combined operation. However, it is forwarded to you under strong reserve.'

197 'Mme Sauvage of Liège ... this side of the Channel': KV 6/10.

198 in Belgium at the time: Hooper was an agent of the SS by March 1939. Twice that spring and summer he met Giskes of the Abwehr at Cologne (Liddell diary, 27 July).

198 liked living in London: Hardy Amies, Imperial War Museum Sound Archive.

198 'Your trouble is ... love your agents: Langley, *Fight Another Day*, p. 202.

Chapter Fourteen: The Viscount

200 Girl Guide leaders: The transcript and details of the court martial are in WO 71/1078.

201 'unique fairy prince of modern life': Biographical details of Evan
    Morgan drawn from Monty Dart and William Cross, *Aspects of Evan*
    (William Cross, 2012) and William Cross, *Not Behind Lace Curtains*
    (William Cross, 2013).
201 enhanced by the industrial revolution: Christopher Wilson, 'The
    devil worshipping viscount and his very naughty party trick with a
    parrot', *Daily Mail*, 18 June 2013.
202 head of the SA, Ernst Rohm: http://www.bbc.co.uk/blogs/
    waleshistory/2010/12/evan_morgan_of_tredegar_house.html;
    http://www.bbc.co.uk/blogs/wales/
    entries/58b3be05-87b7-3fca-b511-2c9c24bc61a8
202–'glorious house ... crucifixes and crocodiles': Dart and Cross, *Aspects
203 of Evan*, p. 96.
203 a job he loved: WO 208/3556.
203 'One Lord Tredegar ... very keen': BBC E2/78, 11 November
    1942.
204 'considerable value ... CX reports': WO 208/3561.
205 a supply of pigeons: Foot, *SOE in the Low Countries*, p. 62.
206 take it over directly: The next day a senior officer wrote to the
    Deputy Director of Military Intelligence backing Melland, saying
    that he viewed the material as of real value. And he stressed that its
    value would increase when the time came to send troops over the
    Channel and back into Europe. 'Then, and not till then, will be the
    time to consider its abolition,' the lieutenant colonel (Hirsch) wrote.
    WO 208/3561 has details of the plans to abolish the service and of
    the impact of Tredegar's arrival.
207 some of the best pigeons: Columba Summary 7, MI14(d), 21
    December 1942, WO 208/3556.
208 details of the agents involved: SOE had already expressed some
    security concerns, dating back to the summer. They used Columba
    pigeons in preference to Air Ministry birds because they performed
    better, but wanted to be sure there was no danger that details of
    operations would leak out. They asked MI5 to keep an eye on
    Columba's security for them.
208 discuss the problems: Columba Summary 8, 21 January 1943, WO
    208/3556.
209 at least thirty birds: McCafferty, *They Had No Choice*, p. 17.
218 without proper permission: WO 208/3563.
218 value of the information: AIR 2/4969, April 1944.
219 'If the whole scheme ... facilitate it': AIR 2/4969, July 1944.

219 did not comply: The NPS was dominated at national and local levels by strong personalities who were accused of using it to serve their own interests. An MI5 report noted that 'the personnel appointed held conspicuous peace-time positions within the fancy and the services were thereby brought into political issues affecting the civilian pigeon world' (KV 4/229).

220 sale of pigeons: WO 32/10681.

220 'not in accordance … patriotic motives': One version has it that Osman failed to offer up his own birds for NPS work, which then led the committee to withdraw his membership. They suggested he had a conflict of interest with his editorship of the *Racing Pigeon* and had generally been obstinate (WO 32/10681).

221 scope of Columba's activities: WO 208/3561.

Chapter Fifteen: Trials and Tribulations

224 tried to break the men: The account of Macq, who survived and provided testimony to the Belgian Sûreté after the war, is the only one we have. The most detailed account of the specific allegations against the men comes in a series of German court documents. One set is in the Leopold Vindictive file in the Belgian Security Service Archives, with other versions obtained from Berlin on microfilm in the same archive (CEGES AA MIC 136). Another copy obtained from Germany is in the papers of Brigitte Raskin.

226 source of every one: Testimony of the German interrogator given after the war, in the Belgian Security Service Archives.

229 never made it out: Details emerged in a packet of information and belongings released to the family after death. Further information from Brigitte Raskin and her papers.

Chapter Sixteen: Deception

237 win it the Dickin Medal: Dickin Medal citation 30: Pigeon NPS.42. NS.7524, bred by C. Dyson, Barnsley. Date of Award: October 1945, 'For bringing important messages three times from enemy-occupied country, viz: July 1942, May 1943 and July 1943, while serving with the Special Service from the continent.' The three flights appear to be: (1) departing 23 July 1942, arrived 28 July from Brittany; this is possibly Columba message 177, which has details of arrivals of minesweepers at Duistieham from Caen, and was received in MI14 on 29 July; (2) from France, 10 May 1943, returned 17 May; (3) from France, released by agent 22 July 1943, arrived 26 July.

237 The Canadian troops involved in Dieppe used their own pigeons, of which four were taken from a loft for the raid. Two were released from Dieppe beach with operational messages from the brigadier. The first bird, 4230, returned in less than three hours; the second, 2707, was presumed killed by heavy flak. A third bird was released from a British destroyer in the middle of the Channel with an operational message from Major General J. H. Roberts and returned at 5 p.m. that day. The last bird was released on return to England.

237 The losses proved terrible: MI14 note 24 September 1942, WO 208/3556; Columba messages 195 and 214 from Pas-de-Calais.

238 'They've always said … aim at an area': Jones, *Most Secret War*, p. 425.

239 spots in northern France: AIR 20/8457.

239 risky for the crews: AIR 20/8457.

239 pigeon section in Palestine: Memo of February 1944, https://worldwar2militaryintelligence.blogspot.co.uk/2016/10/microgram-pigeon-service-1944.html

239 'On one occasion … by this means': KV 4/229, 3a.

240 Bordeaux in southern France: In 1943, 5,814 birds were dropped, of which 634 came back, 378 with messages. Messages of support continued to come in. By 1943 the team had also moved to cardboard message containers, which were less likely to be lost. They also started to drop the birds in pairs to improve the chances of return. No compensation was initially offered to the owners of intelligence pigeons, but in late 1943 pressure from NPS and the Air Ministry led the War Office to adopt a less direct method of selecting civilian fanciers. In 1944 the selection of lofts was no longer permitted to be the sole responsibility of the special section, although the War Office thought this a retrograde step.

241 'She was arrested': Liddell diary, 16 July 1944, KV 4/194.

241 no returns whatsoever: MI14(d) looked at what it might do – for instance asking the Dutch underground to advise contacts through a whispering campaign that pigeons were genuine, perhaps with the addition of a sign such as if the last two numbers of the pigeon ring added up to 4, 7 or 11. They also wondered about having the same newspaper publish a retraction that would be dropped along with the pigeons. The last option was to broadcast a message on the BBC.

241 'smoke the cigarettes – eat the pigeons': WO 208/3561.

242 nine out of ten messages useless: Melland also wondered whether some references to different types of basket might not relate to the Gestapo but to MI6. 'I am just wondering whether the users of the

"petits paniers en osier" are the Gestapo or whether friends [the semi-ironic name often used to refer to MI6] are running a service as well. Do you remember a CX report [issued by MI6] which rather suggested something of the sort?' he asked. It was clear that MI14 were under no illusions that their sister service might keep them informed as to its activities.

242 messages planted by Germans: WO 208/3556.

242 'They are apt ... we know already': WO 208/3561.

243 War Office on 24 June: CAB 154/35.

244 prevent it being too obvious: Minutes of meeting, WO 208/3561.

244 worry about such consequences: https:// worldwar2militaryintelligence.blogspot.co.uk/2015/09/1943- british-correspondence-reveals-use.html; CAB 154/61.

246 over Belgium and the Netherlands: See also Liddell diary, KV 4/193. In November 1944 (29 November according to KV 4/195), Walker says that a pigeon dropped in Belgium with phoney rings and markings had been picked up by the resistance and seemed to have been used by the Germans, as it had another mark on its wing which had not been put there by the British, although there was no message attached. Bert Woodman in Plymouth claimed that the Germans did something similar by putting fake British rings on their own pigeons and sent them to infiltrate British lofts by throwing them out of planes over the south of the country.

246 possibility of deception: KV 4/195.

Chapter Seventeen: The Americans are Coming

Information on US pigeon operations is drawn largely from the US national archives. The primary set of files are RG111 National Archives Identifier 6924019 which are on the US Army Pigeon Service. These boxes also contain significant amounts of information about the German pigeon services, activities in Belgium and also correspondence with the British Army and other services, including a significant amount of MI5 material on stay-behind networks and countering German pigeon operations towards the end of the war. The files also include histories written by some of the US Army Pigeon Signal companies such as the 280th. Within the NSA records at the National Archives, NR 4660 (National Archives Identifier 2765793) has a useful file on pigeon messages. Another set of useful files is RG 498 (National Archives Identifier 5896574) with a box on British organisation records including the role of pigeons.

247 shipped to Iceland: 280th Signal Pigeon Company Report, US
National Archives, Records Relating to Army Pigeons R 611.

248 purchased from American fanciers: Levi, *The Pigeon*.

248 'Cheer up … Drafted': Joe Razes, 'Pigeons of War', American Pigeon
Museum website.

248 emblazoned with a Nazi swastika: US National Archives, Historic
Cryptographic Records RG 457.

249 marked secret and urgent: On 9 May 1943 a pigeon brought
through the very first news of the surrender of the German 10th and
15th Panzer Divisions by almost two hours (WO 204/2930; http://
www.arcre.com/archive/pigeons/pigeonstunis)

250 as well as civilians: WO 204/2930, cited at http://www.arcre.com/
archive/pigeons/pigeonsgijoe

250 age of 18: MI14 had considered trying to use Columba in southern
Italy but found it was relatively easy to get agents through on foot in
both directions, while it was thought that the Italian population
would not be sympathetic enough to provide reliable intelligence. A
service for Greece was also considered but the distances were too far
from the nearest base (WO 208/3561).

250 invasion of the Chinese coast: Levi, *The Pigeon*, pp. 21–2.

251 Dar es Salaam: KV 4/299. On 14 April 1943, a six-month-old
pigeon named Princess was liberated from Crete at 5.30 a.m. and
arrived at the Middle Eastern pigeon loft in Alexandria at 4.30 p.m.
the same day, 285 miles away, but died of exhaustion from the flight.
It received the Dickin Medal. MI5 officers in the Middle East caught
the odd pigeon with a message in Arabic, but when translated found
they were invocations and prayers since some locals thought that a
message would fly straight to God.

251 heard in Europe: The only correspondence and references to the US
questionnaire are in BBC E2/78, August–October 1942. There is a
1993 article – now declassified – in the CIA's classified journal,
Studies in Intelligence, about the US and Columba. However, many of
the details appear to be wrong and based on a partial understanding
of the operation from when the US joined in 1944. The article fails
to appreciate that the operation had already been going on for a
number of years. The article is at https://www.cia.gov/library/
center-for-the-study-of-intelligence/kent-csi/vol5no2/html/
v05i2a11p_0001.htm

252 born in the pub: Woodman, 'War of Little Wings'.

255 fall victim to their talons: HS 8/85.

255 exhausted enemy birds: WO 208/3565.

256 accidentally stepped on him: Another bird was deemed slightly less useful on D-Day. A message made its way back to HQ from a keeper the day after D-Day: 'Pigeon released owing to unsuitable accommodation. Having laid 2 eggs I think she deserves some compassionate leave.'

259 a bridge too far: McCafferty, *They Had No Choice*.

260 group of partisans might be: One short message picked up in West Cork, Ireland, even though the pigeon was sent from Cambridge, was telephoned to MI5. It asked for the bombing of targets in Côtes du Nord with the promise that a battalion of Free French would attack the moment the bombing started. Another pigeon alighted exhausted on a British ship, the HMCS *Kootenay*, on 2 August 1944, and in a reverse of the usual flow, the message was passed from Naval Intelligence to MI14(d). It was filled with useful intelligence about a German naval base and a fortified island (ADM 199/2475). There was also extensive reporting of battle damage – for instance of how twenty American aircraft had bombed trains and railway depots at Bertrix-Libramont, with the result that twelve trains were put out of order, although there were no casualties.

262 sports grounds of a college: Columba message 987, August 1944. 'The following are safe and well and awaiting developments under cover: F/Lt. DM Shanks – RAAF, W/O Capusdin, A., RCAF, Lts V. Dingman – Pensinger, Clements, Bishop, Hansen, McDonald B. – USAAF'.

263 Jean du Coin Larue: Columba message 938.

264 driver and his fireman … were not hit: Columba message 935.

264 'I implore you … low flying aircraft': Columba message 978, 15 August 1944.

265 maintain radio silence: Woodman, 'War of Little Wings'.

266 various messages received: Note from T. A. Robertson, 6 October 1944; note from Paris, 9 November 1944; Counter-measures enemy pigeon service, 25 December 1944; Walker note, 23 January 1945, US National Archives British Organization Records RG 498.

266 forced to retreat: Prisoner of War Interrogation Report, US National Archives Records Relating to Army Pigeons RG 111.

266 then interrogate them: Memo of 30 April 1945, US National Archives British Organization Records RG 498.

266 supplying Nazi networks: KV 4/10.

267 'Every time we halted … greengrocer's shops': Frank William Clarke, WW2 People's War, http://www.bbc.co.uk/history/ww2peopleswar/stories/79/a4801079.shtml

267 run agents into Germany: Jeffery, *MI6*, p. 544.

268 'spicy tit-bit': HS 9/29/2.

269 fly to German lofts: *Special Section 1940–1945, Royal Signals* (The War Office).

Chapter Eighteen: Fates

272 say the rosary and give sermons: Macq letters, Belgian Security Service Archives.

273 working for an escape line: The Australian was Bruce Dowding (WO 311/296).

276 Seventeen were killed in all: http://herinneringmemoire.be/documenten/Knippschild/Rede-Knippschild/index.htm; http://herinneringmemoire.be/documenten/Knippschild/Willkuerjustiz/index.htm

277 the same day as Raskin: Their times of death can be found at http://www.herinneringmemoire.be/lijsten/Gexecuteerden/Dortmund/Dortmund-Hinrichtungen-NN-Belgier.htm

278 'There are empty chairs … in the loft': 'Women, Wartime and the Fancy' in McCafferty, *They Had No Choice*.

278 more naturally timid and nervous than a dog: AIR 2/5036.

279 'This pigeon … delivered the goods': The Director of Signals then presented three medals, bearing the Signals emblem, to Herbie Keys of Ipswich, as the pigeon supply officer who had presented the greatest number of recorded service returns, to Mr Bryant, whose pigeon NURP38BPC6 had homed three times, and to J. H. Catchpole from Ipswich, owner of a bird which had homed 480 miles from northern Denmark, the most outstanding single performance.

280 on behalf of the intelligence services: KV 4/299, minutes of first meeting held on 2 April 1946.

280 to a specific target: Rayner paper, AIR 15/716.

281 'the nearest thing … job for himself': KV 4/466(1), 10 July.

281 'Otherwise … can be obtained': KV 4/229, 3a.

281 did not want to pay for it: KV 4/229, 25a.

281 included Boomerang as standard practice: KV 4/229.

281 from a distance: Jones, *Most Secret War*, pp. 636–7.

282 rather than a permanent establishment: KV 4/229, 14a.

282 work at Fort Monmouth: KV 4/230.
283 lobbied for his removal: KV 4/299.
284 knocked out electronic communications: http://www.telegraph.
     co.uk/news/worldnews/asia/china/8356921/China-trains-army-of-
     messenger-pigeons.html
284 organize its war archives: KV 4/196, 30 May.
285 he and Sanderson agreed: WO 208/3564.

List of Illustrations

Section 1

PAGE 1, TOP: Cover of the 'secret' Columba file (© The National Archives, ref. WO208/3560)

PAGE 1, BOTTOM: The instructions for attaching messages to a Columba pigeon (Courtesy of the Raskin Family)

PAGE 2, TOP: Columba message 37 from Leopold Vindictive (© The National Archives, ref. WO208/3560)

PAGE 2, BOTTOM: Columba message 37 from Leopold Vindictive (© The National Archives, ref. WO208/3560)

PAGE 3, TOP: Michel Debaillie clutches the pigeon destined for Britain (Courtesy of the Debaillie family)

PAGE 3, BOTTOM: The message about to be placed in the container (Courtesy of the Debaillie family)

PAGE 4, TOP: The pigeon with a sign detailing its arrival and departure date (Courtesy of the Debaillie family)

PAGE 4, BOTTOM: The pigeon that carried Columba message 37 (Courtesy of the Debaillie family)

PAGE 5, TOP: The message being placed in the container (Courtesy of the Debaillie family)

PAGE 5, BOTTOM: The pigeon with the Debaillie family (Courtesy of the Debaillie family)

PAGE 6, TOP: Michel Debaillie releases the pigeon from the roof (Courtesy of the Debaillie family)

PAGE 6, BOTTOM: Brian Melland (Courtesy of David Melland)

PAGE 7, TOP: Joseph Raskin, the leader of the Leopold Vindictive network (Courtesy of the Raskin family)

PAGE 7, BOTTOM: Joseph Raskin while serving as a missionary in China (Courtesy of the Raskin family)

PAGE 8, TOP: Hector Joye and family with Joseph Raskin (Courtesy of the Joye family)

PAGE 8, BOTTOM: RAF reconnaissance photo of the field Leopold Vindictive requested for the second pigeon drop (from the Sanderson Papers © Liddell Hart Archive, King's College London)

Section 2

PAGE 1: The map of coastal defences drawn up by Hector Joye and Joseph Raskin (Courtesy of the Joye family)

PAGE 2, TOP: Joseph Raskin's diary, July 1941 (Courtesy of the Raskin family)

PAGE 2, BOTTOM: The scene at Wijnendale on May 27 1940 (Courtesy of the Raskin family)

PAGE 3: The map of coastal defences drawn up by Hector Joye and Joseph Raskin (Courtesy of the Joye family)

PAGE 4, TOP: Hardy Amies (Fred Ramage/Stringer © Getty Images)

PAGE 4, BOTTOM: King Leopold III of Belgium (Hutton Archive/ Stringer © Getty Images)

PAGE 5, TOP: Ursula the Falcon (Keystone Features/Stringer © Getty Images)

PAGE 5, BOTTOM: RAF pilot with pigeons (© IWM, TR 193)

PAGE 6, TOP: Hector Joye (Courtesy of the Joye family)

PAGE 6, BOTTOM: Nancy Price and Lee Rayner (Reg Burkett/ Stringer © Getty Images)

PAGE 7, TOP: Frederick Jempson – also known as Major Page (Courtesy of the Belgian Security Service Archives at CEGESOMA)

PAGE 7, BOTTOM: MI5's Falcon Destruction Unit (Courtesy of The Racing Pigeon Pictorial International)

PAGE 8, TOP: The National Pigeon Service Committee (Courtesy of The Racing Pigeon Pictorial International)

PAGE 8, BOTTOM: Special Section (Carrier Pigeon) in the Army's Royal Corps of Signals (Courtesy of The Racing Pigeon Pictorial International)

Index

Aarschot, Belgium, 47–8, 264

Abwehr: Section IIIF, 109, 124, 152, 156–8, 194; *Hauskapelle* network, 152

Admiralty: co-compiles questionnaire for agents, 23; suspects captured pigeon, 93; denies help to Columba, 114

aerial photographs, 32–3

Air Ministry: coordinates pigeon service, 18; co-compiles questionnaire for agents, 23; antipathy towards Columba team, 218–19; and use of pigeons in invasion of Europe, 253; and post-war role of pigeons, 280

Albert I, King of the Belgians, 69

Amies, Hardy, 129–30, 132, 134, 144, 193, 197–8, 267–8

Annan, Noel, 27

Ardoye, near Lichtervelde, Belgium, 14

Army Group, 21st (Allied), 266

Army Pigeon Service: Special Continental Section, 22, 279; uses anti-hawk unit, 92, 97; conflict with Air Ministry, 218

Arnhem, 258–9

Atlantic Wall, 104

Audacious, SS, 247

Baden-Powell, Olave, Lady, 211

Baldwin, Stanley, 34

Barrett, G., 219

'Battle of the Beams', 35, 116, 281

Battle of Britain (1940), 36

Beach Comber (pigeon), 237

Beaver (intelligence network), 196

Belgium: invaded and occupied by Nazis, 1–3, 7, 53, 67; pigeon racing in, 9; pigeon service in World War I, 16; and German preparations for invasion of Britain, 32, 37, 41, 64, 101; intelligence agents in, 32, 101; food taken by Germans, 40; in World War I, 47–50; resistance organisations, 53–4, 83, 118; coastal defences against potential British attack, 58, 104–6; collapses, 70–1; under German military administration, 109; anti-aircraft defences, 115; escape networks for prisoners and British servicemen, 118–20; low priority for

Belgium (*cont* ...)
  clandestine operations, 130; British
  intelligence services rivalries in,
  133, 190–2; intelligence services in
  exile government in London,
  133–4; agents dropped by
  parachute, 139; Congo revenues,
  139; close-knit population, 148–9;
  agents captured, 174–6, 184–7;
  intelligence networks penetrated
  and collapse, 179, 192–3, 196;
  suspected traitors undiscovered,
  197–8; Allies liberate, 266–7
Berlin: bombed by RAF, 116
Bletchley Park: Enigma decrypts, 31,
  93; pigeons at, 142
Blunt, Anthony, 126
Bochum, Germany, 227
Bodicker (or Boedecker), Georg,
  109–11, 124, 152, 157, 180–1, 223
Bomber Command: losses to German
  night fighters, 15; favours carrying
  pigeons, 163
Boomerang (pigeon technique), 281
Boyle, David, 93
Brautweiler prison, Cologne, 222–4
Brave (intelligence network), 196
Brest, 244
Briel, Le (northern France), 37
Briscoe, Professor, 245
British Army Pigeon Service:
  disbanded after World War I, 16;
  established, 19; cooperates with US
  pigeon service, 247
British Broadcasting Corporation
  (BBC): co-compiles questionnaire
  for agents, 23; broadcasts received
  in France and Belgium, 43, 75–6;
  acknowledges resisters with
  personal messages, 77; broadcasts
  on dropping agents by parachute,

139; exposes collaborators, 169;
  employs Pearson, 217–18; D-Day
  messages to agents, 256
British Expeditionary Force, 67–8
Brodmeier, Walter, 174
Brussels: MI6 station in, 68; liberated,
  267; *see also* Belgium
Burma: pigeons in campaign, 250–1

Caester, Marcel van, 273, 277
Caiger, Captain James, 280, 282; *The
  Secrets of the Eye*, 283
Carhaix, France, 259
Carr, Larry, 159–60, 162, 165, 173, 179
Carruthers, Major, 210–11
Cassart, Jean, 101, 120–2, 139
Cassidy, Major, 210–11, 213–14, 216
Central Intelligence Agency (CIA),
  283
Chamberlain, Neville, 67
Channel Islands: pigeon sender shot,
  86–7
Channon, Sir Henry ('Chips'), 202
China: use of pigeons, 284
Churchill, Winston: in cartoon, 6; and
  German invasion threat, 28–9;
  Jones briefs on radio beam, 35;
  appointed Prime Minister (1940),
  67; and Keyes, 67–8; and Belgian
  collapse, 70–1; sees message 37, 73,
  286; and V for Victory sign, 76;
  advocates attacks on enemy coasts,
  106; and SOE's activities in Europe,
  128, 132; and German V2 attacks,
  261
Claribel, Operation, 65
Cockade, Operation, 243–4
Columba, Operation (Secret Pigeon
  Service): formation and operation,
  5–6, 10–11, 15; under Army
  control, 22; first messages from

continent, 38–9, 44; provides hard intelligence, 41–4; early success, 72–3; acknowledged in BBC messages, 77; organises pigeon drops, 80; casualty rate among pigeons, 86; and difficulty of dropping pigeons precisely, 102; fails to make contact with Leopold Vindictive, 114; poor return of dropped pigeons, 114; suspends operations (Jan–March 1942), 115; questionnaires on location of radar stations, 117; drops pigeons for agents, 142; and locations of German radar installations, 168; message 468, 169–71; Jones praises and promotes, 171; Germans use for deception, 194; under threat, 198–9; speed of transmitting messages, 204; returning birds success rate, 206; termination rumours, 206; and political/interservice wrangling, 217–21; conflict with Air Ministry, 218; closure threat withdrawn, 221; prepares for Allied invasion of Europe, 221; focuses on specific information gathering, 237–8; appraised at 1943 'Pigeon Conference', 240; and German planted pigeons, 241–3; incorporates US pigeon service, 251; and invasion of Europe, 253; proposed move to France, 261; helps locate V1 and V2 sites, 263; pigeons captured by Germans, 269; terminated (14 February 1945), 269; achievements, 285–6

Colvi Vecchia, Italy, 249

Comet (evasion network), 119–20, 156–7, 159

Commandos: used in coastal attacks, 106

Courtrai, Belgium, 86

Croix-Caluyau, France, 170

Crowley, Aleister, 202–3, 216

Cullinan, Lieut Col., 212, 214–17

CX reports, 197, 204

D-Day *see* Europe: Allied invasion plan

Dansey, Claude: character, 19; runs 'Z' organisation, 19; supervises MI6's European operations, 19, 33, 118–19, 131, 144; rivalry with SOE, 31, 132; on paucity of MI6 intelligence, 73; interest in escape work and intelligence, 118, 123; and Page, 131; and Lepage, 133–4; concern over arrests of agents, 196; criticises Langley for overprotecting agents, 198

Debaillie family (Belgium): in Lichtervelde, 2, 45–6, 54–5, 57, 83; photographed, 59–60, 76; awaits further pigeon drops, 80; Raskin stays with, 102; and arrest of Belgian agents, 185, 223

Debaillie, Arseen: and arrival of first pigeon, 45; calls Raskin, 54; gathers intelligence, 56, 105; in family photograph, 59; frustrated in awaiting delivery, 80; contact with Devos, 112; betrayed at Michel's funderal, 186; taken to German prisons, 223, 227–8; survives dysentery in prison, 230; trial, 231–4; vanishes, 270; sentenced to death and executed, 272–3, 276–7, 286; ashes returned to Belgium, 276

Debaillie, Gabriel, 45, 54, 56, 59, 80, 186–7, 270

Debaillie, Margaret, 45, 55, 59, 75, 78, 84, 100, 151, 186, 276

Debaillie, Marie, 45, 55–7, 59, 75, 78, 84, 100, 151, 186, 276

Debaillie, Michel, 2–3, 45, 54, 59–61, 78, 80, 105, 186, 233

Defence Regulation 9, 91

Dehennin, Joseph, 110–11, 117, 188, 224, 226, 231–2, 273, 277

Denmark: pigeon service, 210

Dessain (Belgian clergyman), 172

Deuxième Bureau (Belgian), 134

Devos, Fritz, 112–14, 117, 149–50, 183–4, 188, 223, 233

Dickin Medal, 237, 250, 279

Dieppe raid (August 1942), 107, 162, 237–8

Dortmund, 273, 276

Double Cross (scheme), 178

Duck, Exercise, 252

Dufour, Hélène, 231, 234, 272

Dufrasne, René, 108, 224–6, 228, 231, 234, 272, 277

Duncan-Sandys, Duncan Edwin, 238

Eckardt, Reinhold, 160

El Guettar, battle of (1943), 249

Elizabeth, Belgian Queen Mother, 69, 189

Enigma: decrypted, 31

Esterwegen, 229, 271

Europe: Allied invasion plan, 221, 243, 251–3; Resistance increases, 254; D-Day landings, 256; Allied bombing campaign, 263–4

Falcon Destruction Unit (MI5), 91, 97–8, 255

falcons see hawks

Father Christmas of Normandy, The (codename), 237–8

Favue, Le (French agent), 262

Ferrant, Julien, 87

Fowler, Major General Sir John Sharman, 16

France: intelligence agent in, 32; Resistance activities, 254, 259–60; civilians killed by Allied bombing, 263–4

Freisler, Roland, 231, 277

Freya (German defence unit), 116, 166

Frost, Major (of MI5), 94, 208

Funkabwehr (radio direction-finding), 153

Gaulle, Charles de, 133, 260

Geheime Feldpolizei (GFP), 174, 188

Germany: intelligence on military strength, 25–6; Melland in, 27; invasion threat to Britain, 28–33, 36, 41–2, 64, 93; western advance (1940), 28, 31; bombing campaign against Britain, 34–6; intelligence on new weapons, 34–5; takes food from occupied countries, 39–40; imposes controls on pigeon owners, 54–5; counter-pigeon activities, 86–8; wartime use of pigeons, 92–9; sends undercover agents to Britain, 93; coastal defences against attack, 105–7; counter-intelligence in Belgium, 109; anti-aircraft defences, 115–17; night fighters guided by radar against British bombers, 165–8, 170; penetrates and uses Belgian intelligence network, 179, 192–3; identification of military units, 204; invades Soviet Russia, 222; observes Columba operations, 240–1; plants pigeons for deception, 241–3; and British deception plans, 243–5; low morale of soldiers reported, 254; prepares for Allied invasion, 255–6; use of pigeons after Allied invasion and advance, 264–6; organises resistance in countries conquered by Allies, 265; advanced pigeon techniques, 281

Gestapo: interrogates Leopold Vindictive members, 223–6

GI Joe (US pigeon), 149–50

Giralt, Florentine (aka Florie Dings), 175–6

Goering, Hermann, 89

Grunne, Comte de, 69, 81, 155, 189

Gustav (pigeon), 256

hawks: attack pigeons, 88–90, 96–9; measures against, 91–2

Hess, Rudolf, 27, 40, 202

Himmler, Heinrich, 95

Hitler, Adolf: and Operation Sealion, 30; claims to have secret weapon, 34; orders extended coastal defences (Atlantic Wall), 104

Hockey, Ron, 14, 84

Hooff, Jef van: first drop fails, 125–6; recruited and trained, 126–39; prefers pigeons to radio, 143; second drop attempt succeeds, 144–6; caught in tree on landing, 146–7; activities in Belgium, 148–9, 172; admires Raskin's map, 150; learns of mother's death, 152–3; moves to Liège, 152–3; radios messages to London, 153; cooperates with Raskin, 154; meets Thonus in Brussels, 155–6; and Raskin's contacts with King Leopold, 155; and meeting at Michelli's, 159; captured and imprisoned, 174, 180, 184, 188, 198; reports Leopold Vindictive arrests to London, 190; MI6 sends to Belgium, 196; not tried with Leopold Vindictive members, 233; survives, 277

Hooper (MI6 traitor), 196

Hope, Captain, 245

Horen, Jacques van, 158, 176–8, 192, 193–5, 242

Ichtegem, near Wijnendal, Belgium, 78

India: accuses Pakistan of using pigeons for espionage, 283

Indian Pigeon Service, 251

Intersection (agent), 179

Invasion Warning Committee (MI14), 28

Ipswich, 121, 209–10, 213–14

Italy: pigeons in, 149

Jackson, Ashley, 14

Jean du Coin Larue (French informant), 263

Jean of the Reception Committee, 194–5

Jempson, Frederick John see Page-Jempson, Frederick John, 131

Joint Intelligence Committee: Sub-Committee on Pigeons, 280–3

Jones, R.V. (Reginald): as scientific advisor to Air Ministry, 34–6; briefs Churchill, 35; on German defences, 116; supports use of pigeons, 117, 143; meets Dansey, 132; concern over RAF bomber losses to German night fighters, 165; learns of German radar and interception installations, 166–8, 171, 212, 240; devises anti-radar system using

Jones, R.V. (Reginald) (*cont ...*)
    aluminium foil strips, 169, 171,
    255; success in penetrating German
    defences, 222; learns of German V
    weapons, 238–9; favours
    maintaining pigeon research, 281;
    uses pigeon messages, 285
Jonge, Andrée de ('Dedeee'; 'Little
    Cyclone'), 118–19, 122, 156, 179,
    277
Jonge, Frederick de (Andrée's father),
    156–7
Jonks, Stan, 161
Joye, Hector: in Belgian resistance, 46,
    54–6, 59, 83; seeks aid from Macq,
    102–3; reconnaissance work and
    mapping in Belgium, 105–7; meets
    Thonus and Devos, 149; Raskin
    advises to disappear, 183; family
    arrested, 185; imprisoned in
    Germany and interrogated, 222,
    224–6, 228; fever in German
    prison, 230; trial, 231–2, 234;
    sentenced to death and executed,
    272–3, 276, 286; ashes returned to
    Belgium, 276
Joye, Louise (*née* Legros), 55, 71, 230
Jungle Joe (pigeon), 150

Keyes, Admiral Roger, 66–8, 70–2,
    155
Keys, Herbie, 210, 213, 232
Kirkman, Brigadier, 240
Kleyn, Captain John Leonard:
    appointed to liaise with BBC,
    203–4; clash with Morgan, 205,
    207–8, 217; takes pigeons to
    airfield, 209; keeps log books of
    pigeon use, 210, 214; and Morgan's
    informing Girl Guides of pigeon
    activities, 212; on Pearson's reform

proposals, 218; and search for V1
    sites, 239; writes paper on German
    observation of Columba, 240–1;
    lists priority areas after D-Day, 261
Kleyn, Diana, 205

La Basse, 254
Langley, Jimmy, 119, 198
Leduc, Augustin (codenamed Laurent),
    152, 181–2, 267
Lena, Operation (German), 93
Leopold III, King of the Belgians:
    friendship with Keyes, 66–8, 70;
    Raskin's relations with, 69–70;
    surrenders to Germans, 70–1;
    questioned over Leopold
    Vindictive, 124; mission to make
    contact with, 154–5; remarries,
    154; and Raskin's capture, 189
Leopold Vindictive (codename):
    message 37, 7, 59, 63–5, 72–3, 77,
    285–6; symbol, 59; name, 72; BBC
    acknowledges receipt of message,
    78; requests more pigeons, 78–9,
    103, 150; requests name change,
    81–2, 122; further pigeon drops,
    100–1; gathers intelligence on
    Belgian coastal defences, 104–6;
    reputation in Belgium, 108–9;
    relations with Comet network,
    119; pigeons fail to reach, 123;
    Bodicker pursues, 124; divided on
    use of pigeons, 143; Van Hooff and
    Thonus tasked to contact and
    support, 149; incommunicado, 151;
    Frederick de Jonge's contact with,
    156; survivors from arrest, 183; and
    arrests of agents, 188, 190; contacts
    with MI14, 191–2; MI6 establishes
    contact with, 191; members
    interrogated by Germans, 223–7;

members tried in Germany, 230–4;
uncertain fate of members, 270;
Sûreté investigates at war's end, 277
Lepage, Fernand, 133–5, 138, 196, 267
Le Queux, William, 48
Lichtervelde, Belgium, 2, 13, 15, 45–6,
57, 61, 75, 101–2, 185–6, 270
Liddell, Guy, 93, 96, 98, 245, 246
Liège, 152–3
Lisbon, 120, 122–3
Lockhart, Guy, 162
Long, Leo, 26
Loudun, France, 88
Luc (intelligence network), 119, 188
Lulu (of French resistance), 259
Lysander aircraft, 13, 23

Macq, Clément: Joye negotiates with
to send messages, 102–4, 108; sees
Raskin's maps, 107; arrested, 184;
on Muylaert's boastfulness, 187;
interrogated, 224–6; on Raskin's
self-sacrifice, 227; life in prison,
228; tried, 231, 234; on Raskin's
attitude at trial, 235; prison
sentence, 272; and Raskin's fate,
273; survives, 277
Manfriday/Intersection operation, 193
Manningham-Buller, Mary, 236–8
Manningham-Buller, Reginald, 236,
282
Marc (intelligence network), 119, 188
Meister (German pigeon), 269
Melland, Brian: background and
character, 26–7; oversees Columba,
26, 28, 37; on possible German
invasion plans, 41; receives message
from Lichtervelde, 62; and low
return of dropped pigeons, 114–15;
and non-sending of pigeons to
Raskin, 144; receives message from

Ville de Landrecies, 169, 190;
unaware of MI6's activities, 190–1;
and Kleyn, 205; defends pigeon
service, 206, 207; as witness at
Morgan's court martial, 215–16;
hostility to Morgan, 217; and
Osman's politicking, 220; and
search for V1 sites, 239; attends
1943 Pigeon Conference, 240; on
planted German pigeons, 242;
letter from Pearson after D-Day,
260–1; post-war correspondence
with Sanderson, 284–5; visits post-
war Germany, 284; death, 284
message 37 (from Leopold Vindictive),
7, 59, 62, 64, 72, 77, 190, 285–6
MI3, 26
MI5: counters German pigeon service,
92–6, 98–9; on Abwehr IIIF, 109;
investigates Belgian intelligence
failure, 193–6; and Kleyn-Tredegar
conflict, 207; preserves secrecy of
D-Day plans, 254; and post-war
Sub-Committee on Pigeons, 280,
283
MI6 (Secret Intelligence Service): and
dropping of agents in enemy
territory, 13; in Switzerland, 19–20;
undercover officers, 19; and human
intelligence, 31, 33; reputation and
effectiveness, 31–2; delays in
transmitting reports to London, 33;
scepticism over use of pigeons, 34,
143–4, 195; and German invasion
threat, 37; station in Brussels, 68;
paucity of intelligence, 73; in
Lisbon, 120; takes over Leopold
Vindictive liaison, 123–4; agents
flown into Belgium, 125, 128;
rivalry with SOE, 131–3, 158;
supports Lepage, 135; sends Van

MI6 (*cont* ...)
  Hooff to Belgium, 143; seeks
  contact with Leopold Vindictive,
  144; suspicion of other intelligence
  agencies, 144; agents cooperate
  with SOE in Belgium, 158; keeps
  MI114(d) uninformed, 190–2;
  establishes contact with Leopold
  Vindictive, 191; and collapse of
  Belgian intelligence networks, 192,
  195–6; and MI5 investigation into
  Belgian failures, 196; traitors in,
  198; appreciates value of pigeons,
  239–40; on post-war role of
  pigeons, 281, 283
MI9, 25, 118–20
MI14: organisation and role, 25–6, 28;
  and German invasion threat, 30–2,
  36; requests MI6 agents in potential
  invasion ports, 33; use of pigeons,
  36, 203; unaware of Van Hooff-
  Thonus mission, 144; uninformed
  by MI6, 190–2; fears responsible
  for arrest of Raskin, 192; and
  rumours of termination of
  Columba, 206; and Osman's
  politicking, 220; and German use
  of pigeons to deceive, 242; on post-
  war role of pigeons, 281
MI14(d): 'Special Continental Pigeon
  Service', 25–6; pigeon messages
  from Leopold Vindictive, 80–1;
  lacks influence with Admiralty, 114;
  and Morgan's administration, 207;
  ends threat to close down
  Columba, 221; and search for V1
  sites, 239; keeps cartoon of Hitler
  and pigeon, 284
Michelli, Henri: as agent in Belgium,
  118–20, 123, 150–1, 156, 158–60;
  captured and interrogated, 172–6,

179, 184, 188; and Van Horen, 178,
  193; survives, 277
Middle East Pigeon Service, 251
Military Intelligence: accepts idea of
  using pigeons, 22; co-compiles
  questionnaire for agents, 23
Miller, Lee, 268
Mohring, Major (of Abwehr), 109
Monckton, Sir Walter (*later* Viscount):
  defends Tredegar (Morgan),
  213–16
Mont St Michel, France, 42–3
Montgomery, General Bernard Law,
  263
Montgomery, Lieutenant Colonel,
  252
Morelle, Charles, 173
Murphy, Flight Lieutenant Alan
  ('Sticky'), 121
Muylaert, Maurice, 108, 110–11, 187,
  226, 230, 232–3, 273, 277

National Pigeon Service (NPS),
  17–18, 94–5, 205, 218–19
Netherlands: German radar
  installations in, 167–8; all
  intelligence agents captured, 192;
  German pigeons planted, 241
Newmarket, 12
North Africa: US army pigeons in,
  249
Norway: Germany invades (1940), 30;
  German coastal defences, 104;
  deceit pigeons dropped, 244

Observer Corps, 96
Office of Strategic Services (OSS),
  250
Official Secrets Act, 200, 209
Opperdoes, Belgium, 167
Osman family, 15, 236

Osman, Lieut.-Col. Alfred Henry, 15

Osman, William, 16–17, 219–20

Paddy (pigeon), 256
Page (-Jempson), Frederick John, 130–1, 134–8, 149, 151, 159, 165–6, 193, 267
Panzer Korps, 1st (German), 254
Papenburg convent, 231
Papua New Guinea, 250
Paris: 1870 siege, 9, 88, 94
Parthenay, Deux-Sèvres, 263
Pas-de-Calais: in British deception over invasion plans, 244
Patton, General George S., 249
Pearson, Rex: background, 19–20; proposes separate pigeon Intelligence Service, 20–2, 217; sees message 37, 72; on difficulty of contacting Leopold Vindictive, 114–15; offers use of Columba birds to SOE, 141, 143; on elimination of German radar post, 168; replaced by Morgan, 203–4; shows documents to visitors, 214; employed by BBC, 217–18; and American pigeon service, 251; letter to Melland after D-Day, 260–1
Peenemünde, 238
peregrine falcons see hawks
Periwig, Operation, 84
Petaval, Major, 243
Philby, Kim, 68
Pieren, Eric, 110–11, 226, 267
'Pigeon Conference' (9 July 1943), 240
pigeons: unpopularity, 8–9; early use for message-carrying, 9; fancying (and racing), 9, 15, 206, 209; role in World War II, 10; dropped in enemy territory, 13–15, 21–2; in World War I, 15–16, 21–2, 88; registered in wartime Britain, 17, 92; agents' questionnaire compiled, 23–4, 37; experimental dropping by parachute, 23; first operation, 24–5; messenger service in Blitz, 34; first intelligence messages received from continent, 37–44; ownership controlled in German occupied territories, 54–5; messages handled on arrival, 61; dropped and not found in Belgium, 85; fall into German hands, 86–7; vulnerability to hawks, 88–91, 96, 255; foreign birds slaughtered, 92; German use of, 92–9; at RAF Special Duties airfield, 140; carried by parachuted agents, 140–2; care of, 141–2; carry messages from crashed aircrew, 163–4; and detection of German radar stations, 167–8; MI5 criticises use of, 195; breeding for success, 206; and political/inter-service wrangling, 219–20; awarded Dickin Medal, 236–7, 250, 279; carry microfilms, 239; numbers available, 240; planted by Germans, 241–2; in British deception plans, 243–6; American use of, 247–50; carry D-Day messages, 256–7; captured from Germans, 268–9; treatment and recognition after war, 278–9; role in future war, 280–3; casualties, 286
Plate, Willy (aka Peeters), 152, 157, 180–1
Plymouth, 209, 256
Pontorson, 42–3

Praet, Julian, 184
Prescott, Colonel, 216

Racing Pigeon (magazine), 15, 17–18,
    220
radar: developed, 35; German, 116–17,
    165–8, 170; foiled by dropping
    aluminium strips, 168–9
Ralston, Bill, 179
Raskin family, 267, 271–2, 275
Raskin, Father Joseph: in Lichtervelde,
    46–7; activities in World War I,
    47–51; as missionary priest in
    China and Mongolia, 47, 51–2; in
    Belgian resistance in World War II,
    54–7; drafts messages for pigeon
    despatch, 57–9, 61; message 37
    received in England, 61–3, 286;
    acquaintance with Keyes, 66, 70–2;
    royal connection, 69, 155, 189;
    reports pigeons handed in to
    Germans, 79; requests further
    pigeon drops, 79–81, 84, 150; asks
    for Leopold Vindictive name
    change, 81–2; gathers intelligence,
    81, 102; helps in escape and evasion
    operations, 83; meets Macq, 103–4;
    travels to give religious lectures,
    104–5, 117; draws maps of Belgian
    coastal defences, 106–7; eagerness
    to send maps to London, 108, 110;
    and German counter-intelligence,
    111; passes message to London via
    Devos, 113–14, 118–20; message to
    London never delivered, 122–3;
    and MI6 involvement, 125; Van
    Hooff and Thonus bring no
    pigeons for, 143; meets Thonus and
    Devos, 149; German search for,
    152; Van Hooff cooperates with,
    153–4; and Starck, 180; arrested,
181–2, 188, 191; Laurent meets,
    181; sends messages from Saint-
    Gilles prison, 182–3; messages
    smuggled, 189; treatment after
    arrest, 189–90; arrest known in
    London, 191; imprisoned and
    interrogated in Germany, 222, 224,
    226–8; celebrates mass in prison,
    228; composes messages from
    German prisons, 228–9; life in
    German prisons, 229–30; trial, 230,
    232–5; prepares microfilms, 240;
    fate (execution), 271–5, 286; ashes
    returned to Belgium, 276
Raskin, Justin, 276
'Rat Week' operation, 129
Ray, Man, 268
Ray, Mr (Dutch escapee), 214
Rayner, William Dex Lea: runs Air
    Ministry pigeon section, 18–19;
    and Schneidau, 140; and SOE
    rivalry, 141; conflict with Army
    pigeon service, 218, 252–3, 257,
    280; on qualities of pigeons, 278;
    not informed of Columba success
    rate, 279; clash with Caiger over
    use of pigeons, 280–1, 283
Resistance: nature of, 38; in Belgium,
    53–4, 83; increases for Allied
    invasion and advance, 254, 259–60
Roberts, Jesse, 83
Roberts, Madame (*née* Anna de
    Bruycker): background, 83;
    friendship with Raskin, 108;
    introduces Muylaert to Raskin,
    108; introduces Raskin to Michelli,
    118; collaborates with Michelli,
    150, 156, 173, 175; friendship with
    Florentina Giralt, 175; Raskin
    warns, 183–4; arrested, 184;
    imprisoned and released, 277

Robertson, T.A. ('TAR'), 243, 265, 283

Rohm, Ernst, 202

Royal Air Force (RAF): drops agents in enemy territory, 13–15, 139; uses pigeons, 17, 162–5; Special Duties Squadron, 139–40, 240, 256; crashed crews rescued and helped to escape, 160–4; and conflict with Army over pigeon service, 219; discontinues use of pigeons for search and rescue, 280

Royal Corps of Signals: Carrier Pigeon Section, 22, 203

Royal Victoria Patriotic School, Wandsworth, 127, 130, 132

Saint-Gilles prison, Belgium, 182

Salz, Lieutenant Irwin F., 247, 251–2

Sanderson, L.H.F. ('Sandy'): in MI14(d), 27–8; and German invasion threat, 29–31, 37, 41, 204; sees intelligence reports, 32; and compilation of pigeon questionnaire, 37; and hard intelligence sent by pigeon, 42; receives message 37 from Lichtervelde, 62, 64, 190; and follow-up to message 37, 81; and non-sending of pigeons to Raskin, 144; unaware of MI6's activities, 190; post-war correspondence with Melland, 284–5

Sauvage, Madame (of Liège), 197

Schneidau, Philip (Agent 'Felix'), 140–1

Scotch Lass (pigeon), 239

Scottish Society for the Protection of Wild Birds, 90

Sealion, Operation (German invasion plan), 30

Sequedin, near Lille, 254

SHAEF (Supreme Headquarters Allied Expeditionary Force), 253, 265–6

Shepherd, Major, 276

Shoebridge, Ron, 173, 179

Signal Pigeon Companies (US): 280th, 247, 251–2; 282nd, 268; 285th, 268

'Smokey Joe' (water diviner), 31

Sondell, Friesland, 167

Special Air Service (SAS), 253–8

Special Operations Executive (SOE): formed, 31; in Lisbon, 120; sends agents into Europe, 128; Van Hooff joins, 129; rivalry with MI6, 131–3, 135, 158, 191, 195; bad relations with Lepage, 134–5, 196; agents carry pigeons to acknowledge safe landing, 141–2; agents cooperate with MI6 in Belgium, 158; and collapse of Belgian intelligence networks, 192, 194, 197; unaware of intelligence failures, 193, 195; suspects Belgian Sûreté, 196–7; and Kleyn-Tredegar conflict, 208; coordinated by SHAEF, 253

Spencer, Lieut. Thomas H., 247, 251–2

Starck, Jean, 180, 272

Steinhoff (Catholic priest), 273–5

Sûreté (Belgian), 133, 139, 143, 187, 195–6, 267–8, 277

Swann, Captain G.F., 245, 266

Tackley, Oxfordshire, 236

Tempsford airfield, 139, 144, 205, 244

Thérèse, Countess, 268

Thomas, Selby, 219

Thonus, Marcel: in failed first drop, 125–6, 132; drinking, 138, 151; parachuted into Belgium, 143–5,

Thonus, Marcel (*cont ...*)
147–50; as radio operator, 150–1;
radio fails, 151, 155–6; loses nerve,
156; plans departure from Belgium,
156, 159; captured, 170, 184–5, 188,
233; in Brussels, 173, 272; and Carr,
179; denies denouncing agents after
arrest, 187–8; MI6 sends to
Belgium, 195; survives, 277
Tidworth, Wiltshire, 247
Tillegem chateau, near Bruges, 65, 73
Tommy (pigeon), 167
Totes, Normandy, 262
Tower, Commander Cyril, 168
Tredegar, Evan Morgan, 2nd Viscount:
court martialled and severely
reprimanded, 200, 209–16;
background and lifestyle, 201–3,
207, 215–16; marriage and divorce,
203, 216; takes charge of Carrier
Pigeon Service, 204, 206–7;
relations with Kleyn, 205, 207;
death (1949), 216

United States of America: army
pigeon service, 247–9, 251, 258;
supplied with wartime British
pigeons, 253; First Army uses
pigeons on D-Day, 257; and post-
war role of pigeons, 282

V for Victory campaign, 76–7
V1 flying bombs, 238, 261–2
V2 rockets, 238–9, 261, 267
Valenciennes, 146–7
Vandael, Jean, 119–20, 122–3, 125,
144, 149, 158
Venlo incident (November 1939), 31
Verhaeghe, Father Remi, 107, 183,
189
Ville de Landrecies, France, 169

Walker, Richard Melville, 94, 96,
98, 220–1, 245–6, 255, 265, 269,
282
Wannsee conference (1942), 231
Wauquez, Gérard, 173
Weasel (agent in Belgium), 193
Wells, H.G., 203
White, Dick, 265
Wijnendal, Belgium, 78, 103
William of Orange (pigeon), 258
Window (British counter-radar
system), 170–1
Winkie (pigeon), 164–5
Woodman, Bert: operates in
Plymouth, 17–18, 34, 209; on
cylinder with explosives, 62; and
Falcon Destruction Unit, 91; and
official control and destruction of
pigeons, 93–4; delivers birds to
RAF airfields, 163; and Australians'
consumption of pigeons, 164; refers
to Channel as 'the moat', 207;
cooperates with Americans, 251–2;
sees invasion preparations, 256
World War I (1914–18): pigeons in,
15–16, 21–2, 88
World War II: recruiting of
intelligence agents abroad, 21; ends,
271
Wuppertal, 229
Wurtzburgs (German interception
structure), 166

Yank (US pigeon), 249

'Z' organization, 19
Zero (intelligence network), 119, 188,
196
Zitter, Prosper de, 157, 175
Zurich: British military intelligence
in, 19